China's Legal System:
New Developments, New Challenges

China's Legal System: New Developments, New Challenges

The China Quarterly Special Issues

New Series, No. 8

Edited by

DONALD C. CLARKE

CAMBRIDGE
UNIVERSITY PRESS

CAMBRIDGE UNIVERSITY PRESS
Cambridge, New York, Melbourne, Madrid, Cape Town, Singapore,
São Paulo, Delhi, Dubai, Tokyo, Mexico City

Cambridge University Press
The Edinburgh Building, Cambridge CB2 8RU, UK

Published in the United States of America by Cambridge University Press, New York

www.cambridge.org
Information on this title: www.cambridge.org/9780521719292

First published 2007 (*China Quarterly* 191 September 2007)
This edition 2008

A catalogue record for this publication is available from the British Library

ISBN 978-0-521-71929-2 Paperback

Contents

Cover illustration: Courtesy Thirteen/WNET New York, Xanadu Productions and Independent Television Service

The complete episode of WIDE ANGLE: "The People's Court" can be viewed online at http:www.pbs.org/wnet/wideangle/shows/china2/index.html

Notes on Contributors

DONALD C. CLARKE is a professor at the George Washington University Law School in Washington, DC. His work focuses on legal institutions, law and economic reform, and law and social change in China.

JAMES V. FEINERMAN is James M. Morita professor of Asian legal studies at Georgetown University Law Center. He has also taught as a visitor at both Harvard and Yale Law Schools.

FU HUALING is associate professor and director of the Centre for Comparative and Public Law, Faculty of Law, the University of Hong Kong. He teaches and researches on human rights, constitutional law and the criminal justice system, with a focus on Greater China. With Lison Harris and Simon Young he recently co-edited *The Struggle for Coherence: Constitutional Interpretation in Hong Kong* (forthcoming with Palgrave Macmillan, 2008).

ERIC GREEN recently received his PhD in political science from Western Michigan University.

HE WEIFANG is professor of law at Peking University Faculty of Law and editor-in-chief of *Peking University Law Journal.*

HUANG DONGLI is professor of law and director of the international economic law division of the Institute of Law of Chinese Academy of Social Sciences (CASS). She specializes in international trade law, jurisprudence, and the law and economics.

JAMES LI ZHAOJIE is a professor of international law at Tsinghua University School of Law in Beijing. Prior to joining the faculty at Tsinghua Law School, he taught in the Department of Law at Peking University. He has served as co-chief editor for the *Chinese Yearbook of International Law*, and serves as vice-president of the Chinese Society of International Law.

BENJAMIN L. LIEBMAN is professor of law and the director of the Center for Chinese Legal Studies at Columbia Law School. His current research focuses on the evolution of China's courts, popular access to justice, and civil litigation. His recent publications include "Chinese Network Justice," *Chicago Journal of International Law* (2007) (with Tim Wu); "Evolution through Intimidation? An Empirical Account of Defamation Litigation in China," *Harvard International Law Journal* (2006); and "Watchdog or Demagogue? The Media in the Chinese Legal System," *Columbia Law Review* (2005).

MICHAEL PALMER is professor of law at the University of London. He is a former head of the School of Law, and chair of the Centre of Chinese Studies, at SOAS. At present, he is an associate dean for research and the chair of the Centre of East Asian Law at SOAS, and honorary professor of law at Renmin University, Beijing. His research in progress includes family law reform, human rights, environmental welfare, the refurbishment of people's and judicial mediation, and the use of mediation in criminal and administrative justice systems.

PITMAN B. POTTER is director of the Institute of Asian Research at the University of British Columbia (UBC), and professor of law at UBC Law Faculty. His teaching and research are focused on PRC and Taiwan law and policy in the areas of foreign trade and investment, dispute resolution, intellectual property, contracts, business regulation, and human rights. He has published several books on China, including most recently *From Leninist Discipline to Socialist Legalism: Peng Zhen on Law and Political Authority in the PRC* (Stanford University Press, 2003).

JULIA YA QIN is an associate professor of law at Wayne State University Law School. Her most recent publications include "Defining Nondiscrimination under the Law of the World Trade Organization," in the *Boston University International Law Journal* (2005), and "'WTO-Plus' Obligations and Their Implications for the WTO Legal System – An Appraisal of the China Accession Protocol," in the *Journal of World Trade* (2003).

SHEN KUI is associate professor at Peking University Law School, where he obtained his PhD. His research interests include administrative law, constitutional law, and anti-discrimination law. Recent publications include "On the Approach to the Legitimization of Administrative

© The China Quarterly, 2008 doi:10.1017/S0305741007002147

Organization" (*Journal of Legal Studies*, 2005), "Legitimacy on Openness and Reflexiveness: A Normative Basis for the Change of Public Law in China" (*Social Sciences in China*, 2004), and "Is It the Beginning of the Era of the Rule of the Constitution? Reinterpreting China's "First Constitutional Case" (*Pacific Rim Law & Policy Journal*, 2003).

TANG XIN is an associate professor of law at Tsinghua University Law School in Beijing. His chief interests include corporations and the regulation of financial markets. He is the author of a book named *Takeover of Listed Companies and Corporate Governance*. Dr. Tang has been invited to give consultation opinions to the drafting of numerous laws, administrative decrees and Judicial Interpretations in China, he also serves as independent directors in a listed company and an Investment Fund Management Company.

MURRAY SCOT TANNER recently accepted an appointment as deputy staff director of the United States Congressional-Executive Commission on China. Prior to that, he served as a senior political scientist at the RAND Corporation in Washington, DC, and as professor of political science at Western Michigan University. Dr. Tanner has published extensively on Chinese and politics, in particular on policing and internal security, social unrest, legal reform and human rights, lawmaking, leadership politics, and Chinas relations with Taiwan and North Korea. Among his noteworthy recent publications are *Chinese Economic Coercion Against Taiwan: A Tricky Weapon to Use* (RAND Corporation, 2007), *Chinese Responses to US Military Transformation and Implications for the Department of Defense* (co-authored) (RAND Corporation, 2006), and "China Rethinks Unrest," *The Washington Quarterly* (2004).

ZHANG XIANCHU is a professor of law and associate dean of the Faculty of Law, University of Hong Kong. He specializes in commercial law, Chinese law and comparative law as well as some WTO areas concerned. He currently also serves as the director of the Master of Common Law Programme, co-director of HKU-Peking U Legal Research Centre, and deputy director of the Institute of China and Global Development of the University of Hong Kong. He is an arbitrator of China International Economic and Trade Arbitration Commission (CIETAC) and a trustee of the Legal Education Trust Fund of Hong Kong.

Acknowledgements

This Special Issue is the result of a conference generously funded by All Souls College, Oxford. Special thanks are due to Sir Robert Wade-Gery for his support and to Humaira Erfan-Ahmed for her tremendous organizational skills. The authors would also like to thank Andrew Halper, Perry Keller, Neysun Mahboubi, Vivienne Shue, Frank Upham and Yang Weidong for their contributions and an anonymous reviewer for his or her very conscientious reading and helpful comments.

 doi:10.1017/S0305741007002159

Introduction: The Chinese Legal System Since 1995: Steady Development and Striking Continuities

Donald C. Clarke

In March 1995, *The China Quarterly* published a special issue devoted to developments in the Chinese legal system. That issue canvassed a wide range of subjects: the legislative process,[1] the implementation of legislation via the interpretive practices of courts and administrative agencies[2] as well as through the enforcement of civil judgements,[3] the personnel staffing the system in the role of legal advisers,[4] criminal law and human rights,[5] the key area of foreign trade and investment law,[6] and finally China's place and role in the international legal order.[7]

Over a decade later, it seemed appropriate to revisit the Chinese legal system in order to assess developments since the mid-1990s, and that is what this Special Issue sets out to do. Many of the original authors were invited to submit contributions, and new authors were brought in as well. In addition, a number of legal scholars from China were asked to participate as commentators, and their comments appear here. The authors were not asked to do whatever they had done before; instead, the subject matter of the contributions was dictated by their perceptions of the current important issues in Chinese law as well as their own interests. Although not all subjects of importance are covered here, it is fair to say that all subjects covered here are important.

As Stanley Lubman noted in his introductory essay to the 1995 special issue, "prediction of the future configuration and fate of Chinese legal institutions [is] risky,"[8] and it is interesting to compare how the legal system looked to a group of specialists over ten years ago with how it looks today. Reviewing the essays in

1 Murray Scot Tanner, "How a bill becomes law in China: stages and processes in lawmaking," *The China Quarterly*, No. 141 (1995), pp. 39–64.
2 Anthony R. Dicks, "Compartmentalized law and judicial restraint: an inductive view of some jurisdictional barriers to reform," *The China Quarterly*, No. 141 (1995), pp. 82–109.
3 Donald C. Clarke, "The execution of civil judgments in China," *The China Quarterly*, No. 141 (1995), pp. 65–81.
4 William P. Alford, "Tasselled loafers for barefoot lawyers: transformation and tension in the world of Chinese legal workers," *The China Quarterly*, No. 141 (1995), pp. 22–38.
5 Donald C. Clarke and James V. Feinerman, "Antagonistic contradictions: criminal law and human rights in China," *The China Quarterly*, No. 141 (1995), pp. 135–54.
6 Pitman B. Potter, "Foreign investment law in the People's Republic of China: dilemmas of state control," *The China Quarterly*, No. 141 (1995), pp. 155–85.
7 James V. Feinerman, "Chinese participation in the international legal order: rogue elephant or team player?" *The China Quarterly*, No. 141 (1995), pp. 186–210.
8 Stanley Lubman, "Introduction: The future of Chinese law," *The China Quarterly*, No. 141 (1995), pp. 1–21 at p. 14.

 doi:10.1017/S0305741007001567

the 1995 special issue, Lubman pointed to a number of factors clouding the future of Chinese law reform, in particular the "growing weakness of the Chinese apparatus of state" and the declining power of the central government over the rest of the country.[9] Yet from the vantage point of today it is hard not to be impressed by the staying power of the Chinese state. Murray Scot Tanner's article refers to several studies arguing that "the wave of decentralization of power that occurred in the 1980s has, in important ways, been reversed since the early 1990s, thus reviving the Chinese central state's capacity in finance, administration and personnel, monitoring, and coercion."[10] A decade ago, for example, government revenues were 10 per cent of gross domestic product – a "pathetic figure," in the words of economist Arthur Kroeber. Today they are 20 per cent.[11] If local protectionism has not significantly declined, it does not seem to have significantly worsened either. China has become neither a de jure nor a de facto federal state. Thus, to the extent law reform depends on a strong central state, the prospects are perhaps a little better today – certainly not worse – than they were in 1995.

At the same time, however, certain continuities are striking. My article in 1995, for example, called attention to the severe problems courts faced in enforcing their judgements.[12] Benjamin Liebman in this issue finds the situation essentially unchanged, as are the institutional features of courts, such as local control, that contribute to their problems.[13] Murray Scot Tanner shows that the public security apparatus remains as decentralized today as it was in the mid-1990s. My article finds unchanged the state's suspicion of bottom-up approaches to the solution of legal problems. And Lubman's observation that "legality remains an ideal only inconsistently supported by the leadership, and has still not been clearly distinguished from bureaucratic regularity" could have been written today, as extra-legal detentions of Party officials continue under the *shuanggui* system.

Central and Local Governments: The Police and the Courts

An important aspect of the legal system not examined in the 1995 special issue was precisely the feature that distinguishes a state legal system from other rule systems: the element of enforceability through physical coercion. In this issue, Murray Scot Tanner and Eric Green examine the public security system through the lens of central–local relations. As the authors point out, most studies of central–local relations have focused on economics. Yet coercive force is a core element of state power in general and the legal system in particular, and our

9 *Ibid.* pp. 14–15.
10 See Murray Scot Tanner's article in this issue.
11 Arthur Kroeber, "The underestimated party-state," *Financial Times*, 26 February 2007.
12 Clarke, "The execution of civil judgments in China."
13 See Benjamin L. Liebman's article in this issue.

knowledge is greatly enriched by understanding how central–local dynamics affect its exercise.

The authors begin by observing that in a formally unitary state such as China, one can view local officials, including the police, essentially as agents of the centre. The legitimate right of the centre to direct the actions of local officials is not seriously contested; what is more doubtful is its ability to do so. But the centre's ability and inclination to monitor its local agents is not uniform across sectors. First, some agents and actions are more easily monitored than others. The centre can monitor whether a promised amount of tax revenue has been handed over. But the goals of police work – such as maintaining social order and respecting the rights of citizens – are more difficult to quantify and potentially contradictory. Those that are easily quantified, such as arrests made or proportion of cases solved, may be easily manipulable or not necessarily things one wants to maximize unconditionally.

Secondly, government bureaucracies often operate according to certain stylized "lessons from history," even though the history may be contested. In China, the historical lesson that dominates thinking about central–local relations in police work is the abuses of centralized security forces during the Chinese Soviet Republic in the 1930s. As a result, China did not go down the Soviet road of a centralized police force, and Party leaders remain essentially outside the jurisdiction of the ordinary police.

Tanner and Green conclude that the presence of these two factors has led to "a relatively decentralized and feudal system of law enforcement and state coercion that constitutes a major obstacle to building the rule of law in China."

The authors also point to some specific institutional features of the public security bureaucracy that contribute to local control. While public security organs at superior levels of government are supposed to exercise leadership in "professional" matters over corresponding organs below them, those organs are subject horizontally to local political power in matters of organization, personnel and finance. The local Party committee has the power to resolve disagreements among local courts, police and procurators. Local governments have wide discretion over hiring – sometimes consistently with applicable rules, sometimes not. Unlike senior PLA officers and provincial Party secretaries, provincial public security chiefs are apparently not rotated. And since the late 1950s, the bulk of the budget for public security forces has been paid by local governments.

Entrenched local control makes monitoring difficult, and police misconduct is common. Recently, the spread of the internet and other communication technologies as well as the relaxation of controls over the media has made monitoring outside normal channels more feasible, at least in principle. But as Tanner and Green point out, this confronts the centre with a dilemma: its only choice may be "to accept local Party control and all that these dangerous incentives imply for the Party's future, or risk trying to strengthen non-Party oversight and monitoring institutions and information networks, perhaps even making common cause with social forces that could further erode one-party control over society." So far, they conclude, the centre has chosen to accept the dangers of local Party control: "during the past three years, the Party leadership has, if anything, backed away from building up such hard-to-dominate institutions rather than make a serious effort at mobilizing them to strengthen the centre's monitoring capacity."

I have devoted considerable space to the analysis of Tanner and Green because it resonates strongly with Benjamin Liebman's study of the court system, suggesting that there are important lessons to be drawn here about the legal system as a whole. Liebman's contribution provides a valuable status report on the role of courts in the Chinese legal system, noting both important continuities and incipient developments that may turn out to be quite significant.

The amount that has stayed the same since I looked at courts in the 1995 issue is remarkable, given the scope of change that has occurred elsewhere in Chinese society. The authority of courts remains essentially unchanged; they remain "one of a number of bureaucracies with the power to resolve disputes, and lack significant oversight powers over other state actors."[14] Despite occasional noises made about reform, their funding and personnel remain under local control. Intervention by Party or government officials in a wide range of cases remains common. And despite the vast growth in the scale of economic activity since 1995, there has been no matching growth in litigation. Never important in an absolute sense in the resolution of economic disputes to begin with, courts have in the last dozen years perhaps become even less important relative to other institutions.

At the same time, however, change is evident. Courts have become increasingly used for rights-based litigation[15]; judges increasingly look horizontally to other judges, rather than vertically to political authorities, for guidance in deciding cases[16]; and courts have increasingly come into conflicts with other institutions, such as the media.[17] None of these trends is inexorable or means that the Chinese legal system will become like that of Western countries. But as Liebman points out, the very fact that the role of courts in Chinese society is increasingly contested is itself a significant development.

A central question driving Liebman's analysis is that of why the party-state has allowed the developments he describes to occur. What role does it expect courts to play, and what role *can* courts play in a non-democratic political system?

14 *Ibid.*

15 By "rights-based litigation" I mean litigation designed to vindicate certain political, economic or social rights against powerful institutions, whether state or non-state – essentially the programme of the *weiquan* movement. I do not mean litigation designed to enforce, say, contract rights against a breaching party.

16 Benjamin L. Liebman and Tim Wu, "China's network justice" (9 January 2007), available at http://ssrn.com/abstract=956310.

17 Interestingly, Liebman (in this issue) reports that when courts and media have conflicting understandings of a case, political authorities typically trust the media more than the courts – or at least, for whatever reason, accept the media's view as determinative.

Here Liebman's discussion parallels in important ways that of Tanner and Green. Like the police, the courts are an organ of state power largely outside the control of the central government. They answer to local government in almost all matters. At the same time, however, they play a role that is useful to the centre. In addition to serving as institutions for the resolution of grievances, the proper handling of which can reduce dangerous social tensions, courts are also one of many state institutions used by the government for the supervision of other state institutions. Thus, the state is willing to allow courts a modest increase in power if it enhances their supervisory function.

But as Tanner and Green show, the state willingly gives up monitoring capacity if it carries with it the danger of evading control and challenging the Party's political monopoly. Just as the state has forgone the possibility of citizen supervision over the police through, for example, the internet, so it rejects the possibility of enhanced court supervision of other branches of government through increased independence for the judiciary.

While not fundamentally disagreeing with the story told in Liebman's article, Shen Kui in his comments offers an alternative interpretation. Certainly, he agrees, "judicial reform has not yet brought about any significant change in the position or role of courts in China's political system." Yet he suggests that the yardstick of judicial independence is not the only one against which the court system should be measured. He notes that court reform has in fact gone further than reform of people's congresses[18] or the Communist Party, and that this success has bred expectations of even more progress. Indeed, courts do seem to be special in the sense that they are one institution of which the expectations of a generally cynical society remain remarkably high – and well above performance. Shen agrees that the role of courts is increasingly contested, but sees this as a great achievement of reform.

Law and the Economy: What Role for Non-State Institutions?

My own contribution to this special issue is a review of legislation relating to commercial activity in the past few years. As with many of the other aspects of the legal system covered in this issue, rapid change in some areas coexists with surprising continuities in others.

China's legislative institutions have been extremely busy, and the work of foundational legislation seems almost complete. There are laws and regulations providing for a variety of business organizations; there are laws and regulations about contracts, banking, secured lending, bankruptcy, real estate and securities.

18 Although it is common to say that the people's congresses are no longer the meaningless rubber stamp they once were, this is not the same as saying they have moved very far away from that position. See, for example, Peter Ford, "China's congress follows the script, literally," *Christian Science Monitor*, 12 March 2007; Kristine Kwok, "'Fake' representatives need training: deputy," *South China Morning Post*, 13 March 2007 (quoting complaint of NPC deputy that many representatives lack the training to do their job of reviewing legislation, and that once bills come to the NPC it is already too late to make any major changes).

The missing pieces – such as a comprehensive law on competition – are almost there.

At the same time, however, an important feature of a commerce-friendly legal system is missing: a good, bottom-up system for filling the gaps that will inevitably occur. The state institutions that come into regular contact with the gaps and ambiguities in the law are courts and low-level administrative agencies. It is true that the administrative agencies can and do fill in the gaps by simply making up a rule. This is a system, but not an especially good one, since there is no good way of ensuring that they act within their proper sphere of authority and without conflicting with other rules. Court decisions, by contrast, are subject to the unifying pressure of review by superior courts, but the power of courts to fill in gaps by making up provisional rules is quite limited. Often the response of courts is simply to decline to hear a troublesome case.

At the same time, there does not exist a legal environment in which non-state institutions can readily arise in response to market forces in order to deal with the infinite number of problems that state legislation does not anticipate or cannot handle very efficiently. The state remains suspicious of institutions not under its control and tends to suppress them. But the returns to formal state legislative activity are much less than they used to be; a greater appreciation of the role that could be played by non-state institutions is now called for.

Zhang Xianchu in his comment agrees that there is an impressive legal framework, but points out that a major problem remains in the implementation of this framework. He ties implementation problems precisely to the model of state-driven development: because the state has dictated all the rules in a heavy-handed, top-down manner with little sensitivity to business realities, it has in fact invited violations. He also notes that implementation is stymied by the state's flouting of its own rules, as when the State Council passed regulations overriding the distribution rules of the Bankruptcy Law. Perhaps most importantly, Zhang reminds us that the narrative of commercial legislation has recently changed in a significant way. At the time of the first special issue, this kind of legislation was not particularly controversial among the public. But economic and commercial legislation has now become subject to political debates and strongly opposed feelings.

James Feinerman's contribution looks at recent developments in a specific realm of the commercial legal system: corporate governance. Corporate governance in China's economic reform programme is a term with significance in two quite different areas. First, one can speak of it in the context of state-owned enterprise (SOE) reform. Although SOE reform had been on the government's agenda since the very beginning of the post-Third Plenum era of economic reform, it was in 1993, with the passage of the Company Law, that the government shifted to a policy of SOE reform through fundamental organizational changes. The Company Law passed in 1993 was not primarily about enabling the efficient formation of entities for the conduct of business; it was instead essentially about reforming existing SOEs. To the extent the Company Law had something to say about internal corporate governance, it contemplated a company in which the state's equity interest and voice was dominant.

By contrast, one can also speak of corporate governance as applied to all business entities in the corporate form, particularly those listed on public stock exchanges. The public policy concerns in this case are different: instead of being another way of thinking about the state's internal procedures governing the management of its assets, corporate governance becomes a way of thinking about – and perhaps, although not necessarily, prescribing in law – the relationship between enterprise managers, large stockholders and small stockholders.

In the decade-plus since the Company Law came into effect, the significance of corporate governance has shifted largely from the first conception to the second. In particular, recent reforms to the state shareholding system have made it possible (in a way it was not before) for the state to divest itself completely of its interest in publicly listed companies by selling its shares into the market, thus increasing the importance of thinking about corporate governance separately from the issue of SOE management.

Both Feinerman and commentator Tang Xin agree that there are many problems with China's corporate governance regime. Shareholder protections have been limited; boards are dominated by management, with independent directors few and weak; and information disclosure is unreliable. Although Feinerman finds that the 2005 revisions to the Company Law and the Securities Law offer some new protections, Tang notes in his comments the importance of actual implementation on the ground of these paper rights.

Particularly interesting is the congruence of both writers' observations with those of other writers in this issue on the question of the role of unofficial or non-state institutions in monitoring legal compliance. From 2001 to 2003, the Supreme People's Court issued a series of three documents governing shareholder suits against corporations and their managers for various violations of the Securities Law. The cumulative effect of these documents has been to limit severely the right of shareholders to bring suit for violations. No suits may be brought at all for violations of rules against market manipulation or insider trading. Shareholders may bring suit for violations of disclosure rules, but only where a government body – an administrative agency such as the China Securities Regulatory Commission or a criminal court – has already found a violation of law. In short, would-be private plaintiffs must first get a key to the courthouse from a government agency.

In addition perhaps to causing injustice in particular cases, this requirement closes off what in some countries can be an important supplement to government regulation: the promotion of public policy goals through private litigation. In this as in many other areas of law, the state has consistently opted for less effective enforcement if it could be bought only with the coin of increased and difficult-to-control public participation.

The State and the Family: Paradoxes of a New Relationship

Michael Palmer's contribution, as in the 1995 special issue, surveys developments in family law. As the economy has changed in the last dozen years, so have the family and social relationships in general. As important as these changes is the fact that there has emerged considerable open debate about the proper scope and content of the state's rules about family and sexual life. While debate over the state's birth control policy is still stifled, almost everything else seems to be fair game, with one NPC deputy even advocating the legalization of prostitution.[19]

Unlike in some of the other fields of law surveyed here, the state seems willing to withdraw in the realm of family life and interfere less. Parties wishing to marry may now simply declare that they have the capacity to do so; the requirement of a letter from the work unit, which effectively imposed on the marriage a condition of work unit consent, has been abolished. The matching requirement of a letter from the work unit for parties wishing to divorce has similarly been abolished. In short, family law has acknowledged, and perhaps reinforced, the decline of the *danwei* as the essential intermediary between the urban citizen and the state.

At the same time, however, Palmer points out that the state has begun to insert itself into an area that until recently it had (like many Western states until recent decades) left essentially private: the sphere of domestic violence. Both the retreat and the advance of the state can, however, be explained by the rise of a single principle: that of the abstract citizen largely separated from a social context. In other words, Chinese law sees farmers who wish to marry as identical *for those purposes* to urban government workers, state-owned enterprise employees and the self-employed. It increasingly says that assault is assault, without regard for the identity of or relationship between the parties to the act. This notion of the abstract citizen is, of course, quite different from the view that traditionally prevailed in Mao-era China, when individuals were typically viewed by the law as existing within a particular social context – most notoriously, of course, class background.

Fu Hualing's comment to Palmer's contribution echoes some of these themes. He finds that Chinese legal reform largely follows a liberal paradigm, with the goal being to separate the Chinese Communist Party from the state and to limit the role of the state in the economy and society. He calls attention, however, to the paradox of Chinese political and legal reform: severe repression in core policy areas combined with freedom in peripheral areas. In family law, this paradox is reflected in the strict controls over the decision to have children, beside which the freedom of marriage and divorce "pales and becomes marginalized."[20] Thus, it is clear that the legal system's growing acceptance of the notion of the abstract citizen does not necessarily mean more freedoms for

19 Daniel Bell, "Sexual development," 28 January 2007, at http://commentisfree.guardian.co.uk/daniel_a_bell/2007/01/sexual_development.html.

20 See Hualing Fu's commentary in this issue.

that citizen; it reflects a different principle of governance, but is as consistent with greater state control as with less.

Fu also points out that greater freedom for some in areas where the state retreats may mean less freedom for others. Many of the traditional social welfare mechanisms have been weakened by economic reform; those who are hurt by the increased social and legal acceptance of divorce, for example, have less to fall back on than before.

The Domestic and International Legal Orders: A Two-Way Street

Pitman Potter's contribution examines China's participation in the international legal order. In the 1995 special issue, James Feinerman entitled his article "Chinese participation in the international legal order: rogue elephant or team player?" Today there is little doubt that China wants at least to be seen as a team player. Potter examines two key areas of China's participation in the international legal order: its participation in human rights diplomacy and its membership in the World Trade Organization.

As Potter points out, China's participation in the international legal order cannot be separated from aspects of its domestic legal order. The norms of the international human rights and trade regimes must find some resonance domestically for participation to be meaningful. At the same time, complete congruence is neither to be expected nor even possible. China's policy of engagement reflects a conscious decision to be a part of the international norm-creation process instead of being faced with the choice of simply accepting or rejecting norms made by others. China wants to influence norm-creation precisely because its government does not accept the current norm structure *in toto*. Yet it must accept some parts of that structure, even parts it does not like, in order to be on the inside.

That much could perhaps be said for any country that participates in international legal institutions. But for China there is an additional element: in some areas and to some degree, international participation is a tool used by the central government to enhance its power over local governments. This is most clearly the case with China's WTO membership. Although China is a unitary state in which all power is formally in the hands of the central government, local governments often have considerable de facto powers of their own. While WTO membership does not, of course, give the central government any powers over local governments that it did not already have, it is still meaningful in that it gives added legitimacy to certain claims of the central government. Moreover, by placing itself under WTO disciplines and in effect tying its own hands, the central government can enhance its bargaining power with local governments in trying, for example, to remove local trade barriers.

In common with many of the other authors in this issue, Potter shows that while major changes have occurred in some areas, customs and practices in others remain remarkably resilient. For example, principles of transparency and accountability have made little headway over the years. While they have received much publicity as good policy, mandatory standards are virtually non-existent,[21] and where they exist, not observed.[22] Thus, while some WTO standards may be easily accepted, others will face much more resistance of an almost cultural kind.

In his comments, Li Zhaojie confirms Potter's observation that the PRC has essentially moved from the position of "victim-minded underdog" to that of "active status-quo keeper." The system as a whole is viewed as conforming to China's interests. He also notes the important role that international norms play in shaping China's domestic legal system. While many legal and policy reforms might have taken place even without WTO membership, it seems clear that it made them happen sooner. Even apart from the mandatory norms of the WTO, international norms are having their effect: Li observes that many proposals made and measures taken in the reform of China's criminal procedure law have their roots in the standards of international human rights law. Whether in the field of trade or that of human rights, Chinese political culture seems generally to accept an appeal to international law norms as a legitimate (if not necessarily overwhelming) argument in favour of a policy position. This certainly represents a sea change from just a few decades ago.

Julia Qin's contribution to this issue also addresses the interaction between domestic and international legal norms in a specific area: she looks at the way China's membership in the World Trade Organization and its concomitant international law obligations have affected its domestic legal system.

Assessing the significance of China's WTO membership requires an analysis of several issues. First, just how extensive are China's commitments, both relative to its pre-membership economic and political structure and relative to what has been demanded of other entering members? Secondly, to the extent that these commitments go beyond what has been required of other entering members, is their imposition unfair or otherwise undesirable, or is it an appropriate response to legitimate concerns about China's impact on world trading patterns once inside the WTO? Thirdly, to what extent will China's commitments dictate its domestic policies, and to what extent are the commitments themselves the result of domestic policies of economic reform

21 Even in such an apparently non-sensitive area such as real estate, the recently passed Property Law states in Article 18 that only right-holders and "parties with an interest" (*lihai guanxi ren*) may inspect ownership records. In effect, registration authorities have the power to refuse access if they determine that an individual's interest is not legitimate. A similar reluctance to allow unfettered public access to corporate registration records prevails at offices of the State Administration of Industry and Commerce. Law-making is similarly opaque: while various regulations call for public participation, no specific format is required and the obligation is vague. Article 12 of the State Council's 2001 Regulations on the Procedure for the Formulation of Administrative Regulations (*Xingzheng fagui zhiding chengxu tiaoli*), for example, calls for the seeking of citizen comments through such methods as discussion groups and hearings. Yet ironically, the draft text of the State Council's own regulations on transparency was kept a close secret, making meaningful citizen comment impossible. Mure Dickie, "China refuses to be open on transparency," *Financial Times*, 18 January 2007.

22 The most obvious example here is that of trials, which – almost 30 years after the 1979 Court Organization Law called for open trials – are still not truly open in the sense that courts are obliged to allow access impartially, even to those they would prefer to keep out.

– that is, policies that would have been adopted even without the spur of WTO membership? Finally, what is the domestic legal effect of China's WTO commitments?

The last question is perhaps the easiest to answer. Although Chinese law has not been crystal-clear on the point, Qin notes that a consensus has emerged that the WTO agreements do not have a direct legal effect domestically, and must instead be implemented through enabling legislation – the same position adopted by, among others, the United States.

The first question is also relatively uncontroversial: the scope of China's commitments is remarkable, exceeding in many cases the basic requirements of the various WTO agreements and going beyond what has been required of other entering members. For example, although the WTO is generally about trade and is not an investment agreement, China made extensive commitments to liberalize its rules on foreign investment through undertaking obligations under the General Agreement on Trade in Services. It agreed to provide foreign investors and foreign-invested enterprises with national treatment in certain respects, such as the procurement of goods and services necessary for production, a commitment not made by any other WTO member. China has also agreed to be liable to safeguard measures directed specifically at Chinese products in case of export surges; safeguard measures directed at products from any other country must be applied on a non-discriminatory basis against all like products from any source.

What is more controversial is whether the imposition of these commitments is justified by China's unique size and the huge role of the state in its economy, or whether the so-called "WTO-plus" commitments represent nothing more than protectionist forces in China's trading partners taking whatever they have the practical power to take. There is also room for controversy over whether certain government policies can in a sense be blamed on the WTO accession agreement, or whether they would have been adopted by the government in any case as unavoidable components of economic reform.

However one looks at these questions, Qin shows clearly that China's commitments have had a large impact on its domestic legal system even without being directly enforceable. Indeed, she argues that China's commitments have in a sense constitutionalized the current policy of economic reform and made reversal of this course not only difficult domestically but also a violation of China's international law obligations. While such obligations are admittedly only indifferently enforced, they nevertheless are not without weight. In particular, not only have policies such as marketization and free pricing been constitutionalized, but certain procedural values such as transparency have also been widely publicized and, if not yet the norm in practice, have become yardsticks against which the actions of government are measured.

In short, Qin's argument leads to the conclusion that to ask whether China's WTO obligations are directly enforceable in domestic law may be to miss the point. Enforceable or not, they are having an effect on the domestic economic and political system and on the discourse of state regulation of the economy.

Commentator Huang Dongli endorses Qin's argument that China's WTO obligations have had a genuine effect on domestic political discourse, making it less acceptable to argue, as have some in the controversy over the Property Law, that economic reforms are contrary to socialism or should be rolled back.[23] Like Qin, she observes that China's WTO obligations, even if unenforceable domestically and of limited enforceability internationally,[24] have important domestic legal effects. For example, the WTO's requirement of independent judicial review of administrative agency actions triggered a discussion in China about existing practices of judicial review. Whether or not China's courts can be called independent, WTO membership has made genuine independence a legitimate standard against which to measure them.

Conclusion

The years since the 1995 special issue have been years of extraordinary change within the Chinese legal system – as perhaps could be said about any 12-year span in the post-Mao era. But a key theme emerging from the contributions to this special issue is the high degree of continuity in many areas – perhaps equally extraordinary, given the great changes taking place in other parts of Chinese society. A similar resilience can be seen, of course, in China's political institutions. The observation that the Chinese legal system is tightly politically controlled is not new. These contributions reinforce that observation; more intriguingly, they suggest by implication that significant changes in the legal system might be signs of truly significant changes in the political system as well.

23 Mure Dickie, "China delays property law amid rights dispute," *Financial Times*, 9 March 2006 (discussing Beijing University law professor Gong Xiantian's criticism of the draft Property Law on constitutional grounds).

24 An aggrieved WTO member must go through an extended dispute settlement process; even if it wins, the most it can do is to take WTO-sanctioned retaliatory countermeasures against the offending country, something it could do freely if either party were not a WTO member. In this sense, WTO membership does not expose a country to greater coercion from its trading partners than it would face outside the WTO.

Legislating for a Market Economy in China

Donald C. Clarke

ABSTRACT Since the early 1990s, China has come a long way in legislating the foundational rules for its reformed economy. Virtually all of the important areas – contracts, business organizations, securities, bankruptcy and secured transactions, to name a few – are now covered by national legislation as well as lower-level regulations. Yet an important feature of a legal structure suited to a market economy is missing: the ability of the system to generate from below solutions to problems not adequately dealt with by existing legislation. The top-down model that has dominated Chinese law reform efforts to date can only do so much. What is needed now is a more welcoming attitude to market-generated solutions to the gaps and other problems that will invariably exist in legislation. The state's distrust of civil-society institutions and other bottom-up initiatives suggests, however, that this different approach will not come easily.

This article aims to provide a review and assessment of developments since the early 1990s in the realm of legal regulation of economic activity in China. This regulation has two aspects: first, the substantive content of the rules themselves (for example, norms that discourage monopoly and promote competition), and second, the institutions, both legal and non-legal, that make state rulemaking effective or obviate the need for it through alternative mechanisms. The main thesis of this article is that in the era under review, China has accomplished far more by way of rulemaking than it has by way of institution-building.

In assessing developments in any realm of activity, one must have a standard against which to measure those developments. One cannot speak of incompleteness or gaps without having a picture of completeness or gaplessness, but where does the picture come from? When economic reform began, it is unlikely that Deng Xiaoping or anyone else in the Chinese leadership imagined what China some three decades later would look like; it is not plausible to posit today's China as a goal of economic reform from the very beginning.

Yet it seems that certain goals have developed in the course of economic reform itself. While it would be difficult at present to identify a single goal for economic and institutional reform held by virtually all China's leaders, it is probably safe to say that most would support further marketization of the economy and greater scope for China's private sector, at least to the extent that it did not affect the Party's political monopoly. Thus, this article will look at developments in the legal regulation of economic activity primarily through that

 doi:10.1017/S0305741007001579

lens: how they have promoted or obstructed the further development of China's market economy and opened up space for its private sector. It will also assess China's approach generally to promotion of the market economy through legal institution-building. The focus will be on developments since 1992, because that year marked the end of the post-June 4th retrenchment and the beginning of a new period of economic reform that is still with us.

A useful way of thinking about government's involvement in economic development is via the models of state-driven and market-driven development.[1] In state-driven development, the state plays a leading role in law reform. It attempts to enact comprehensive laws, often with the advice of foreign experts. In market-driven development, the state establishes the initial conditions necessary to promote the development of the market economy – such as recognizing private property rights and liberalizing trade – but looks largely to non-governmental actors to devise specific legal principles and institutions that will serve the market. This model does not require state efforts to construct a comprehensive legal framework at the beginning of the reform process, and stresses gradual, piecemeal approval by courts and legislatures of privately created norms.[2] Moreover, it is not law-centred. If legal institutions can perform some function more efficiently than non-legal institutions then they may do so, but there is no inherent bias in favour of or against them. In the concluding section of this article, I will argue that China's path so far has been almost exclusively that of the model of state-driven development, and that more balance is desirable.

Finally, it must be noted that there are perspectives other than that of market economy development from which one could assess changes in the economic legal regime in the era under examination. From the perspective of market economy development, I conclude that while a few gaps remain, and complaints could be made about specific provisions in various statutes and regulations, the work of foundational legislating is almost complete (certainly more so than the work of institution-building). Ironically, however, the growth of the market economy has exposed a number of gaps in other areas of the legal system, such as labour and environmental protection and the social safety net. These gaps mattered little in the pre-reform era because they could be addressed, at least in theory, through bureaucratic directives internal to the state-owned economy without the need for a legal system external to the actors. Market-oriented reform has arguably heightened the need for regulation at the same time that it has made regulation by traditional methods ineffective.

1 These models are based on Cooter's models of political modernization and market modernization. The former term does not mean modernization of the political system. See Robert D. Cooter, "Market modernization of law: economic development through decentralized law," in Jagdeep S. Bhandari and Alan O. Sykes (eds.), *Economic Dimensions in International Law: Comparative and Empirical Perspectives* (Cambridge: Cambridge University Press, 1997), pp. 275–316.

2 See William E. Kovacic, "Institutional foundations for economic legal reform in transition economies: the case of competition policy and antitrust enforcement," *Chicago-Kent Law Review*, Vol. 77, No. 1 (2001), p. 265.

Chronology

1978–1992

The post-Mao era of economic reform began with the December 1978 decision of the Third Plenum of the 11th Central Committee of the Communist Party of China to jettison class struggle as the main task of the Party and to adopt a programme of economic reform in its place. The government reoriented its development strategy to reduce investment in heavy industry and to shift resources to agriculture and consumption.

The first phase of economic reform, lasting from 1979 until approximately 1984, did not involve a commitment to markets. Instead, it was essentially an attempt to make the planning system work better. A new Constitution was adopted in December 1984 that was a complete reworking of its 1978 predecessor, but contained no radical innovations in the realm of economic policy. It declared that the basis of China's economic system was socialist public ownership of the means of production, and that the state sector was to be the leading sector of the economy. The "individual economy" – that is, economic activities by self-employed individual entrepreneurs with fewer than eight employees – was called a "supplement" (补充 *buchong*) to the socialist publicly owned economy (Article 11); market activities were ad hoc and provisional. Socialist public property was declared sacred and inviolable, but there was no parallel declaration respecting private property.[3]

Not surprisingly, market-oriented legislation was sparse in this period. The Economic Contract Law was adopted in December 1981, but it was intended largely to regulate relations between state-owned enterprises. Indeed, contracts between individuals were specifically excluded from its ambit. Foreign investment was officially welcomed with the adoption of the Law on Sino-Foreign Equity Joint Ventures in July 1979, but this very short law is better understood as a policy statement for the guidance of foreign investors than as part of a market-oriented legal system. Its rules functioned more as starting points for negotiation than as mandatory norms.

From 1985 to 1989, China saw a second stage of economic reform in which the market was more fully and openly embraced as a critical component of the economy. This stage also saw the emergence of the private sector, with a rise in the number of privately run and "red hat" enterprises.[4] In October 1987, the 13th Congress of the CCP recognized the private economy (not just the economy of individual entrepreneurs) as a necessary supplement to the state sector, and in 1988 the Constitution was revised: to the existing acceptance of the "individual" economy was added the acceptance of the "private" (*siying* 私营) economy.

3 A great deal of controversy was caused by the 2007 Property Law's giving of equal status to public and private property.

4 Barbara Krug and Hans Hendrischke, "Entrepreneurship in China: institutions, organisational identity and survival. Empirical results from two provinces," *Erasmus Research Institute of Management Report Series*, Reference No. ERS-2002-14-ORG (January 2002), available on http://ssrn.com/abstract=370955.

In 1986, the General Principles of Civil Law were adopted. This statute was an important contribution to the provision of basic legal principles for the operation of a market economy, since it presupposes a universe of individual actors making decisions based upon free will – the antithesis of the universe of the planned economy. It did not, however, contain detailed rules in important areas such as contract, tort and property. The legal regime in those areas continues to be composed of separate regulations promulgated by various bodies.

Contract law continued to develop with the adoption in March 1985 of the Foreign Economic Contract Law, which covered contracts between Chinese entities and foreign parties. The following year saw the adoption of the Law on Wholly Foreign-Owned Enterprises, which for the first time allowed an enterprise organized under Chinese law to be wholly owned by one or more foreign investors, with no Chinese equity participation. In 1988, the basic legal landscape for foreign-invested enterprises was completed with the adoption of the Law on Sino-Foreign Co-operative Joint Ventures, which allowed for a joint venture with more flexible features than were allowed under the Law on Sino-Foreign Equity Joint Ventures.

In the realm of domestic enterprise law, in December 1986 China adopted the Enterprise Bankruptcy Law (effective in 1988). Despite its name, this is less a law about bankruptcy than a statement of policy about closing down SOEs in certain circumstances. Its main purpose, as contemporary commentary made clear, was not to protect creditors or to assist in the reallocation of inefficiently used capital, but to improve SOE performance through the threat of closure. After many years of controversy and false starts, this law was substantially revised in August 2006; the revisions are discussed further below.

An important legislative step was made in improving the business environment for private entrepreneurship with the adoption in August 1987 of the Provisional Regulations on the Administration of Urban and Township Individual Industrial and Commercial Households. These regulations provided some legal form to small sole proprietorships in addition to signifying state approval of their existence. In addition to stipulating some limitations in the form of needed permits, the regulations also provided some protections.

June 1988 saw the adoption by the State Council of the Provisional Regulations on Private Enterprises. These regulations, still in effect today although seriously dated, legitimize sole proprietorships, partnerships, and limited liability companies with eight or more employees. However, only a limited class of persons is eligible to form such enterprises, such as farmers, the urban unemployed and the retired. Over the years, local implementing regulations have for all practical purposes largely abolished these limitations. At the time of their adoption, however, the regulations reflected a view that private enterprises are not a normal part of economic life, but a supplementary part to be operated by those who are not fully participating members of the urban socialist economy. Thus, their organizational problems were not seen as the concern of a major legislative body such as the National People's Congress; they were more of a technical problem to be solved by administrators at the State Council.

An important step in the marketization of the economy, from both a legal-system and a policy perspective, came with the April 1988 amendment of the Constitution to sanction the granting of long-term land leases in state-owned land. This was a key step in the commoditization of land and allowed governments at various levels to reap significant revenues. At the same time, it made land use more subject to market forces and less subject to bureaucratic priorities.

The third stage of economic reform, from 1989 to 1992, is in fact more a period of post-June 4th retrenchment. This stage saw an attempt to undertake a significant rollback of economic reforms, recentralize, and strengthen economic planning. The attempt did not last long, however, and momentum for reform had begun to build anew by the end of 1990. Already in May 1990, for example, the Provisional Regulations on the Grant and Transfer of Use Rights in Urban Land provided the statutory framework for the commoditization of urban land. The regulations provided that long-term leases from the state of up to 70 years could be granted and subsequently transferred relatively freely.

1992 to the present

The fourth and current stage of economic reform dates from the end of the retrenchment period, marked most explicitly by Deng Xiaoping's Southern Tour in early 1992. During this period, economic reform and markets have been fully embraced once more, and China has taken major steps to create an economic and legal system that fully and explicitly embraces the private sector as an important component of the economy. The system envisages a rules-based market operating through the institutionalization of property rights, and this period has seen the rapid development of private firms and the building of market institutions and associated laws. The tenor of the period is aptly symbolized by the CCP's endorsement of the "socialist market economy" at its 14th Congress in October 1992 and by the March 1993 amendment of Article 15 of the Constitution, which replaced the reference to the "supplementary role" of the market with the straightforward declaration that "the state practises the socialist market economy." Articles 16 and 17 were also amended to eliminate the duty of SOEs and collective enterprises to fulfil the state plan. While these constitutional duties had never been legally binding in a realistic sense, their elimination was nevertheless symbolically important.

The Constitution was further revised in March 1999 in two other symbolically important ways. First, the concept of "rule of law" was written into it. The words, of course, do not by themselves mean any change in the role of the legal system. But they do represent a policy declaration by the government that the legal system is to be given greater weight as a technique of governing.

Second, Article 6 was amended to acknowledge the contribution of "diverse sectors" of the economy in addition to the publicly owned sector. The amendment also blessed "a variety of modes of distribution" in addition to distribution according to work; this legitimized income such as interest and dividends (which had not been unlawful before, but lacked such high-level sanction). Article 11 was amended to label the private, individual and other non-public sectors "major components" of the socialist market economy.

In addition to having a more welcoming attitude towards the private sector – perhaps symbolized most strongly by Jiang Zemin's announcement in 2001 that private entrepreneurs could become Party members – legal reform in this era has been distinctive in that it has seen the construction of the legal infrastructure of a rules-based market system in which distinctions between state and non-state actors, as well as between Chinese and foreign actors, are gradually being eroded.

In May 1992, China took an important step forward in the law of business organization when the State Commission on Reform of the Economic System (SCRES) adopted its Normative Opinion on Joint Stock Companies. This document was in effect half of China's first post-1949 general company law, and provided an organizational vehicle for enterprises – SCRES had state-owned enterprises in mind – that wished to restructure and list shares on the stock exchanges. One year later, in April 1993, the State Council issued the Provisional Regulations on the Administration of the Issuance and Trading of Stock, in effect China's first law on securities and a necessary complement to the Normative Opinion. The Provisional Regulations were supplemented but (rather curiously) not abolished by the Securities Law, adopted in December 1998 and substantially revised in October 2005.

The second half of China's proto-company law was the Normative Opinion on Limited Liability Companies adopted by SCRES at the same time. This document provided an organizational vehicle for enterprises that wished to restructure into companies with investors holding equity shares, but did not wish to list on the stock exchanges. Both Normative Opinions were superseded by the Company Law, adopted in December 1993 and substantially amended in October 2005. This law formalized the classification of companies into two types: the joint stock company (*gufen youxian gongsi* 股份有限公司), intended for large pools of assets with liquid and tradable equity interests, and the limited liability company (*youxian zeren gongsi* 有限责任公司), intended for smaller entities in which the investors could be more like partners than mutually anonymous shareholders.

The Company Law was followed in February 1997 by the Law on Partnership Enterprises (Partnership Law). Partnership law has an important role to play in an economy that wishes to encourage entrepreneurship and small business. Among other things, it provides a set of default rules for the type of informal organization that springs up any time two or more people decide to go into business together when they have neither the time nor the expertise to think hard about the precise governance rules they desire.

The 1997 Partnership Law was not business-friendly. It contemplated partnerships as relatively formal organizations, and its provisions tended to be mandatory rules instead of default rules that could be changed at the will of the partners. It was never clear whether entities other than natural persons could be partners,[5] and partnerships were taxed like corporations until 2000.[6] Perhaps as a result, as of early 2006 only some 60,000 partnerships had been formed since the law came into effect in August 1997.[7]

In response to the market's lack of enthusiasm, the Partnership Law was substantially revised in August 2006. The revisions clarify that legal persons can indeed be partners and that partnership income shall be taxable only to the partners and not to the partnership. Perhaps more importantly, the revisions allow for limited partnerships and, in certain sectors, something akin to a limited liability partnership.[8] In short, the new law is clearly an attempt to foster business activity through providing a larger menu of organizational forms.[9]

China also adopted a Law on Individual Wholly-Owned Enterprises in August 1999 in order to provide a legal framework for certain types of sole proprietorships. Like the Partnership Law, this law specifies that investors shall *not* enjoy limited liability. Also like the original Partnership Law, it seems designed to regulate more than to enable, and it is not clear that it fills a pressing business need.

An important legal institution in promoting flexibility in private and business relationships is the trust. The law of trusts provides a set of background rules when for various reasons it makes sense to have assets legally owned by one person but managed for the benefit of another. China adopted a Law on Trusts in April 2001; while the law leaves some important questions unanswered – who, for example, is responsible for taxes on income earned by trust assets? – and is necessarily vague with respect to fiduciary standards, nevertheless it represents

5 Although the original Partnership Law was not unambiguously clear on this point, the consensus of subsequent practice was that partners had to be natural persons. See Zhu Shaoping, "Tan hehuo qiye fa xiugai" ("A discussion of the revision of the Partnership Law"), *Zhongguo renda wang* (*China National People's Congress Net*), 26 April 2006, available on http://www.npc.gov.cn/zgrdw/common/zw.jsp?label=WXZLK&id=348775&pdmc=1131; see also Wang Xiang, "Hehuo qiye fa xiugai qingkuang jieshao" ("An introduction to the circumstances of the revision of the Partnership Law"), *Zhongguo renda wang* (*China National People's Congress Net*), 29 August 2006, available on http://www.npc.gov.cn/cwh/common/zw.jsp?label=WXZLK&id=352015&pdmc=hyjc?=undefined.

6 State Council, "Guanyu geren duzi qiye he hehuo qiye zhengshou suodeshui wenti de tongzhi" ("Notice on the question of levying income tax on sole proprietorship enterprises and partnership enterprises"), 20 June 2000, available on http://www.law-lib.com/law/law_view.asp?id=72144. In the United States and many other jurisdictions, partnership income is taxed once, directly to the partners, and not also at the partnership level. In the United States and China, corporate income is generally taxed once when received by the corporation and again when it is distributed to shareholders as a dividend.

7 Zhu Shaoping, "Revision of the Partnership Law."

8 A limited partnership consists of general partners (although there is usually only one) and limited partners. The general partner exercises management power and bears unlimited liability for partnership obligations; the limited partners are passive investors similar to corporate stockholders who are not liable for partnership obligations. A limited liability partnership is internally like an ordinary partnership, but the partners are not liable for the debts of the partnership.

9 Wang Xiang, "Circumstances of the revision of the partnership law."

an important foundation that can be built on through subsequent rulemaking and jurisprudence.

During this period China also adopted a number of laws and regulations establishing some basic market institutions and rules of the game. In March 1999, Chinese contract law was finally unified with the adoption of the Contract Law. This superseded three prior laws: the Economic Contract Law (covering contracts between domestic businesses but not individuals), the Foreign Economic Contract Law (covering contracts in which one party was a foreigner) and the Technology Contract Law (covering technology transfers such as licensing). The Contract Law by and large follows international practice; as with many other Chinese statutes the problem areas are less in the content of the norms than in their implementation.

In May 1995, a Negotiable Instruments Law was passed. Such a law is critical to the smooth functioning of a market economy, since it establishes the rules without which payment systems such as cheques cannot function, thereby reducing the transaction cost of commerce. On the other hand, such a law alone is not sufficient to induce the widespread use of cheques, as their continued relative rarity in China demonstrates. The appropriate accompanying institutions are also needed, such as a central bank like the Federal Reserve Bank that guarantees cheques to its member banks. Because no bank performs this function in China, cheques take much longer to clear.

Further legal support for modern methods of financing was provided by the Security Law, adopted in June 1995. This law made secured lending possible. As with negotiable instruments, however, a law alone is not sufficient and there have been a number of problems with the implementation of the Security Law. Because borrowers may attempt to secure many loans with the same asset, a secured lending regime must provide a means for prior lenders to give, and subsequent lenders to receive, fair notice of the prior lender's interest in the asset so that the prior lender can enjoy priority in repayment. China does not yet have a uniform and unambiguous system for doing this.

Price reform was advanced by the Price Law, adopted in December 1997. It established the principle that the great majority of prices should be set by the market, that is, decided by producers themselves. At the same time, however, the Price Law retains significant vestiges of the producer-oriented planned economy: it contains provisions designed not just to regulate the process by which prices come to be set (as any anti-monopoly law might be said to do), but to ensure that prices are neither too high nor too low.

China also passed several regulations in the field of foreign trade. In May 1994, the Foreign Trade Law was adopted. It provided an important default rule that any good was tradable unless regulations provided otherwise, but was still restrictive in prohibiting natural persons from engaging in foreign trade. It authorized various restrictions on imports and exports, some GATT-compatible and some not. It also provided in principle for anti-dumping and countervailing duties, but with no details as to procedure. Regulations on anti-dumping and countervailing duties were not passed until March 1997; they contained some WTO-incompatible elements and were superseded by WTO-compatible regulations in November 2001, just before China's entry into the WTO in December 2001.

On the eve of WTO entry, China also passed several laws and regulations aimed at regularizing the lawmaking procedure itself, among them the 2000 Law on Legislation. This established in statutory form a hierarchy of legal norms as well as certain procedures.

In December 2001, China finally entered the World Trade Organization. Although some analysts view WTO entry as a major driver of further economic and legal reform in China, it has not been the occasion for major policy changes and is perhaps better seen as a manifestation or effect of China's ongoing economic and legal reforms. WTO accession has affected patterns of business organization and foreign investment, even though neither is covered *per se* by China's commitments. Requirements for local sourcing and export orientation applicable to wholly foreign-owned enterprises but not to joint ventures had to be dropped, with the result that wholly foreign-owned enterprises now dominate new foreign investment projects.[10]

The current era saw another revision to the Constitution in March 2004 giving yet more ideological protection to markets: Article 11 was revised to include the term "non-publicly owned economy" and to provide that this sector was not only permitted but encouraged. Further rhetorical protection for private property was also provided. Nevertheless, progress in the realm of legal acknowledgment and protection of private property rights has been slow. Constitutional provisions by themselves mean little in the Chinese legal system; they are not directly enforceable against the government and are implemented, if at all, only through legislation.

A Rural Land Contracting Law was passed in August 2002. This law – long overdue in a realm that had previously been governed by policy pronouncements – is important both as a policy document and as an element of legal system reform. In terms of policy, it strengthened considerably the rights of farmers against ad hoc readjustments of their contracted land holdings by local officials. In terms of market-oriented legal system reform, its significance lies in furthering the commoditization of rural land by making it easier for farmers to transfer their contract rights. While such contract rights were not, until the passage of the Property Law in March 2007, viewed by the legal system as unambiguous and robust real rights, and land use rights transferred by farmers must still be used for agricultural purposes, the law still increased the potential for circulation of land use rights in a way that encourages their flow to the highest-value user.

Further progress in the commoditization of urban industrial assets was achieved with the establishment in 2003 of the State Asset Supervision and Administration Commission and the adoption by the State Council in March

10 See Organization for Economic Co-operation and Development, *OECD Economic Surveys: China*, Vol. 2005, No. 13 (Paris: OECD Publishing, 2005), p. 85.

2003 of the Provisional Regulations on the Supervision and Administration of Enterprise State-Owned Assets. As a policy matter, the establishment of the Commission was important because it represented the furthest step yet taken in bringing under a single administrative umbrella the state's activities as enterprise owner (as opposed to economic regulator).

In December 2003, the government made important progress in the realm of banking sector reform. First, the Banking Regulation Law established the China Bank Regulatory Commission as the regulator for all banking activities within China. Second, amendments to the Central Banking Law recast the role of the People's Bank of China, following transfer of its regulatory power to the China Bank Regulatory Commission, as that of "setting and implementing monetary policy, preventing and resolving financial risk, and maintaining financial stability."

In the realm of commercial regulation, the Administrative Licensing Law was passed in August 2003. This law established the important principle that the licensing of business activities should be justified only by public necessity – in other words, the mere existence of a business activity is no longer sufficient justification for requiring it to be licensed; some public benefit from a licensing scheme must be shown. There does not yet exist, however, any institutional method of realistically challenging local government determinations that a particular licensing scheme has a public benefit. While the law may over time change the general culture of administrative licensing, then, its immediate effects are likely to be small.

Important legislative support for the private sector came in February 2005 with the State Council's Guidelines on Encouraging and Supporting the Development of the Non-Public Sector Including Individual and Private Enterprises. This policy document provides greater market access to private companies in previously restricted industries, including public utilities, financial services, social services and national defence. In addition – and very importantly – it requires authorities to give equal access in financing to private enterprises.

On the other hand, economic liberalization suffered an important symbolic setback in August 2005, when the progress of the draft Property Law (*wuquan fa* 物权法) towards enactment was derailed following the publication on the internet of an open letter to the Standing Committee of the National People's Congress by Gong Xiantian (巩献田) of the Beijing University Faculty of Law.[11] Professor Gong denounced the draft as unconstitutional and contrary to principles of socialism. Nevertheless, despite continuing opposition and controversy, the Property Law was finally passed at the March 2007 session of the National People's Congress.[12]

11 See Gong Xiantian, "Yibu weibei xianfa de 'wuquan fa (caoan)': wei 'xianfa' di 12 tiao he 86 nian 'minfa tongze' di 73 tiao de feichu xie de gongkai xin" ("A draft Property Law that violates the Constitution: open letter written upon the abolition of Article 12 of the Constitution and Article 73 of the 1986 General Principles of Civil Law"), 12 August 2005, available on http://www.chinaelections.org/NewsInfo.asp?NewsID=45986.

12 Joseph Kahn, "China approves property law, strengthening its middle class," *New York Times*, 16 March 2007, available on http://www.nytimes.com.

At the same time as the debate over the draft Property Law, voices calling for more controls over foreign investment were also getting a sympathetic hearing,[13] and in August 2006 the Ministry of Commerce published rules governing foreign takeovers of Chinese companies that provide for extensive review powers in the interest of protecting "national economic security."[14]

Taken together, these developments hint that it is too early to assume that the path to further reform is clear and largely uncontested. Opposition to further reforms in the direction of markets and increased openings for the private sector may be more deep-rooted than hitherto supposed, and this opposition might be able to link up with the strain of economic nationalism demonstrated in the controversy over foreign acquisitions of Chinese firms. At the time of this writing, these developments are little more than straws in the wind. But they bear further watching.

Assessment of Recent Developments

The relationship between legal institutions and economic development

Much of China's work in the establishment of laws and legal institutions related to the economy has doubtless been intended to promote economic growth. Although it has long been posited – since at least the time of Weber – that the right legal institutions promote growth,[15] it has proven surprisingly difficult to demonstrate a causal relationship through empirical research or to shed light on the specific details of what is required.[16]

The relationship between law and economic development is, to say the least, not simple, as the growth of China and other countries that typically score (or in

13 Mure Dickie, "China calls to restrict foreign takeovers," *Financial Times*, 3 August 2006, available on http://www.ft.com. The objections have been phrased in terms of preventing foreign control of strategic industrial sectors and use the language of national security. Ironically, however, the particular case that was a focus of controversy involved a proposed acquisition by Carlyle, an American firm, of Xugong, a Chinese manufacturer of construction equipment – hardly a sector many would view as strategically critical. Geoff Dyer, Sundeep Tucker, and Tom Mitchell, "Foreign deals in China hit new resistance," *Financial Times*, 7 August 2006, available on http://www.ft.com.

14 Mure Dickie and Sundeep Tucker, "Beijing seeks to clarify foreign takeover rules," *Financial Times*, 11 August 2006, available on http://www.ft.com; Li Xiran, "New rule curbs mergers by foreign firms," *Shanghai Daily*, 10 August 2006, available on http://www.shanghaidaily.com/art/2006/08/10/288748/New_rule_curbs_mergers_by_foreign_firms.htm; Guo Qiong, Hu Wang, He Huafeng and Ning Yu, "Waizi bingguo xin gui chongjibo" ("The shock wave of the new rules on acquisitions by foreign investors"), *Caijing zazhi* (*Finance and Economy*), No. 16 (7 August 2006), pp. 80–82.

15 The literature is too vast to be fully cited here. See, among others, Max Rheinstein (ed.), *Max Weber on Law in Economy and Society* (Cambridge, MA: Harvard University Press, 1954), and Douglass C. North, *Institutions, Institutional Change and Economic Performance* (New York: Cambridge University Press, 1990).

16 For good reviews of the literature and the evidence, see Kevin E. Davis and Michael J. Trebilcock, "Legal reforms and development," *Third World Quarterly*, Vol. 22, No. 1 (2001), pp. 21–36; Tom Ginsburg, "Does law matter for economic development? Evidence from East Asia," *Law and Society Review*, Vol. 34, No. 3 (2000), pp. 829–56; and Richard E. Messick, "Judicial reform and economic development: a survey of the issues," *The World Bank Research Observer*, Vol. 14, No. 1 (1999), pp. 117–36.

the past scored) low on various rule-of-law indices demonstrates.[17] Economies can achieve significant growth (at least to a point) without well-functioning markets – consider, for example, the Soviet Union and China itself prior to reform – and informal institutions can go a long way towards making up for the lack of a well-functioning legal system.[18]

On the other hand, perhaps they cannot go the whole way. A study of entrepreneurs in transition economies argues that the scope of transactions beyond what can be achieved through reliance on non-legal institutions is substantial and important.[19] Social networks cost resources to establish, and the trusted middlemen who facilitate transactions don't work for free.

A practical problem for legal system reformers is that while it is plausible that legal institutions matter, it is not clear what their exact shape should be. For example, arbitrariness is bad, but it is simply the other side of the coin of discretion and flexibility, which are often good. Institutions that make it difficult for government to change policy rapidly may help economic development by making government commitments credible; they may also hurt it by hindering the government's ability to respond effectively to economic crises or rapid change.[20] Nor can there be a single right answer: particularly in some developing countries, maintaining credibility may be worth paying a price in terms of flexibility, but the right balance will always be context-dependent.

Given the variety of local circumstances and institutions, while policy makers should certainly be aware of what are generally considered international "best practices" in many areas of law, they should also be sensitive to local conditions. Moreover, the key is less getting the rules and institutions right at any given time than having a system that allows institutions to change and adapt over time to meet new circumstances.[21]

Thus, while we can of course assess China's current economic legislation and institution-building in terms of their current regulatory content, we should also contemplate whether China is creating an environment that will allow new institutions to arise and existing institutions to adapt or disappear.

17 See, for example, Table 1 in Hiroshi Matsuo, "The rule of law and economic development: a cause or a result?" 2003, available on http://cale.nomolog.nagoya-u.ac.jp/en/files/matsuo/en. Consider also the cases of Japan, South Korea and Taiwan; see Curtis J. Milhaupt, "Law, judicial systems, and economic growth: notes on the uneasy case of Japan," 2000, available on http://www.worldbank.org/wdr/2001/wkshppapers/summer/milhaupt.pdf; John K. Ohnesorge, "Developing development theory: law & development orthodoxies and northeast Asian experience," *University of Wisconsin Law School Legal Studies Research Paper Series*, Paper No. 1024 (2006), available on http://ssrn.com/abstract=916781.

18 See, for example, John McMillan and Christopher Woodruff, "Dispute prevention without courts in Vietnam," *Journal of Law, Economics, and Organization*, Vol. 15, No. 3 (1999), p. 637.

19 John McMillan and Christopher Woodruff, "The central role of entrepreneurs in transition economies," *Journal of Economic Perspectives*, Vol. 16, No. 3 (2002), pp. 153–70.

20 Zhang Xiaobo, "Asymmetric property rights in China's economic growth," *DSGD Discussion Paper No. 28* (Washington, DC: International Food Policy Research Institute, 2006), available on http://ssrn.com/abstract-882446; Matthew Stephenson, "Economic development and the quality of legal institutions," *The World Bank Online*, 2001, available on www1.worldbank.org/publicsector/legal/institutional.htm; Mancur Olsen, *The Rise and Decline of Nations: Economic Growth, Stagflation, and Social Rigidities* (New Haven: Yale University Press, 1982).

21 Lewis S. Davis, "Institutional flexibility and economic growth," 5 December 2005, available on http://ssrn.com/abstract=871759.

Notwithstanding the lack of definitive guidelines offered by empirical research, few would disagree that a modern market economy generally requires the provision of a certain set of functions, whether or not such functions are provided by legal institutions. The sections below examine particular areas of economic regulation discussed in the chronology and evaluate where China stands.

Definition of property rights

Because a market economy is about exchange between freely contracting parties, there must be a set of rules or common understandings governing what can be owned and exchanged. These rules include provisions on property in general, real estate, securities, corporate mergers and acquisitions, and intellectual property.

At the level of ordinary commodities, there is little confusion about what can or cannot be owned, and similarly China's laws on intellectual property establish an adequate definitional framework. On the other hand, there is still work to be done on rights over urban and rural land and over ownership rights in "collectively owned" enterprises; the long-awaited Property Law did little to clarify such rights.

Reduction of barriers to entry and exit

A key step governments can take to promote a market economy is to promote competition by eliminating unnecessary barriers to entry in various sectors of the economy. Significant obstacles to entrepreneurship exist in the form of business licence requirements and high initial capitalization requirements for companies.[22] Until the 2005 revisions to the Company Law, a joint stock company (*gufen youxian gongsi* 股份有限公司) (the form required when there are more than 50 shareholders) was required to have an initial non-withdrawable investment of at least ten million yuan (five million yuan following the revisions).[23] Although the law's goal of striking a balance between the interests of creditors and the facilitation of business activity is unexceptionable, this particular obstacle could be removed without damage to the interests of creditors because they are not in fact significantly protected by initial capitalization requirements.[24]

Institutions enabling market actors to structure transactions as they desire

No government can foresee the various forms that socially beneficial transactions might take, and therefore contract law, while providing some

22 *OECD Economic Surveys: China*, pp. 90 ff.

23 At the exchange rate prevailing during the 12 years the provision was in effect, 10 million yuan amounted to about $1.28 million. During this period, the minimum capitalization required for companies of this kind in the OECD countries was far less: about $42,000 in Germany, and in Delaware, of course, nothing at all. About one-third of OECD countries have no minimum capitalization requirements. *Ibid*. p. 91.

24 Jonathan R. Macey and Luca Enriques, "Creditors versus capital formation: the case against the European legal capital rules," *Cornell Law Review*, Vol. 86, No. 6 (2001).

necessary default rules, should give as much flexibility to the parties as possible. Contract law is different from many other areas of law in that it can assist co-operation and not just resolve conflicts. At the time of contracting, the parties have a common interest in maximizing the size of the pie; their conflict of interest is over how to divide it. In property and tort law, by contrast, the law's concern at any given moment is with the division of an existing pie.[25] Thus there is a strong argument in favour of minimizing state interference in contracting activities if the goal is economic growth.

China's current Contract Law achieves a reasonable balance between flexibility and predictability. But an important way of minimizing problems in any system of contract law and enforcement is to encourage, or at least not restrict, the growth of non-legal institutions that promote the same beneficial exchanges contract law does by providing information and facilitating the free flow of capital, goods and services.

Such institutions can be established by government, and indeed government action may be helpful in overcoming certain market failures.[26] But there is no good economic reason for governments at the same time to block the establishment of competing institutions by non-state actors. Important information, for example, can be provided by accountants and other gate-keepers; credit bureaus tell potential lenders about the reputation of borrowers; and media organizations can provide various kinds of useful information.

At present, the information industry in China is subject to considerable barriers to entry and restrictions on operations. The government has stopped, for example, issuing permits for new periodicals (that is, periodical numbers) and a trade has thus sprung up in existing numbers. The limitation of supply, of course, raises costs. The courts have also tended to apply defamation law in a way unfriendly to the free flow of information. *Caijing* (财经), a well-known business journal, lost a libel suit after questioning a firm's accounting practices,[27] and a journalism professor recently won a case against a website that published a blogger's unflattering opinion of him.[28]

The picture is not completely bleak: in a recent libel case based on unfavourable press coverage, the court found that journalists should be immune from suit if their reporting is backed by a source that is reasonable and credible

25 Paul H. Rubin, "Growing a legal system in the post-communist economies," *Cornell International Law Journal*, Vol. 27, No. 1 (1994), p. 4. I am grateful to an anonymous reader for pointing out that property and tort law, properly designed, can spur activities that enlarge the social pie. The innovation encouraged by protection for intellectual property is one example.

26 On the potential for helpful government action in credit reporting, for example, see Messick, "Judicial reform and economic development," p. 21, and the sources cited therein.

27 Benjamin Liebman, "Innovation through intimidation: an empirical account of defamation litigation in China," *Harvard International Law Journal*, Vol. 47, No. 1 (2006), p. 69.

28 See "'Zhongguo boke di yi an': fu jiaoshou xiang wangluo manma xuanzhan" ("First Chinese blog case: assistant professor declares war on web vituperation"), *Xinhuanet*, 2 February 2006, available on http://news.xinhuanet.com/legal/2006-02/10/content_4161160.htm; "Professor wins suit against blog site," *Associated Press*, 4 August 2006, available on http://www.breitbart.com/news/2006/08/04/D8J9JK602.html; Donald C. Clarke, "Journalism professor wins defamation suit against blog host," *Chinese Law Prof Blog*, 10 November 2006, available on http://tinyurl.com/tc65s.

and not based simply on rumours.[29] Nevertheless, while different views may legitimately exist on the appropriate trade-off between the value of freely flowing information and the value of protecting reputation and dignity, courts and commentators in China continue to pay inadequate attention to the costs of a system that protects plaintiffs from the publication even of merely unflattering opinions.

Institutions imposing standards on the market in the public interest

Not all market transactions serve the public interest. For example, agreements between producers not to compete are market transactions but are prohibited in many jurisdictions. As in many realms of market regulation, state prohibitions have a mix of costs and benefits that are unique to each country. Nevertheless, some clarity in the rules as well as adaptability to new circumstances would seem to have only benefits.

In this realm, there is still a substantial amount of work to be done in lawmaking in China. In the realm of competition policy, several drafts of an Anti-Monopoly Law have been circulated but so far no final law has been promulgated. There is disagreement about how the competition policy regulator should be constituted as well as over substantive provisions in the law. It may be that it is trying to do too much, and should instead start with basic problems such as collusion to fix prices before attempting to regulate more complex (and from a welfare standpoint more ambiguous) arrangements such as vertical restraints or price discrimination.[30] And commentators have pointed out that various drafts, instead of focusing solely on competition issues, attempt to ensure "fair" prices (including prices that are not "too low") and to achieve other social objectives as well that would be better accomplished through separate legislation.[31]

While state policy makers naturally tend to think of lawmaking as a solution to problems, in fact many pro-competition objectives can be achieved without anti-monopoly regulation and an enforcement bureaucracy at all. As discussed above, trade liberalization measures such as reducing barriers to domestic entry and to imported goods and services, as well as enhancing the flow of

29 The case in question pitted the Guangzhou Huaqiao Real Estate Development Company against the journal *China Reform*. Excerpts from the text of the judgement as well as commentary by prominent attorney Pu Zhiqiang, who appeared for the defendants, can be found at http://www.epochtimes.com/gb/4/10/18/n694419.htm. For further sources, see Liebman, "Innovation through intimidation," appendix B, case 185.

30 Kovacic, "Foundations for economic legal reform."

31 See American Bar Association (ABA) Sections of Antitrust Law and International Law and Practice, "Joint submission on the proposed anti-monopoly law of the People's Republic of China," 15 July 2003, available on http://www.abanet.org/intlaw/committees/business_regulation/antitrust/abaprcatfinalcombo.pdf; see also ABA Sections of Antitrust Law, Intellectual Property Law and International Law, "Joint submission on the proposed anti-monopoly law of the People's Republic of China," 15 May 2005, available on http://www.abanet.org/intlaw/committees/business_regulation/antitrust/chinacommentsantimonopoly.pdf.

information, will generally be far more effective than legal regulation through prohibitions and penalties.

Bankruptcy law was until quite recently mired in controversy, although in serious need of updating. A minimal set of rules was in place for several years: the Enterprise Bankruptcy Law, adopted in late 1986 and effective in 1988, covered state-owned enterprises, and a chapter of the Civil Procedure Law covered other legal persons. However, such laws did not appear to apply to actual bankruptcies, which were governed far more by state policy than by legal rules. In August 2006, a substantially revised Enterprise Bankruptcy Law was finally adopted by the NPC's Standing Committee, to come into effect on 1 January 2007. Somewhat surprisingly, the final version of the law – contrary to provisions in preceding drafts – reaffirmed the principle of priority for secured creditors over claims for unpaid wages. Although this principle was also explicit in previously applicable NPC legislation, it had been seriously compromised through a series of State Council directives providing otherwise.[32] It is still too soon to know whether the new law will, like its predecessor, be overridden in practice by administrative directives and political imperatives.

Two more types of mandatory regulation that should be discussed are the regulation of securities and organizational laws for business. Securities regulation could be handled entirely as a matter of contract between the seller of securities and the buyer, but no modern economy has taken this route and there is a public-good element to securities regulation. For this and other reasons, China's Securities Law can be considered a useful framework. Without discussing it in detail, the main point is that China's securities regulatory regime is still heavily oriented to serving the interests of state-owned enterprises that convert to joint stock companies and list securities on one of China's two stock exchanges.[33] Thus, an important even if unstated part of the mission of the China Securities Regulatory Commission is to keep stock prices up, and not simply to ensure the fair, orderly and transparent operation of securities markets. But the former goal may conflict with the latter. While China need not import wholesale any country's model of securities regulation, its own model should indeed be about *securities regulation*, and not the quite different goal of facilitating the reform of state-owned enterprises. The institutions and policies that might serve the former goal well – such as a relatively independent administrative agency, an emphasis on disclosure as opposed to substantive regulation, or decentralized enforcement through citizen lawsuits – might be quite unsuited to the latter.

32 In 1994 and 1997, the State Council issued two Notices, the collective effect of which was to override certain priorities and rights provided in the Bankruptcy Law and the Security Law. Although formally subordinate to NPC legislation, State Council directives will in practice override it in case of conflict. For a discussion of these issues, see Donald C. Clarke, "State council notice nullifies statutory rights of creditors," *East Asian Executive Reports*, Vol. 19, No. 1 (15 April 1997), pp. 9–15.

33 Sebastian Heilmann, "The Chinese stock market: pitfalls of a policy-driven market," *China Analysis*, No. 15 (2002), available on http://www.chinapolitik.de/studien/china_analysis/no_15.pdf.

Corporate law is also about more than simply voluntary associations among individuals; without state law, it would be impossible for the institution of limited liability to function as it does.[34] Moreover, law for business organizations – whether corporations, partnerships or some other form – can reduce the transaction costs of organizing by providing a set of default rules of governance.

While China's Company Law provides limited liability to properly organized companies, legislation on business organizations generally – including laws on partnerships and other business forms – does less well in providing a low-cost vehicle for the conduct of business. As discussed above, barriers to corporate formation are unnecessarily high. Creditors are protected by a business's current net assets and future success, not by the amount of cash originally invested. The August 2006 revisions to the Partnership Law, however, do add to the menu of business vehicles and thus constitute progress from this perspective.

Conclusion

The introduction to this article identified the models of state-driven and market-driven development. Neither model in its extreme form is appropriate for China or any other country. At the same time, however, it must be recognized that in China market-driven development has not been attempted at all. In both models, the goal is to serve the needs of the market economy. In state-driven development, that is the whole point of seeking foreign advice on lawmaking. But as Alford points out, while multilateral financial institutions and economists are sceptical of the ability of Western politicians to get it right when they regulate economic activity, they seem oddly to have more faith in the ability of Chinese politicians, who after all have much less direct experience of a market economy and the workings of civil society, to put their prescriptions into effect.[35]

China has so far followed state-driven development almost exclusively. This model has by no means been a failure, in that it does not seem to have stifled growth significantly. But neither can it be conclusively be called a success, since the degree to which the laws passed and legal institutions established really mattered for China's development has not been demonstrated. The key challenge ahead is not simply to decide what laws are missing and to put them in place, but to establish a set of institutions – or more precisely, to *enable* the establishment of a set of institutions by state or non-state actors – that will be able to respond flexibly to the needs of the market economy. Many of these

34 Henry Hansmann and Reinier Kraakman, "The essential role of organizational law," *Yale Law Journal*, Vol. 110, No. 3 (2000), pp. 387–440.

35 William Alford, "The more law, the more …? Measuring legal reform in the People's Republic of China," in Nicholas C. Hope, Dennis Tao Yang and Mu Yang Li (eds.), *How Far Across the River? Chinese Policy Reform at the Millennium* (Stanford: Stanford University Press, 2003), pp. 122–49.

institutions almost by definition cannot be created by the state; they should be enabled and permitted, but not forced into existence.

What concrete steps might China take? First, institutions that collect and disseminate information contribute to flexibility and adaptability in other institutions, since one cannot adjust to a change one cannot even observe. The unrestricted flow of information has costs: for example, privacy may be compromised. But the suppression of information does as well, and it is important in policymaking to recognize both sets of costs. Whether institutions are being created from the top down or from the bottom up, in general they will function better if the supply of information is better. A policy of furthering information flow is consistent with either approach.

Second, Chinese legislators, legal officials and academics need to be more willing to take local conditions into account. While government officials frequently speak of this need in many contexts, in the realm of lawmaking and legal institutions one often encounters an unwillingness to move beyond existing models. The purpose of China's legal system is to serve China's needs. Legal reforms in continental Europe or the United States are not discussed in terms of whether or not they conform with the civil law or the common law model, and there is no reason for Chinese policy makers to think about legal reforms in such terms, either.

Third, more flexibility in lawmaking would be helpful. At present, there are few if any good ways of discovering and rectifying problems in legislation. The result is that inappropriate and inefficient rules are not weeded out. But because they are widely recognized as inappropriate, actors within the legal system tend simply to ignore them. Although this kind of disobedience by consensus may help the system move forward despite its inefficiencies, it severely hampers the creation of a culture of legality.

Fourth, greater scope should be allowed for contractually agreed dispute settlement procedures between businesses and individuals. At present, dispute settlement is essentially monopolized by the state. Parties must use either courts or state-approved arbitration bodies; ad hoc arbitration bodies have no legal standing and their awards are not enforceable in courts.[36] But government and quasi-government institutions may not be the best fora for dispute settlement; indeed, the number of first-instance civil cases declined from 1999 to 2004, a trend that Liebman plausibly attributes to the public's lack of confidence in courts and not to an increase in social harmony.[37]

If there is indeed a demand for non-court, and by extension non-state, dispute resolution institutions, is it sound policy to satisfy it? Given that China (like other states) does not allow complete freedom of contract, it could be argued that state control over dispute resolution is necessary in order to ensure

36 Article 14 of the Civil Procedure Law states that courts may enforce awards made by arbitration bodies established "according to law." Article 10 of the Arbitration Law requires in effect that arbitration bodies be state-certified.

37 Benjamin Liebman, "China's courts: restricted reform," in this volume.

enforcement of substantive state contract norms. Otherwise, parties not allowed to agree on (for example) a wage below a state-mandated minimum could simply agree to a dispute resolution procedure that would not enforce the state rule. At the same time, however, there are probably many instances where there is no such policy cost to allowing market actors to decide for themselves – provided they agree – on the best way to resolve their disputes. If the state-sponsored institutions are the best venue, they will certainly be used; if they are not the best venue, it does not serve the market economy to force them to be used and to prohibit competition.

China has come an extraordinary distance – further than anyone could have foreseen – since the beginning of economic reform in the late 1970s. Its legislative and administrative bodies have shown remarkable diligence and energy in formulating and adopting rules on a wide variety of subjects, many technically complex. But precisely because of the vast amount of work that has already been done, the returns to yet more work of the same type – consulting experts and enacting comprehensive statutes – are much less than they were. Many laws and institutions are now in place; what the state must now do is to adopt "policies that will allow the law to evolve efficiently. In this scheme, no one need decide ex ante what the outcome of the process will be."[38] Ideally, the outcome will reflect local conditions in China; international best practices may be a reference but should not be a target.

38 Rubin, "Growing a legal system," p. 2.

Commentary on "Legislating for a Market Economy in China"

Xianchu Zhang

Donald Clarke's article provides a pretty full and accurate review of legislative activities in the course of China's economic developments since 1992. His perceptive analysis not only reflects the important achievements of economic legislation and its undeniable contribution to market developments in China, but also critically conceptualizes the many-featured legislative practice within an established theoretic framework with an emphasis on institutional capacity building.

I agree with Clarke on his finding that lawmaking in China, while impressive and dynamic, may only be part of its capacity building, and more developments are needed to allow the institutions of law and market to function effectively. Also, given the size and complexity of China and its unprecedented practice of the so-called "socialist market economy," it is difficult to find a commonly accepted standard to measure China's legislative and economic developments and a candid theory to explain them accurately. I particularly appreciate Clarke's argument that the "political modernization" model as almost the exclusive path of legal reform in China thus far is not law centred. As a result, more legal institutions, rather than bureaucratic measures, should be built up in order to fill the gap between the adopted rules and the challenges of the rapidly developing market. On this basis I would like to make some critical and complementary points on some "Chinese characteristics" in China's transition towards a market economy[1] and a rule of law state.[2]

First, although there is no doubt that a preliminary legal framework for a market economy in China has been established and has fuelled economic growth, the laws adopted are still limited and there is a considerable gap between them and what happens in practice. While this kind of gap may exist in any legal system, the specific Chinese characteristic in this case is that the gap is more because of the party-state's limited willingness to "permit law to function as a framework to facilitate private transactions" than for other social or economic reasons.[3] The speed of lawmaking has been impressive, but the extent of violations, including counter-measures invented by local governments and corrupt means commonly deployed by private entrepreneurs to circumvent the

1 Article 7 of the 1993 Amendment to the PRC Constitution states that China will practise a socialist market economy.
2 Article 13 of the 1999 Amendment to the PRC Constitution states that China will build up a socialist country under the rule of law.
3 Stanley B. Lubman, *Bird in a Cage: Legal Reform in China after Mao* (Stanford: Stanford University Press, 1999), pp. 300–09.

 doi:10.1017/S0305741007001580

laws and regulations, is equally striking. It is against this background that rapid economic development has been maintained in China. Legal order is definitely needed to streamline market activities, but it needs to be established on a rational basis. In China the "political modernization model" often leads to economic legislation with excessive government control, over-restrictive measures and hostile political ideology. These irrational regulations have invited "violations." Lack of a level playing field between domestic and foreign investors, leading to false foreign investments through foreign entities established by domestic investors,[4] and the high threshold of market access under the Company Law of 1993, causing extensive false corporate registration,[5] are two telling examples. In this context, it may be argued that the economy in China thus far has been dynamically developed on a game-playing basis. Despite the advocacy of the new institutional economics that a good market economy requires "getting institutions right,"[6] some recent studies have shown that considerable economic growth is possible without strong legal institutions, although sustainable development would require their further development.[7]

Secondly, in terms of establishing the legal framework for a market economy in China, the major problem thus far is not legislation but enforcement. There are some infrastructural issues, such as limited financial resources, under-developed professional standards and lack of training and experience. But a more important concern for effective enforcement is the political will of the central and local governments, as well as the Communist Party, to abide by the law and respect market discipline themselves. The second decade of economic reform and legislation continues to see governments' ideological struggle and their strong "instrumentalist" approach. Using government policy to trump the distribution order stipulated by the Bankruptcy Law,[8] carrying out ownership reallocation on the securities market without allowing open debates on the justice and fairness issues,[9] and a recent amendment to the Company Law

4 Angel K. Yan, "China cracks down on false foreign investment," *China News*, 15 June 2006, available at http://english.rednet.cn/c/2006/06/15/916562.htm.

5 Zhu Ciyun, "Statutory minimum capital requirement and adequacy of corporate capital," *Fashang yanjiu* (*Studies in Law and Business*), No. 1 (2004), pp. 17–21.

6 Ronald Coase, "The institutional structure of production," *American Economic Review* (September 1992), pp. 713–19; and Douglas North, "The contribution of the new institutional economics to an understanding of the transition problem," WIDER Annual Lectures, March 1997.

7 Dani Rodrik, "Introduction: what do we learn from country narratives?" in Dani Rodrik (ed.), *In Search of Prosperity: Analytic Narratives on Economic Growth* (Princeton: Princeton University Press, 2003), pp. 15–16; John Ohnesorge, "The rule of law, economic development, and the developmental states of Northeast Asia," in Christoph Antons (ed.), *Law and Development in East and Southeast Asia* (London: Routledge, 2003), pp. 91–130; and Kenneth W. Dam, "China as a test case: is the rule of law essential for economic growth?" John M. Olin Law and Economics Working Paper No. 275 (The Law School of the University of Chicago, 2006), available at http://www.law.uchicago.edu/Lawecon/index.html.

8 The State Council by an administrative decree dated 2 March 1997 provided the top priority for labour claims and settlement over secured creditors, contradicting the rule of the Bankruptcy Law of 1986.

9 In The Joint Guiding Opinion of the China Securities Regulatory Commission, the State Assets Supervisory and Management Commission, the Ministry of Finance, the People's Bank and the Ministry of Commerce dated 23 August 2005 concerning unloading state shares on the market, all the news media were required to "adhere to the correct direction" and to "observe the media disciplines."

mandating companies to provide necessary conditions for the activities of Communist Party branches may be considered the examples of this kind.[10] It may be further noted that a recent report of the World Bank Institute concludes that all major areas of governance in China, including rule of law, regulatory quality and accountability, have deteriorated over the last eight years.[11] Clearly, as marketization and reform develop further the fundamental intrinsic contradiction of the "socialist market economy" will become more obvious.

Thirdly, in the past decade, particularly after China acceded to the WTO, certain aspects of economic legislation seem to have reversed. In the first stage of economic reform the major themes of legislation were decentralization and deregulation. However, in recent years, the legislative tone seems to be more in favour of government control over the market. Since the beginning of the 21st century the Chinese government has been firmly implementing its "national champion" policy to form large state-owned or controlled companies in order to compete with foreign firms in China and internationally. As a result, state-controlled companies have again become a dominant force.[12] Between 2002 and 2005 the number of state-owned enterprises decreased by 20 per cent, to only 11 per cent of total industrial enterprises, but their sales turnover, realized profits and tax revenue contribution to the country's economy reached 35, 45 and 57 per cent respectively.[13] A national plan to form 30–50 super-sized state-owned enterprise groups by 2020 is being implemented.[14] Against this backdrop the struggle of the government to maintain its market monopoly and restrict foreign competition has caused a further delay in the adoption of some urgently needed enactments, such as the Anti-Trust Law, the Telecommunication Law and the Law of State Assets Management, which have all been drafted for more than a decade.

Another important and worrying aspect is the continuing discrimination against the private sector. As compared with the first decade of reform, the development of private business slowed down in the second decade. For example, more than 8 million commercial households have disappeared as a result of government restrictions such as limited market access, excessive approval procedures, financing difficulties and biased policy.[15] Although the

10 See Article 19 of the Company Law of 2005.

11 The Report on Governance and Social Policy of the World Bank Institute is available at http://www.worldbank.org/wbi/governance/pubs/govmatters4.html. The Hong Kong based Political & Economic Risk Consultancy in its 2005 Asian Intelligence Report also showed that the quality of China's legal system slipped back considerably. See the presentation of the Report at http://app.subcourt.gov.sg.

12 Chao Xi, "Transforming Chinese enterprises: ideology, efficiency and instrumentalism in the process of reform," in John Gillespie and Pip Nicholson (eds.), *Socialism and Legal Change: The Dynamics of Vietnamese Renewal and Chinese Reform* (Canberra: Asia Pacific Press, 2005), pp. 91–110.

13 See the answers of the State-Owned Assets Supervision and Administration Commission of the State Council to questions concerning the strategic adjustment of the state capital and reorganization of state-owned enterprises on 18 December 2006, available at http://gov.cn/jrzg/2006-12/18/content_472293.htm (in Chinese).

14 See the report of the website of Ministry of Commerce of 18 November 2005 at http://search.mofcom.gov.cn (in Chinese).

15 See the report in *Zhongguo shangbao* (*China Commercial Daily*), 22 August 2006.

Law of Promoting Small and Mid-Sized Enterprises was promulgated in 2002 and the State Council issued an administrative decree in 2005 further promoting the development of the private sector, progress so far seems very limited. As a result, in some areas private business is even decreasing.[16]

Last but not least, reform over the past 20 years has sent legislation in China, particularly economic legislation, into a new political environment. Twenty years ago the reform policy was widely supported by virtually everyone in the country, but now the polarization of the society with all kinds of conflicting interests has subjected more and more enactments to political controversies. The Property Rights Law and the Enterprise Bankruptcy Law are two good examples in recent years where the issues have been taken out of their legal and commercial context to become political debates.[17] This course has been clearly developed as China increasingly becomes a society with diversified and conflicting interests. In fact, besides the recent official admission of the failure of reform in public health care, education and the power industry, legal reform in China has also come to a crossroads.[18] In this context the current conditions of economic legislation apparently add weight mandating for further political reform.

16 See Ke Liang, "The difficult situation of private enterprises in the period of interest reallocation," *Faren* (*Legal Person Magazine*), No. 8 (2006), pp. 33–35. A recent survey shows that financial support to mid-sized or small private enterprises counted for less than 20% of all the banks' lending in China; available at http://www.cctv.com/program/jjbxs/20060920/101045.shtml (in Chinese).

17 Mure Dickie, " China delays property law amid rights dispute," *Financial Times*, 9 March 2006; Wang Xinxin, "Analytical review on major issues of the new bankruptcy (law) legislation," *Frontiers of Law in China*, No. 1 (2006), pp. 287–91;and Simon Elegant, "China gets a property rights law," Time/CNN report, available at http://www.time.com/time/world/articles/0,8599,1599932,00.html.

18 Jerome A Cohen, "China's legal reform at the crossroads," *Far East Economic Review*, March 2006, pp. 23–27.

New Hope for Corporate Governance in China?

James V. Feinerman

ABSTRACT China's recent revisions to its Company Law and Securities Law have brought new attention to issues of corporate governance in Chinese companies and financial markets. Among the chief criticisms of the earlier laws – in both their provisions and application – were the lack of protection for minority shareholders, the paucity of independent directors, the absence of transparency and inadequate financial disclosure. The acknowledged need for greater congruence between Chinese law and practice and that of countries with more developed capital markets led to the proposal of amendments to China's legislation during the first half of this decade. This article highlights several improvements resulting from the revisions as well as remaining weaknesses in the regulatory framework for corporate enterprises in China.

Corporate governance, *gongsi zhili* (公司治理) has become an increasingly important topic in academic, business and policy discussions in China in the last few years. It is closely related to ongoing economic reform, especially of state-owned enterprises (SOEs), and development of the securities and financial market. Recent revisions of China's Company Law and Securities Law have focused new attention on various aspects of corporate governance, including shareholder voting rights and fiduciary duties. These laws will determine the proper roles of a corporate board and its directors, the rights of shareholders, the fiduciary duties of directors and officers, and the balance between directors' responsibilities and the reasonable protection of directors. While it was not the primary goal in their revision, in their current form they hold out some promise for improving corporate governance in China. Of potentially larger significance are changes they imply for other arenas of life and politics there.

How is corporate governance important for China? Better corporate governance is a vital link in bringing capital to China; affordable capital creates jobs, increases tax revenue, increases shareholder wealth – all leading to an increase in the standard of living. Full disclosure and transparency also serve to promote good corporate governance and capital mobility. In China today it is not possible for any sizeable enterprise to ignore the ramifications of globalization and implications for corporate governance. But there is a conundrum: looking at China, and what it has been able to achieve with relatively poor corporate governance, is there still an argument for a good, or at least better, system? China may present a unique "high risk–high reward"

 doi:10.1017/S0305741007001592

scenario in global corporate governance, with a singular combination of 1.3 billion people, vast resources and economic momentum. Yet the emphasis on the acquisition and deployment of capital raises a question with some salience for China. What makes capital "unaffordable"? In China's case, there are several countervailing forces: scarcity due to policy loans made to underperforming state-owned enterprises; corruption premiums ranging from 20 per cent to as high as 50 per cent for non-transparency[1]; and the basic fact that global demand for capital is greater than the supply.

While there are many factors which influence corporate governance, several important pillars include respect for (and legal protection of): a wide range of stakeholders in the enterprise; the board of directors and its responsibilities; disclosure and transparency; and the rights of shareholders, including their equitable treatment. Yet the essence of corporate governance is doing the right thing whether or not anyone is watching; not doing it because the law says so, but doing it because it's right. Of course, good corporate governance also promotes increased regional and international recognition for Chinese corporations and overall greater prosperity.

As a practical matter, however, there must be incentives to change. For Chinese enterprises, these may include an increasing perception of better performance, higher earnings, more access to affordable capital, reduced tension among stakeholders and other benefits. Legal adjustments may also lead to less government interference with the market mechanisms, which in turn builds trust and confidence by the stakeholders, who will then contribute money, talent and greater vitality to civic life.

This article begins by trying to define (generically and in the Chinese context) corporate governance. A few particular Chinese issues are highlighted, including board issues, shareholders' issues, transparency and disclosure, and monitoring. The article also attempts some preliminary evaluation of the effectiveness of the recently revised Chinese Company Law and Securities Law in dealing with these corporate governance questions.

1 Transparency International, National Integrity System, Transparency International Country Study Report, *China 2006*: "As China is in the process of unprecedented reform and transition in its economic, political and social systems and a proper legal anti-corruption framework is yet to develop, there are still huge opportunities for corruption. Corruption remains a big challenge in China. ... Over-regulation of the economy has impeded the private sector and civil society. Extra-budgetary funds provide opportunities for corruption, and government transparency is limited" (http://www.transparency.org/policy_research/nis/regional/asia_pacific China_nis_2006.pdf, p. 8). Cf. Bernard Black, "The corporate governance behavior and market value of Russian firms," *Emerging Markets Review*, Vol. 2, No. 2 (2001), pp. 89–108. (Study of Russian firms showed that a worst-to-best improvement in corporate governance predicted an astronomical 700-fold (70,000%) increase in firm value!) See also International Finance Corporation, "The irresistible case for corporate governance," March 2006, http://www.ifc.org/ifcext/pepse.nsf/AttachmentsByTitle/IrresistibleCase4CG.pdf/$FILE/IrresistibleCase4CG.pdf.

Defining Objective Corporate Governance Standards

Corporate governance relates to the internal means by which corporations are operated and controlled. In the formulation of the Organization for Economic Co-operation and Development (OECD), an international organization of developed countries that accept the principles of representative democracy and a free market economy:

> Corporate governance is the system by which business corporations are directed and controlled. The corporate governance structure specifies the distribution of rights and responsibilities among different participants in the corporation, such as the board, managers, shareholders and other stakeholders, and spells out the rules and procedures for making decisions on corporate affairs. By doing this, it also provides the structure through which the company objectives are set, and the means of attaining those objectives and monitoring performance.

The corporate governance principles of the OECD[2] are recognized as an influential, objective set of corporate governance principles and represent the first initiative by an inter-governmental organization to develop the core elements of a good corporate governance regime. The principles can be used as a benchmark by governments as they evaluate and improve their laws and regulations. They have also been used by private sector parties that have a role in developing corporate governance systems and best practices.

The OECD principles comprise five themes: protection of shareholders' rights; equitable treatment of all shareholders, including minority and foreign shareholders; recognition of the rights of stakeholders as established by law; ensuring timely and accurate disclosure of all material matters regarding the corporation; and effective monitoring of management by the board, with board accountability to the company and the shareholders. Each of these principles has salience for the current situation in China, since every one of them has proven problematic since the inception of China's corporatizing reforms over the past two decades.

General Observations on Corporate Governance in China

Since China's first Company Law,[3] enacted in 1993 to come into effect in 1994, much has been accomplished in establishing the basic features of corporate governance; however, there is still much to do. While various laws had existed before the Company Law to deal with state, collective and private enterprises and those with foreign investment, the Company Law was the first attempt since 1949 to create limited liability companies without regard to the nature of

2 Available at http://www.oecd.org/dataoecd/32/18/31557724.pdf.

3 The Company Law of the People's Republic of China, *Zhonghua renmin gongheguo gongsi fa*, adopted by the Fifth Session of the Standing Committee of the Eighth National People's Congress, 29 December 1993, effective 1 July 1994; revised at the 18th Meeting of the Standing Committee of the Tenth National People's Congress, 27 October 2005, according to the Decision on Revising the Company Law of the People's Republic of China, at the 11th Meeting of the Standing Committee of the Tenth People's Congress, 28 August 2004.

ownership as part of a modern economic system.[4] In little more than a decade, corporate governance has moved to the centre stage of Chinese enterprise reform. The Fourth Plenum of the Chinese Communist Party's 15th Central Committee held in September 1999 adopted a decision that identified corporate governance as the core of the modern enterprise system. Commitments under the World Trade Organization add some urgency to tackle corporate governance issues in a comprehensive and systematic manner.[5]

However, the current legal framework – even after the recent revisions of the Company Law[6] and the Securities Law[7] – still provides rather limited shareholder protection. In the light of continuing majority government ownership of enterprises, corporations with concentrated ownership still predominate. Small shareholders are inactive in company oversight; government influences management appointments and corporate operations. Too much power remains concentrated in the hands of a few shareholders, and there is – in many instances – a lack of accountability for corporate actions or omissions.

Major issues of corporate governance in Chinese listed companies

The biggest single factor affecting corporate governance in China is state ownership: the Chinese state owns about 50 per cent of all the shares of listed companies. Moreover, during the economy's transition from command to market it is often unclear who represents the state as a shareholder in the listed companies. In addition, transactions between the controlling shareholder (or a group company) and the listed company often disadvantage minority shareholders.

Other issues for corporate governance relate to the directors and officers of Chinese listed companies. For example, most directors are "inside" or executive directors; few companies have many independent directors, leading to insider control. Although Chinese securities regulators attempted to overhaul insider-

4 But see James Feinerman, "Backwards into the future (Securities Law in the People's Republic of China)," *Law and Contemporary Problems*, Vol. 52, No. 3 (1989) pp. 169–84, describing institutions in existence before the enactment of enabling legislation such as the 1994 Company Law and 1999 Securities Law.

5 A study based on empirical evidence and survey data on Shanghai's publicly listed companies concluded that China's approach to corporate governance development may be failing to achieve its objectives and outcomes. These data – gathered before Chinese accession to the WTO – showed the adoption of Anglo-American external market-based models: i.e. a top-down legalistic approach to mandate formal corporate governance structures as the major means to develop modern corporate forms. It remains to be seen whether the problem lies in choosing the wrong model or incomplete implementation of the model chosen. O.K. Tam, "Models of corporate governance for Chinese companies," *Corporate Governance: An International Review*, Vol. 8, No. 1 (2000), pp. 52–64.

6 Revised for the third time at the 18th Session of the Tenth National People's Congress, 27 October 2005.

7 The Securities Law of the People's Republic of China, *Zhonghua renmin gongheguo zhengquan fa*, adopted at the Sixth Meeting of the Standing Committee of the Ninth National People's Congress, 29 December 1998, effective 1 July 1999; revised at the 18th Meeting of the Standing Committee of the Tenth National People's Congress, 27 October 2005 according to the Decision on Revising the Securities Law of the People's Republic of China, at the 11th Meeting of the Standing Committee of the Tenth People's Congress, 28 August 2004.

controlled boards by requiring every listed company to have independent directors forming at least a third of the board, majority power remains extremely concentrated.

Traditionally, executives of PRC companies and other enterprises have been underpaid.[8] Managers of major listed SOEs, still chosen by the government, are often appointed more for political reliability than managerial skill.[9] Lack of a market for professional managers and proper incentives for rewarding performance also influence the quality of management.[10] Information disclosure in many cases is not timely and accurate, and not easily understandable to investors, making it difficult to monitor board and management performance.

The increasing importance of corporate governance reform in China

An overview of China's securities market shows that in December 2006 there were 1,461 companies listed in China.[11] There are two stock exchanges, the Shanghai Stock Exchange and the Shenzhen Stock Exchange, both established in 1990. Total market capitalization reached US$520 billion at the end of 2001, and about US$516 billion by the end of 2002; at the end of 2006, the Shanghai Stock Exchange's capitalization alone was US$915 billion. There were over 65 million investor accounts (5 per cent of the population), 118 securities firms and dozens of fund management firms in China as of mid-2003.[12]

As for the regulatory system, the China Securities Regulatory Commission (CSRC), established in 1992, oversees all the securities business activities in China (including futures). Its headquarters are in Beijing, with 36 regional offices in each province and many major municipalities, and 1,500 employees. The original Securities Law, enacted in July 1999 and significantly amended in 2005 along with the revised Company Law, provides a legal framework for securities regulation. The CSRC's recent and ongoing measures to improve corporate governance include encouraging public companies to get independent

8 Oliver Rui, Michael Firth and Peter Fung, "Corporate governance and CEO compensation in China" (September 2002). Available at SSRN: http://ssrn.com/abstract=337841.

9 Despite attempts to export Western management techniques and training, it has been suggested that the nature of management tasks and the skills required to run Chinese enterprises may entail different learning. Sue Newell, "The transfer of management knowledge to China: building learning communities rather than translating Western textbooks?" *Education & Training*, Vol. 41, No. 67 (1999), pp. 28–29.

10 While in many cases in other countries the primary problem is excessive executive compensation, in China the opposite problem may be more significant: under-compensation of senior managers which would provide a greater incentive to maximize returns for all shareholders. Takao Kato and Cheryl Long, "Executive compensation, firm performance, and corporate governance in China: evidence from firms listed in the Shanghai and Shenzhen Stock Exchanges," IZA Discussion Papers 1767, Institute for the Study of Labor (IZA) (2005).

11 China Securities Regulatory Commission, Statistical Information, http://211.154.210.238/en/statinfo/index_en. China Enterprise Confederation and China Enterprise Directors Association, *China Top 500 Enterprises 2006 Analysis Report*, revealed that 349 enterprises were state owned, nearly 70% of the total. Their combined assets reached 39 trillion yuan (US$4.87 trillion) at the end of 2005, 95% of the total. The state-owned economy remains dominant and controls the leading industries in the national economy. 2 September 2006 http://news3.xinhuanet.com/english/2006-09/02/content_5040531.htm.

12 OECD, "China's securities market," http://www.oecd.org/dataoecd/5/32/18469881.pdf.

directors on board, to adopt a Code of Corporate Governance and to provide better information disclosure. Legal reform protecting shareholder rights through lawsuits, accounting reform and supervision of auditors have also been promoted by the CSRC.

As noted above, one of the chief policies of CSRC regulation was to increase the number of independent directors to company boards.[13] By 30 June 2002, 2,414 independent directors had been elected and appointed by shareholder meetings of listed companies. In a survey of 1,084 firms, 80 per cent appointed two independent directors to their board of directors, and 70 per cent had at least one accounting professional as an independent director.[14]

In 2001, just as the United States was beginning to experience the collapse of a series of corporations from Enron to WorldCom to Global Crossing as a result of corporate governance failures, the exposure of several major Enron-type scandals highlighted the urgency of corporate governance reform in China. The companies involved were leading enterprises and their stock prices performed extremely well before they collapsed. It turns out that profit figures were highly inflated or even fabricated by the directors and management to support the high stock prices and for the purpose of secondary offerings. Subsequent abuses from just one year (2004) included the implosion of the conglomerate D'Long group, the arrest of the chairman and six senior executives of Guangdong Kelon Electrical Holdings for overstating revenues and profits by over 2 billion yuan and a three-year prison sentence for one of China's richest citizens, Zhou Zhengyi, for manipulating share prices and falsifying the registered capital of his company, Nongkai Development Group. Zhou's case also proved an embarrassing setback for the Bank of China's then-recently listed Hong Kong branch and revealed internal-control and governance lapses in the Bank of China Hong Kong branch.[15]

In mid-2006, Guangdong Securities Co. was liquidated after the CSRC lifted its business permit and ordered its closure because of "severe irregularities." The CSRC assigned the China Securities Investors Protection Fund the task of trusteeship and liquidation of Guangdong Securities after share transactions were halted on 4 November 2005. Guangdong Securities was the fifteenth

13 Donald Clarke, "The independent director in Chinese corporate governance," *Delaware Journal of Corporate Law*, Vol. 36, No. 1 (2006) pp. 125–228.

14 See also "China issues new guidelines for listed companies," www.chinaview.cn, 21 March 2006. The China Securities Regulatory Commission (CSRC) issued amended guidelines for the charters of listed companies, first published in 1997. The new guidelines seek to improve corporate governance by limiting the power of executives in order to prevent power abuse or fraudulent transactions. It states that the highest authority in a listed company is the shareholders' meeting, not the board chairman, and that any major decisions must be approved by the shareholders' meeting. Senior managers and employees' representatives must not account for more than half of the directors. Shareholders cannot vote on transactions in which they are involved, and only the shareholders' meeting can appoint accounting firms. Board members, supervisors and senior executives were formerly banned from selling their shares during their tenure. Now they are allowed to sell them one year after the stocks are listed or six months after termination of service. In any given year, they cannot sell more than 25% of their shares.

15 M. O'Neill, "Shame and scandal on the road to riches," *South China Morning Post*, 7 August 2006.

securities firm the CSRC had shut down since August 2004, when it launched a nationwide campaign to crack down on irregularities in the country's problem-plagued securities sector "to protect legitimate rights of investors and creditors."[16]

Even before some of these occurrences, a Code of Corporate Governance for Listed Companies in China had been developed and enforced from January 2002. The Code is mandatory for all listed companies and has been melded into the listing rules of the two stock exchanges. It stipulates the rights and responsibilities of shareholders, directors, the management and stakeholders.[17] In addition, information disclosure is an ongoing responsibility of all the listed companies. All the shareholders have an equal right to receive correct, timely and complete information, and regular disclosure of audited annual reports, mid-year reports and unaudited quarterly reports. Disclosure of corporate governance practices is required in the annual report, along with disclosure of information on the controlling shareholder or the actual controller of the company.[18]

Legal and accounting reform has also been coming to China.[19] Lawsuits have been brought against directors and management. The Supreme People's Court issued provisions in 2001 about procedures for shareholders suing directors and management for losses due to false company disclosure, and the courts have started to accept such cases. Chinese accounting standards are being revised according to international accounting standards.[20] The regulators have strengthened the supervision of auditors, even revoking the licence for the securities business of one of the largest auditing firms in China because of its involvement in a scandal.

Stronger enforcement of existing law and regulations has led to more regular on-site inspection of listed companies concerning accounting, disclosure, related-party transactions and so on. In a given year about 300 firms go through regular inspection; special inspection on compliance with the Code of Corporate Governance has also been enacted. Stronger sanctions include public criticism against violations of laws and regulations; stock exchanges have been given the

16 Xinhua "Liquidation going on with Guangdong Securities Co.," http://english.people.com.cn/200511/08/eng20051108_219901.html.

17 CSRC, "Code of corporate governance for listed companies in China," 7 January 2001 (Zhengjianfa No.1 of 2002). Available in English at http://www.csrc.gov.cn.

18 Yet as Benjamin Liebman has pointed out, the Chinese media, including the business press, often fail to provide an independent source of information despite some de facto autonomy. Commercialization of the media may create conflicting pressures to highlight sensational cases of abuse and at the same time to suppress unfavourable information about potential advertisers and locally important enterprises. Liebman, "Watchdog or demagogue? The media in the Chinese legal system," *Columbia Law Review*, Vol. 105, No. 1 (2005), pp. 1–157.

19 Jason Z. Xiao, Yikuan Zhang and Zhihua Xie, "The making of independent auditing standards in China," *Accounting Horizons*, Vol. 14, No. 1 (2000), p. 69.

20 Nevertheless, studies have found that China's efforts to improve auditing standards were resisted by companies that prefer small local auditors whose political connections may be helpful in gaining regulatory approvals. Qian Wang, T.J. Wong and Lijun Xia, "State ownership, institutional environment and auditor choice: evidence from China" (September 2005), http://www.baf.cuhk.edu.hk/research/cig/pdf_download/WangWongXia.pdf.

power to reprimand listed companies publicly for violations of their listing rules. The CSRC has also established a joint Bureau for Investigation of Securities Crimes with the Ministry of Public Security to prosecute violations of the Securities Law.[21]

Training of directors and investor education is also a focus of recent reforms. Monthly classes for independent director candidates in Shanghai and Beijing train about 5,000 candidates during a typical year. Monthly training courses for existing directors were organized by the two stock exchanges in 2003 to train all directors over three years. The CSRC also sponsors investor education sessions in major cities and through the media, including the internet.

Key Areas for Reform

Comparison of the Chinese market with mature global markets suggests a need for more reform of the system of state asset management to broaden ownership structures and to transform the enterprise management techniques employed by the government from administrative fiat to contract. Easier prospects for listing non-state controlled companies and better procedures for mergers and acquisitions would also be welcome. Regardless of their ownership, listed companies need increased incentives for their management, to expand the management talent pool in China by providing more effective compensation schemes.

Concentrated ownership[22]

In recent years, the three largest shareholders held, on average, about 58 per cent of total shares in listed Chinese companies. In almost half of all firms, the three largest shareholders accounted for 60 to 80 per cent of total shares. In PRC listed companies, the largest shareholder accounts for slightly less than 50 per cent of all shares but controls more than 50 per cent of board seats. Directly or indirectly, the state selects almost 70 per cent of directors of all PRC listed companies. Other jurisdictions recognize a duty of fair dealing by majority shareholders in relation to minority shareholders. Until the most recent reform (and perhaps even afterwards), fiduciary duties of controlling shareholders have not been clearly stipulated in relevant law, and their liabilities for losses incurred by minority shareholders are not obvious.

Recent PRC regulations may introduce this principle implicitly, however, without spelling out liabilities, penalties or the procedures for invoking them.

21 The CSRC has been quick to impose fines under the new Securities Law, which came into effect on 1 January 2006. Maximum fines are between 300,000 and 600,000 yuan. More specifically, in early July 2006, Kelon was fined 600,000 yuan (US$75,000) for providing false information and other offences; its former chairman, Gu Chujun, was fined 300,000 yuan (US$37,500) in mid-July 2006 for a number of "economic crimes."

22 Grace Hu and Marc Goergen, "A study of ownership concentration, control and evolution of Chinese IPO companies," available at SSRN: http://ssrn.com/abstract=286612.

Thus, there continue to be documented abuses by controlling shareholders: taking out soft loans from listed companies on a long-term basis; using listed companies as guarantors for bank loans; and selling assets at unfair prices, usually without an appraisal by an independent evaluator. As noted below, the recently revised Company Law attempts to address these abuses.

Board issues

In general, Chinese directors are insulated from responsibility for their company's economic performance. Their compensation is not linked to it, and they cannot be dismissed prior to the expiration of their terms without "cause," although what constitutes "cause" is not defined. Directors owe duties of good faith and due diligence and care towards the company and its shareholders, although the law does not define these concepts further or create enforcement mechanisms. Compared with practices in other markets, Chinese boards have less decision-making power within the existing legislative framework, while government ministries and commissions, as well as securities regulatory authorities, have substantial decision-making power. Indeed, the range of decisions which must be made by the shareholders' meeting is extraordinarily large by comparison with the corporate law of other jurisdictions, and the discretion left to the board correspondingly narrow.

The Company Law does not stipulate any disclosure obligation on the part of directors or any specific liabilities for directors who fail to perform their obligations. On 16 August 2001 the CSRC issued the Establishment of Independent Director Systems by Listed Companies Guiding Opinion (the Guiding Opinion), requiring that one-third of Board directors be independent. A 1999 survey showed that only about 3 per cent of all directors had some degree of independence; in 2003, following issuance of the Guiding Opinion, the average company still had only three independent directors.[23] Moreover, most listed Chinese companies have no system for establishing board committees, and only a few plan to establish them. Companies that do have them usually have an investment or finance committee, an audit committee, a financial management committee, and/or a strategy committee. They lack nominating committees for directors and corporate governance committees; listed companies do not disclose their procedures for nominating directors or their corporate governance principles. The main functions of the committees that do exist are to decide on major investment projects. Independent committees with supervisory and auditing functions are at an early stage of development. Thus, independent directors would have few opportunities to exercise their independent judgement.

23 Cf. Tong Lu, "Development of system of independent directors and the Chinese experience," http://www.cipe.org/china/development.htm. The author suggests companies facing the new rules established by the CSRC were seeking methods for nominal compliance without implementing the system completely.

Shareholders' issues

The Company Law requires every company to hold an annual shareholders' general meeting. While every shareholder may attend a general meeting, recent data indicate that most attendees are state representatives and representatives of legal persons. Not all companies comply with this requirement, and there are indications that some boards simply ignore the meeting's decisions. Shareholders' general meetings sometimes check decisions with the board before taking action. Anecdotal evidence suggests that only about 20 per cent of company actions are voted upon at the shareholders' general meeting, despite the very wide range of situations in which such a vote seems to be legally required.

A major disincentive for shareholder protection is the fact that the Supreme People's Court allows courts to hear only a very limited class of securities-related claims as class actions.[24] The remedy the Company Law provides to minority shareholders is application to the courts to prevent the continuation of unlawful conduct by directors and majority shareholders. Existing laws and regulations do not specify penalties for corporations and officers that obstruct shareholders' rights to access information. The Securities Law is unclear as to when and whether investors can take civil action against directors and investment professionals for false or negligent disclosures that result in losses.

On 26 December 2002, the Supreme People's Court promulgated the Several Provisions on Trial of Civil Damages Cases Arising from Misrepresentation in the Securities Market (the Provisions),[25] which entered into effect on 1 February 2003. The Provisions extend the Notice on Questions Concerning the Acceptance of Civil Tort Dispute Cases Arising from Misrepresentation in the Securities Market,[26] issued and effective on 15 January 2002. The Provisions discuss acceptance of cases and jurisdictions, methods of bringing lawsuits, determination of misrepresentation, liabilities determination and exemption, joint tort liability and calculation of loss. As defined in the Provisions, misrepresentation can include fraudulent records, misleading statements, material omissions and improper disclosure. The Provisions deal only with misrepresentation made by public companies and not share price manipulation or insider trading.

24 Binglan Xu, "Securities legislation protects investors," *China Daily*, 28 February 2005, http://www.chinadaily.com.cn/english/doc/2005-02/28/content_419958.htm. "In 2003, the Supreme People's Court promulgated a set of guidelines on [class actions], which said the local courts can only accept cases about fabricated statements, which basically ruled out investors' chances for taking listed companies to court for other misbehaviour."

25 "Zuigao renmin fayuan guanyu shenli zhengquan shichang yin xujia chenshu yinfade minshi peichang anjian de ruogan guiding" ("Several provisions on civil compensation cases arising from misrepresentation in the securities market"), 26 December 2002, available at http://xinhuanet.org.

26 "Zuigao renmin fayuan guanyu shouli zhengzhuan shichang yin xujia chenshu yinfa de minshi qinfan jiufen anjian youguan wenti de tongzhi" ("Notice on questions concerning the acceptance of civil tort dispute cases arising from misrepresentation in the securities market"), *Fazhi ribao* (*Legal Daily*), 16 January 2002.

The greatest criticism of the Provisions is that they require the Ministry of Finance, the CSRC or other administrative agencies first to determine an administrative penalty declaring that directors, officers or other corporate actors have misbehaved. Once this decision is issued by the appropriate administrative agency the courts are then empowered to take the civil case. As a result, obtaining a civil remedy is so cumbersome that private enforcement may be all but impossible.

Recent Amendments to the Company Law

The dilemma in Chinese company law, as in corporate law around the world, is that a majority shareholder or majority of the shareholders have the power to control a company. Corporate law has long recognized the need to counter this right so that majority shareholders do not exercise their control to gain disproportionate benefits at the expense of the corporation or non-controlling shareholders.[27] At the same time, opportunistic behaviour by minority shareholders must also be checked. Therefore, corporate law seeks to provide a sensible balance between the control rights of majority shareholders and protecting minority shareholders from abuse.[28]

Protection of shareholders' rights

The recently amended Company Law makes some considerable progress in this direction but still falls short of protecting minority shareholders in some important respects. This is partly the result of the relatively brief corporate history of post-Mao China: companies are few and only very recently established; most public companies' shares are highly concentrated and have a controlling shareholder (or joint controlling shareholders)[29]; the board of directors is controlled by majority shareholders; PRC courts are inexperienced, ineffective and often corrupt; and market and cultural constraints on the controlling shareholders are weak or absent.[30] Most importantly – and not surprisingly – the managers, directors and controlling shareholders of these new companies remain sheltered with the power of the state, since in most cases these companies are reformulated SOEs or parts thereof. If corporate law reform is to have the transformational effect on Chinese society for which some reformers hope, these features will have to change.

27 See e.g. James Cox, Thomas Hazen and F. Hodge O'Neal, *Corporations* (New York: Aspen Law & Business, 1997), pp. 250–58.

28 Bernard Black and Reinier Kraakman, "A self-enforcing model of corporate law," *Harvard Law Review*, Vol. 109, No. 8 (1996) pp. 1911–82.

29 In June 2004, CSRC statistics stated that China had 1,324 listed companies. Of those, one shareholder held more than 50% of the issued shares of 486 companies, and one shareholder held between 20 and 50% of 724 companies. Nicholas C. Howson, "Regulation of companies with publicly listed share capital in the People's Republic of China," *Cornell International Law Journal*, Vol. 38, No. 1 (2005) pp. 237–49.

30 Xiaonian Xu and Yan Wang, "Ownership structure and corporate governance in Chinese stock companies," *China Economic Review*, Vol. 10, No. 1 (1999) pp. 75–98.

Improved corporate governance is a goal of several adjustments in the new Company Law. In general, the revised Company Law creates better rules about shareholders' meetings; it regulates related-party transactions; it provides minority shareholders with some remedies if they are abused; it ensures information rights for minority shareholders; and it reinforces the power of the board of supervisors or other supervisory authorities. Despite these achievements, the revised Company Law also has several failings. Some are continuing lapses and gaps; others are missed opportunities to remedy deficiencies noted in the earlier Company Law. Some of these are detrimental to the protection of the minority shareholders; others do not improve the lot of the majority who control the company.

Article 20 establishes the fiduciary duty[31] owed by the majority shareholders to the minority shareholders by providing a cause of action for the minority shareholders against controlling shareholders. It provides: "Where any of the shareholders of a company causes any loss to the company or to other shareholders by abusing shareholder's rights, it shall be liable for compensation." These fiduciary duties are owed to all shareholders; elsewhere, Article 152 allows any shareholder "to bring a suit against any person [including controlling shareholders] who encroaches on the lawful rights and interests of the company and causes losses to the company." Despite a failure to list in the new law what acts constitute "encroachment," it provides both a standard and a legal basis for explicit rights to sue, a conspicuous failing of the earlier law which was even more ambiguous as to whether such a right even existed.

The new Company Law also imposes "duties of loyalty and diligence" upon directors, supervisors and senior managers. Article 149 of the revised law prohibits specific acts, mainly involving self-dealing and the usurpation of corporate opportunities as well as ordinary misappropriation, classic duty-of-loyalty problems. These fiduciary principles are alternatives to precatory language or more specific regulatory monitoring. They also shift from criminal and administrative penalties to the private enforcement (by other shareholders) model found in the United States and other developed countries. They substitute deterrence for prior supervision, resetting the balance between majority and minority shareholders.

Equitable treatment for all shareholders

The revised Company Law seeks to ensure that there are regular shareholders' meetings. Chinese experience has shown that scheduled regular and ad hoc interim meetings can be very useful devices to constrain the board of directors and managers. The original Company Law stipulated that the shareholders'

31 A fiduciary is held to a standard of conduct above that of a stranger or casual business person and must avoid "self-dealing" or "conflicts of interests" where his potential benefit conflicts with what is best for the person who trusts him. Commonly as a legal matter, these are duties of care and loyalty on the part of the fiduciary.

meeting could only be convened by the board of directors and had to be presided over by the chairman of the board of directors.[32] Majority shareholders could refuse to convene or to preside over a meeting to suppress expressions of dissent by minority shareholders. Articles 41 and 102 of the revised Company Law entitle the shareholders above a certain threshold, when the board of directors and board of supervisors do not convene or preside over an interim meeting, to do so themselves. Because an interim meeting convened by other shareholders may affect the majority shareholders adversely, this new rule creates in effect a "demand provision" for the board of directors chosen by majority vote to convene shareholders' meetings or else face the prospect that others might convene one.[33] Article 22 further provides shareholders the right to petition a court to revoke any shareholder or board resolution within 60 days of the resolution's passage, where the procedure for convening that shareholders' meeting violates any law, administrative regulation or the articles of association. So both majority and minority shareholders have an incentive to hold shareholders' meetings in an orderly, predictable and lawful fashion, to avoid unnecessary disputes.[34] In a shareholders' meeting with all parties present, each party wishing to pass a proposal must create mutually acceptable conditions, conducive to a sensible balance between them.

By providing minority shareholders above certain thresholds with the rights to propose an interim meeting[35] and with proposal rights,[36] the revised Company Law may encourage minority shareholders to use the shareholders' meeting to check the illegitimate behaviour of a dominant majority.

The revised law allows shareholders to bring an action against the directors, supervisors or officers of a company for both work-related and non-work-related acts harmful to the company committed in violation of the articles of association, regulations or laws. Shareholders may also bring an action against third parties whose actions damage the interests of the company. Furthermore, the rules provide the means for minority shareholders to oust directors who

32 The 1994 Company Law of China, Articles 10(1) and 43(3).

33 In most legal systems, company law requires that before shareholders can sue derivatively or on their own behalf they must make an explicit written demand that the board of directors take appropriate legal action to safeguard the corporation's and shareholders' interests. The demand may be excused if to do so would be futile.

34 Stephen Green and Ming He, "China's stock market: out of the valley in 2004?" Royal Institute of International Affairs, Briefing Paper No. 1, February 2004.

35 Article 40 reduces the threshold from 25% to 10% of voting rights to call a special meeting in a close corporation. Article 101 further enables the articles of association of a company to specify the requirements for calling a special meeting of a public company. Articles 41 and 102 designate that in case the board of directors and board of supervisors does not convene or preside over the shareholders' meeting, any shareholder possessing 10% or more voting rights and the shareholders separately or aggregately holding 10% of the shares can do so.

36 Article 103(2): The shareholders separately or aggregately holding 3% or more of the shares of the company may put forward a written interim proposal to the board of directors ten days before a shareholders' meeting is held. The board of directors may notify other shareholders within two days and submit the interim proposal to the shareholders' meeting for deliberation. The contents of an interim proposal shall fall within the scope to be decided by the shareholders' meeting, and the interim proposal shall have a clear topic for discussion and matters to be decided.

injure overall company rights by favouring the majority, helpful in creating a disincentive for majority shareholders' abuse of their power.

The proposal rights give minority shareholders the chance to raise their concerns in the shareholders' meeting,[37] without which the agenda and content of the shareholders' meeting might be completely controlled by board of directors. As with the rights to propose an interim meeting, the proposal rights also make it possible for outsiders to acquire some shares and replace directors without having to wait until the directors' tenure expires at the next annual shareholders' meeting, reducing the costs of acquisition and creating market power constraints.

Enabling public companies to adopt cumulative voting, set out in Article 106, provides another important protection for shareholders. Under a straight voting system, any person or bloc who controls a majority of the votes in a particular election can elect all the directors. Cumulative voting allows shareholders to multiply their votes by the number of directors and supervisors to be elected.[38] Furthermore, where a listed company within one year purchases or sells material assets or provides a guarantee in excess of 30 per cent of its total assets, approval of shareholders with no less than two-thirds of voting rights must be obtained. These revised voting rights provide shareholders with large minority stakes a chance to elect at least one or more directors, to affect board and management decisions, and may lead to better corporate governance.

This ability to elect "representative" directors is particularly important in China. There have been many cases where majority shareholders overrode minority shareholders' interests notwithstanding a board with independent directors, the oversight of the board of supervisors and shareholder rights to sue. The root failures lie in the weakness and lack of independence of the judiciary and the high costs of shareholders' suits.[39] Furthermore, independent directors and supervisors are not in the position of shareholders: they have no motivation to supervise a majority-dominated company.[40] In contrast, the directors elected by cumulative voting who represent the minority shareholders have greater incentives to exercise their rights. Minority representation on the board may add independent, critical scrutiny of majority-dominated companies and sometimes presents a prior constraint on illegal behaviour, enhancing the protection of minority shareholders.

37 Frank Easterbrook and Daniel Fischel, "Voting in corporate law," *Journal of Law & Economics*, Vol. 26 (1983) pp. 395–427.

38 Cumulative voting helps strengthen the ability of minority shareholders to elect a director, allowing shareholders to cast all their votes for a single nominee for the board of directors when the company has multiple openings on its board. For example, if an election is for four directors and a shareholder holds 500 shares (one vote per share), under straight voting they have a maximum of 500 shares for any one candidate (2,000 votes total, 500 votes for each of the four candidates). With cumulative voting, all 2,000 votes could be for one candidate, 1,000 each to two candidates, or otherwise divided whichever way they chose.

39 The minority shareholders need to bear costs of the suit, and have the burden of proof, as a matter of Chinese civil procedure.

40 See Armen Alchian and Harold Demsetz, "Production, information costs, and economic organization," *American Economic Review*, Vol. 62, No. 5 (1972), pp. 777–95.

Regulation of related-party transactions[41] provides protection from the risk that a corporation may be treated unfairly in such transactions.[42] Legislators cannot expect self-interested directors, for example, to afford primacy to other shareholders' interests.[43] In recent years, many Chinese companies, especially listed companies, have provided illegal guarantees. Article 16 requires that guarantees or investing by a company in related entities must be subject to the determination of the shareholders' meeting, in which the related parties are not eligible to vote.

Normally the majority shareholders hold a high percentage of voting rights; minority shareholders (due to rational apathy) fail to vote; and there is no minimum quorum for a shareholders' meeting of a public company. Thus, even though an investment or a guarantee will substantially injure the interests of the company and minority shareholders, the proposal will be passed. Excluding the votes of related parties can prevent the majority shareholders from engaging in misconduct. If majority shareholders want the company to provide a guarantee, they must provide the same conditions as, or more favourable conditions than, the market requires. For similar reasons, Article 125 states directors of listed companies are ineligible to vote on matters in which they have an interest.

Providing these remedies to aggrieved minority shareholders not only serves to compensate them but may also deter misconduct by majority shareholders. At the same time, to guard against minority shareholders' opportunism and possible harassment of the majority, the Company Law stipulates certain requirements for the minority to exercise their rights.

Article 106 allows cumulative voting as a choice for public companies,[44] but boards of directors will probably continue to be controlled by majority shareholders, allowing continuing injury to a company's interests. Most of the articles of association of the company are determined by the controlling shareholders, and companies may "opt out" of cumulative voting, so majority shareholders can veto a decision in favour of cumulative voting. Some object that cumulative voting may polarize a board and transform it into a contentious group, where constant bickering deflects energies from rational efforts to identify and respond to the corporation's problems and opportunities.[45] Nevertheless, China has introduced independent directors for listed companies to supervise majority shareholders.[46] The independent directors may also fight with inside directors, and supervision may lead to arguments. On the other hand, minority and majority shareholders' interests may "converge to a

41 Transactions conducted between related parties are sometimes called "connected transactions" in Chinese parlance.

42 Cox, Hazen and O'Neal, *Corporations*, pp. 204–15.

43 Huan, "Shareholders' rights in China: an analysis of private equity in former state-owned enterprises," *Singapore Academy of Law Journal*, Vol. 12 (2000), p. 428.

44 Article 106: When the shareholders' assembly elects directors or supervisors, it may, under the articles of association or resolution of the shareholders' assembly, adopt a cumulative voting system.

45 See Robert Charles Clark, *Corporate Law* (Boston: Little, Brown 1986), pp. 362–64.

46 See China Securities Regulatory Commission, "Guanyu zai shangshi gongsi jianli duli dongshi zhidu de zhidao yijian" ("Guidelines regarding establishing the rule of independent directors"), 21 August 2001, http://www.cas.cn/html/Dir/2001/08/21/5860.htm.

significant extent."[47] Hence, contention within the board is unlikely to lead to bad results. Moreover, empirical and historical evidence from the United States shows that the elimination of cumulative voting in large public firms has reduced shareholder wealth on average.[48] The benefits brought by cumulative voting will definitely outweigh its costs.

Derivative suits; appraisal rights

Since those controlling a company are unlikely to authorize it to sue them personally, Article 152 establishes a system of derivative suits. It provides a device by which shareholders may enforce claims of the corporation against managing officers and directors of the corporation, who may be dominated by the majority shareholders. In China, where majority shareholders' illegal behaviour is rampant,[49] the derivative suit may prove a very useful weapon for minority shareholders to protect their interests and deter majority shareholders' oppressive behaviour. To provide a minimal basis for standing to sue, Article 152 requires that the minority shareholders must hold 1 per cent or more of the total shares of the company for more than 180 days and must make a demand on the company first. The reason for the demand requirement is to re-emphasize the basic principle that the board of directors, not the shareholders, manages the corporation, and to protect the directors or supervisors from harassment by litigious shareholders.[50]

Article 75 entitles the shareholders in close companies to appraisal rights when they vote against a shareholders' meeting resolution concerning matters which seriously affect shareholders' rights or suffer other arguably oppressive behaviour.[51] These appraisal rights liberalize the rules related to shareholders' approval of fundamental transactions. They may also overcome a requirement for unanimous consent that permits a small minority to block a decision desired by the majority.[52] It gives the majority the right to control the company, while at

47 See Melvin Eisenberg, "The structure of corporation law," *Columbia Law Review*, Vol. 89, No. 7 (1989), pp. 1461–1525.

48 See Jeffery Gordon, "Institutions as relational investors: a new look at cumulative voting," *Columbia Law Review*, Vol. 94, No. 1 (1994), pp. 124–92.

49 Gregory Chow, "Corruption and China's economic reform in the early 21st century," Princeton University CEPS Working Paper No. 116, October 2005, http://www.princeton.edu/~ceps/workingpapers/116chow.pdf.

50 See Clark, *Corporate Law*, p. 641. In the United States, the demand requirement, minimum shareholdings and posting of bond as security for the expenses of litigation are all features of shareholder derivative litigation.

51 Article 75: Under any of the following circumstances, a shareholder who votes against the resolution of the shareholders' meeting may request the company to purchase its stock rights at a reasonable price: (1) The company has not distributed any profit to the shareholders for five consecutive years, but it has made profits for five consecutive years and conforms to the profit distribution conditions as prescribed in this Law; (2) The merger, split-up, or transfer of the main properties of the company; (3) When the business term as specified in the articles of association expires or other reasons for dissolution as prescribed in the articles of association occur, the shareholders' meeting makes the company continue existing by adopting a resolution on modifying the articles of association.

52 See Cox, Hazen and O'Neal, *Corporations*, pp. 595–606. In corporate law, the appraisal remedy – typically viewed as a form of protection for minority shareholders – gives shareholders the right to dissent from corporate transactions and to obtain payment for their shares from the corporation.

the same time creating a means for the dissenting shareholders to exit. These appraisal claims, while enhancing fairness, may siphon cash from the corporation; thus, the Company Law stipulates the dissenting shareholders may only exercise the rights in designated circumstances.[53]

Article 183[54] empowers shareholders to apply for the company's dissolution to a People's Court, so long as they successfully prove that the company is encountering serious operating difficulties which will cause substantial and irreparable losses,[55] and the problems cannot be solved by any other means. The remedy of involuntary dissolution serves as protection against majority oppression as well as an incentive for the majority shareholders to exercise their control so as to maintain minority confidence.[56] Since involuntary dissolution may cause hardship to other parties, the Article designates that only in the event of serious deadlock with no other solutions may shareholders invoke the remedy. Moreover, to prevent strike suits,[57] it permits only shareholders who have 10 per cent or more of the shares outstanding to exercise the rights.

To ensure shareholders' rights to information, Article 34(1) and Article 98 entitle the shareholder to consult and copy the articles of association, minutes of the shareholders' meetings, resolutions of the board of directors, resolutions of the board of supervisors, and financial reports.[58] Article 151 empowers the shareholders to elicit accurate information from the directors, the senior officials and supervisors. To protect their interests, the shareholders need to ascertain how the majority-controlled directors and officers conduct the company's business. Without access to information, the deterrent effects of shareholder oversight would be reduced. To prevent harassment of management or theft of corporate secrets, Article 34 requires that shareholders in limited liability companies cannot consult the accounting books unless they make a request in writing which states a "proper purpose."

Effective monitoring of management

The revised Company Law intends to reinforce the power of the board of supervisors. The board of supervisors in China – following the model established in German commercial law and employed in other civil law jurisdictions – was supposed to oversee the work of the board of directors and to provide an

53 See Article 75.

54 Article 183: Where any company meets any serious difficulty in its operations or management so that the interests of the shareholders will face heavy loss if it continues to exist and it cannot be solved by any other means, the shareholders who hold 10% or more of the voting rights of all the shareholders of the company may plead the people's court to dissolve the company.

55 See Alan Wang, "Redressing the rights of shareholders in corporate fraud," http://www.chinalawandpractice.com/default.asp.

56 See Cox, Hazen and O'Neal, *Corporations*, pp. 679–89.

57 The purpose of a strike suit, brought by someone who owns very few shares, is to gain a private settlement before going to court that would cost the company less than defending the suit. The suit itself does not benefit the company or other shareholders.

58 Article 98 also entitles shareholders to consult records relating to corporate bonds.

additional layer of checks on management. In the past, it played little role as a watchdog and fell short of the expectations of investors and legislators. Thus, the new Company Law provides the board of supervisors with more powers to make it work properly.

Articles 54, 55 and 119 – which give the board of supervisors the right of inquiry and the right to hire an accounting firm (with the relevant expenses being born by the company) – enhance the board of supervisors' ability to get information about the company, help the board better understand corporate information, and set priorities for supervision.[59] Articles 40 and 101 entrust the board of supervisors in close and public companies to propose an interim meeting, and Articles 41 and 102 vest the right to convene a shareholders' meeting in the board of supervisors in the event the board of directors or executive directors fail to do so. These rules make it possible for the board of supervisors to propose, convene and preside over a shareholders' meeting and report what it has found, augmenting the links between it and the shareholders, indirectly increasing the board of supervisors' role as a watchdog, providing greater deterrence to illegal behaviour by the majority and more weapons to protect the minority shareholders.

Nevertheless, the new Company Law has not altered situations where the watchdog functions of the board of supervisors can be stymied. Articles 52 and 118 still require that at least one-third of the board of supervisors must be employee supervisors, elected by employees. Theoretically employee supervisors know the operation better than other supervisors, and are thus better able to supervise the board of directors. In practice, the situation is quite different.[60] Employee supervisors are more likely to be employees whose salaries and promotion are determined by the directors and managers. While employee supervisors have been successful in Europe (in Germany, for example), Asian nations such as South Korea and Taiwan prohibit employees from being supervisors. This is because of the fear that such supervisors, given the hierarchies of Asian societies, would not be able to exercise their rights neutrally.

In addition, Articles 99 and 104 stipulate that supervisors elected by shareholders should be elected by straight voting in public companies, which may also lead to a majority-controlled board of supervisors. Unlike the supervisors in companies in some other Asian countries (Taiwan, Japan and South Korea) those in the PRC cannot act separately and independently.[61] Because of majority shareholders' control of the board of supervisors, the board may not meaningfully protect minority shareholders.

59 Under provisions of the US Sarbanes-Oxley legislation, a corporation's audit committee also has the authority to retain independent legal, accounting and other consultants to advise the committee.

60 Articles 52 and 124 of the 1994 Company Law also required that some supervisors be employees, but in public companies there were few employee supervisors who fulfilled their responsibility to protect minority shareholders from oppression.

61 Articles 54, 55, 56, 57,118, 119 and 120 of the Company Law require the supervisors in a company to act collectively, except when attending the meeting of the board of directors.

Voting rules still provide various loopholes. The revised Company Law does not mandate cumulative voting and the manner of election of auditors for public companies. Minority shareholders sometimes do not vote in their best interests as a result of information asymmetry, collective action problems or difficulty in judging what arrangements will best suit their interests.[62] Mandatory structural rules may not only help ensure outside directors and large minority shareholders participate in the decision-making process but also protect them against opportunism by insiders.[63]

Article 170 enables a public company to choose the shareholders' meeting or the board of directors to hire or dismiss the accounting firm which audits the company.[64] Independent auditors play a "gatekeeper" role in protecting minority shareholders' interests. Regrettably, in China, there have been many instances where the independent auditors have "cooked the books,"[65] providing further support for the proposition that the watchdogs should not be chosen by those they are supposed to watch.[66] Indeed, mandating that independent auditors must be chosen by the shareholders' meetings does nothing to prevent majority shareholders' opportunistic amendment of the articles to allow the majority-dominated board of directors to choose the independent auditors. It is hard to imagine how the auditors thus chosen will fulfil their gate-keeping responsibility

Article 152 stipulates that defendants in a derivative suit can only be the directors, senior managers and supervisors of a company. An outsider who adversely affects the company's interests – for instance, one who does not pay a debt to the company on time and is not sued by the directors and the supervisors – cannot be sued by the shareholders. As a result, this rule cannot prohibit majority shareholders from utilizing other companies as intermediaries to transfer interests in public companies.

Some elements of the revised Company Law could harm the company and majority shareholders. Article 151[67] demands that directors, senior managers and supervisors must answer shareholders' enquiries. Yet sometimes honest, complete public responses by a director or supervisor may injure the interests of the company; for example, these may involve trade secrets or business strategy. Despite provisions of the Company Law which might hold shareholders liable,

62 Eisenberg, "The structure of corporation law," p. 1461.

63 Jeffery Gordon, "The mandatory structure of corporate law," *Columbia Law Review*, Vol. 89, No. 7 (1989) pp. 1549–98.

64 Article 170 enables both close companies and public companies to choose whether the shareholders' meeting or the board of directors determines hiring or dismissing independent auditors.

65 Yuan Ding, Hua Zhang and Honghui Zhu, "Accounting failures in Chinese listed firms: origins and typology," *International Journal of Disclosure and Governance*, Vol. 2, No. 4, (2005) pp. 395–412. Z. Jun Lin and Feng Chen, "An empirical study of audit 'expectation gap' in the People's Republic of China," *International Journal of Auditing*, Vol. 8, No. 2 (2004), pp. 93–115.

66 See Clark, *Corporate Law*, p. 375.

67 Article 151: If the shareholders' meeting or shareholders' assembly demands a director, supervisor or senior manager attend the meeting as a non-voting representative, he shall do so and shall answer shareholders' inquiries.

the weakness of the courts, the expense of lawsuits and unpredictability of results make any threat of liability highly unlikely.[68]

Articles 34 and 98 give shareholders the right to consult resolutions of meetings of the board of directors, which may also provide access to trade secrets of the company. Minority shareholders may use this right to affect adversely the interests of the company. The Company Law now does not require that shareholders who want to review resolutions of the meetings of the board of directors have a proper purpose.

Executive compensation

Among the issues related to effective monitoring of management by the board of directors, perhaps the most important is executive compensation. Recently this has become a major issue, not only in the United States but in other developed countries. In the United States it is hardly new; as early as 1939, the SEC enacted regulations regarding disclosure of executive compensation.[69] Recently, corporate scandals such as those involving Enron, WorldCom, HealthSouth and Tyco have focused on executive compensation as an important factor in eroding corporate governance. The primary complaint against excessive executive compensation is that in many cases – despite the mantra of pay for performance – executive pay simply does not correlate with performance.[70] The widespread view is that chief executive officers are grossly overpaid[71]: senior managers' pay has increased significantly faster than that of ordinary workers.[72] Moreover, the range of perquisites for high-level executives, including bonuses and special payments, has become excessive.

In China, the development of capital markets and increase in the number of large companies had brought new attention to executive compensation.[73] As in other economies, directors and officers of Chinese companies do not own corporate assets; thus, the economic consequences of their management are felt not by them but by shareholders. To align their interests with those of shareholders and to reduce agency costs, companies create incentives for directors and executives. The most effective, but most often misapplied, incentive is executive compensation.[74]

68 Cindy Schipani and Junhai Liu, "Corporate governance in China: then and now," *Columbia Business Law Review*, Vol. 2002 (2002), pp. 1–69.

69 Tracy Scott Johnson, "Pay for performance: corporate executive compensation in the 1990s," *Delaware Journal of Corporate Law*, Vol. 20 (1995), p. 183.

70 *Ibid.* p. 214.

71 Stephen M. Bainbridge, "Book review essay: executive compensation: who decides? Pay without performance: the unfulfilled promise of executive compensation," *Texas Law Review*, Vol. 83 (2005), pp. 1615–62.

72 According to the Institute for Policy Studies, the ratio in pay between CEOs covered in *Business Week's* survey and the average production worker reached 301 to 1 in 2003. In 2002, the ratio stood at 282 to 1. Estimates more recently suggest the ratio is now over 400 to 1. Institute for Policy Studies and United for a Fair Economy, *Executive Excess 2004* (2004).

73 Kato and Long, "Executive compensation, firm performance, and corporate governance," pp. 945–83.

74 See e.g. D. Quinn Mills, "Paradigm lost: the imperial CEO," *Directors and Boards*, Vol. 27, No. 4 (2003), pp. 41–42.

The revised Chinese Company Law provides that directors, supervisors and management executives must comply with the laws, administrative regulations and corporate charters, and that they owe the duties of loyalty and care. Directors, supervisors and executives may not utilize their power for bribes or other illegal income and may not make personal use of corporate assets.[75] The law further provides that they and controlling shareholders should compensate the company for any losses resulting from abuse of their control positions.[76] As noted above, shareholders' right to file derivative suits is recognized by the law; Article 152 of the Company Law entitles shareholders to sue directors and executives for illegal use of corporate assets.

In most American jurisdictions, suits against executives for excessive compensation rarely succeed. Only where plaintiffs can prove that compensation is unreasonable for the services provided will the courts intervene with their equity power to "prevent a waste of the corporation's assets."[77] If equity requires it, the court will award recovery of excess compensation directly to harmed minority shareholders. The provisions of China's revised Company Law do not explicitly allow a parallel action, so it is difficult to determine whether or not Chinese courts can sustain similar claims.

Increased disclosure of executive compensation has become the norm in developed countries in recent years. The United States Congress passed the Sarbanes-Oxley Act in 2002 which, inter alia, prohibits corporate loans to executives.[78] British and Canadian laws also impose some restrictions on executive compensation; for example, a British corporate reform regulation also passed in 2002 requires an annual shareholder vote on executive compensation practices.[79]

Compared with the law in North America and the United Kingdom, Chinese law has much room for development. Despite China's traditions of centralization and government regulation, the law hardly regulates executive compensation at all. The Company Law treats it entirely as an internal corporate issue, only providing that compensation of directors and supervisors shall be decided by the shareholders' meeting[80] and that compensation of executives shall be decided by the board of directors.[81] After recent revisions, the law prohibits companies from offering loans directly or indirectly through subsidiaries to

75 Article 148.

76 Article 21.

77 Such lawsuits were successfully prosecuted in the Tyco case. Yet courts often uphold huge compensation for executives. See *In re The Walt Disney Co. Derivative Litigation*, Delaware No 411, 2005 (8 June 2006), where the Delaware Supreme Court upheld a severance package of $130 million after only 14 months' work for Michael Ovitz, which withstood a shareholder challenge, *In re The Walt Disney Co. Derivative. Litigation*, Delaware No. 15452 (9 August 2005) (Chandler, C.).

78 Sean A. Power, "Comment, Sarbanes-Oxley ends corporate lending to insiders: some interpretive issues for executive compensation surrounding the Section 402 loan prohibition," *University of Missouri Kansas City Law Review*, Vol. 71 (2003), p. 911.

79 Joanna L. Ossinger, "Regarding CEO pay, why are the British so different?" *Wall Street Journal*, 10 April 2006.

80 Article 37 (2).

81 Article 46 (9).

directors, supervisors and executives.[82] It also requires that companies disclose the compensation of directors, supervisors and executives regularly, similar to provisions of the US Sarbanes-Oxley Act.[83] Yet there have been no implementing rules promulgated by the State Council, the CSRC or other relevant government agencies. It is clear that the system for regulating executive compensation in China will have to be improved in the future, as incentive systems are adopted which attempt to tie managers' take-home pay with job performance. While excessive executive compensation in Chinese listed companies has not proven to be a major problem thus far, experience elsewhere makes clear the need for government regulation of executive compensation to protect vulnerable shareholders – especially small shareholders.[84] Such reforms should do much to increase public confidence in corporate governance and the capital market in China.

Conclusion

Although they fail to address all concerns, the revised Company Law and Securities Law do endeavour to stipulate better rules by taking account of the actual situation of corporate governance in PRC and making use of foreign legislative experience. As for balancing the interests of majority and minority shareholders, especially in attempting to enhance the protection of minority shareholder's interests, the new laws do make some progress. It remains to be seen how effective they will turn out to be in practice.

In the long term, better corporate governance in China will require: clear rules and regulations, including implementing rules for these new laws; certainty in the application of these rules and regulations; fair and consistent enforcement, combined with strong sanction against breaches; and policy initiatives to co-ordinate reforms necessitated by market developments. Not every observer necessarily applauds the recent trends in China of adopting foreign models of corporate governance to achieve results in the context of the business culture of Chinese enterprises.[85] It remains to be seen how a more characteristically Chinese corporate governance system might evolve.

Moreover, there may be many twists and turns in the process of improving and adjusting the corporate governance regime in China. For example, in 2004

82 Article 116.

83 Article 117.

84 But see Dapeng Cai and Jie Li, "A theoretical investigation of agent corruption in Chinese SOEs: causes, effects, and its prevention," taweb.aichi-u.ac.jp/kurihara/jsie8ab.pdf. The authors find increasingly pervasive corruption by SOE managers, especially in large and medium-sized SOEs which have begun to access global capital markets. Others suggest that Chinese managers may need different incentives, such as stock options (which are rarely granted in China), as an inducement to better corporate governance. See Rui, Firth and Fung, "Corporate governance and CEO compensation," p. 20.

85 See e.g. Yu Guanghua, "Takeovers in China: the case against uniformity in corporate governance," *Common Law World Review*, Vol. 34, No. 2 (2005) pp. 169–98. Hui Huang, "The regulation of insider trading in China: a critical review and proposals for reform," *Australian Journal of Corporate Law*, Vol. 17 (2005), pp. 281–322.

the contentious issue of management buyouts (MBOs) of SOEs was clarified. New State Asset Supervision and Administration Commission (SASAC) regulations temporarily prohibited MBOs at large SOEs, closed a number of loopholes and clarified under which conditions MBOs of smaller enterprises could be carried out.[86] At the time, fears were expressed about the possible abuse of insider information by managers to acquire shares of SOEs at bargain prices. By 2006, however, the government was promising to introduce a stock option scheme for managers at China's overseas-listed SOEs, which analysts then said would be an important step in promoting the healthy growth of Chinese companies in the long run. A management incentive stock option programme for overseas-listed SOEs, drafted by SASAC, was to take effect from 1 March 2006.[87] SASAC relaxed the previous ban on management buyouts in large-scale SOEs, allowing executives in those companies to purchase limited shares of the company in which they work. The relationship between policy experimentation and law reform remains unclear and suggests that transition from the command economy to a market environment will combine legal, economic and policy reforms in unstable combinations until a new model suited to Chinese circumstances is developed.

86 Barry Naughton, "SASAC rising," *China Leadership Monitor*, No. 14 (2005), Hoover Institution, http://www.chinaleadershipmonitor.org/20052/bn.html.

87 Zheng Lifei, "State firm executives to get stock options from March 1," *China Daily*, 23 February 2006. "The application of (the management stock options incentive) scheme in overseas-listed SOEs is an important step to improve their corporate governance," said Wang Zhigang, director of the Company Reform and Development Studies at a think-tank affiliated to SASAC.

Commentary on "New Hope for Corporate Governance in China?"

Tang Xin

The concept of corporate governance was not discussed in Chinese academic literature until the year when the first Company Law of the People's Republic was enacted.[1] From scholarship to practice, corporate governance saw great progress throughout the following decade.

James Feinerman gives a general observation about corporate governance in China, highlighting those high-profile elements of (among others) shareholders' issues, transparency and disclosure, and monitoring of controlling shareholders and management. Concerning the newest revisions of China's Company Law, he gives a generous appraisal of legal reforms in the following areas: the fiduciary duties of controlling shareholders; shareholders' rights to challenge the resolution of a shareholders' or board meeting; shareholders' proposal rights and rights to propose an interim meeting; shareholders' rights to information; constraints on related-party transactions; ex post remedies to aggrieved minority shareholders; the appraisal rights of dissenting shareholders; and the reinforcement of powers for boards of supervisors. The author also points out the lapses and gaps of the recent Company Law reform. For example, the watchdog functions of the board of supervisors may still be paralysed and cumulative voting to elect directors and auditors for public companies is not yet mandated.

Some items deserve to be added to both the lists of achievements and failures. In the aggregate, the revisions (although only on paper) will help raise China's scores in the "shareholder protection" index developed by LaPorta and his

1 See Company Law of the People's Republic of China (adopted by the Fifth Session of the Standing Committee of the Eighth National People's Congress on 29 December 1993, and effective 1 July 1994). China's first Company Law (*Gongsilu*) was issued as early as 1904; in many ways, this resembles corporate governance legislation being adopted today in the world's emerging markets, but the modern theories of corporate governance were not introduced to China until 90 years later. For the *Gongsilu* and its implications to the development of China's business organizations and their ownership in China, see William K. Kirby, "China unincorporated: company law and business enterprise in 20th-century China," *Journal of Asian Studies*, No. 54 (1995), p. 43; see also, William N. Goetzmann and Elisabeth Köll, "The history of corporate ownership in China: state patronage, company legislation, and the issue of control," Yale ICF Working Paper No. 04-29, June 2004, available at SSRN: http://ssrn.com/abstract=572122. For the seminal researches of "corporate governance" in China, see Wu Jinglian, *Xiandai gongsi yu qiye gaige* (*The Modern Companies and Enterprise Reform*) (Tianjin: Tianjin People's Publishing House, 1994); Zhang Weiying, "Xifang qiye lilun de yanjin yu zuixin fazhan" ("The evolvement and newest development of Western enterprise theories"), *Economics Review*, Vol. 11 (1994); Qian Yingyi, "Zhongguo de gongsizhili gaige he rongzi gaige" ("The corporate governance structure and financing reform"), in Aoki (ed.), *Zhuangui jingji zhong de gongsi zhili jiegou* (*Corporate Governance Structure in Transition Economies*) (Beijing: The China Economy Publishing House, 1995).

 doi:10.1017/S0305741007001609

colleagues in their law and finance literature.[2] They may also increase the welfare of minority shareholders of listed companies.[3] But a critical question remains: to what extent will the "law on the paper," on which Feinerman concentrates, improve China's corporate governance in the real world?

Formal Enforcement Measures

As commentators have found, enforcement problems plague corporate governance and shareholder protection efforts in transition economies, where weaknesses in legal and market constraints are prevalent. China provides a vivid example of the impotence of formal enforcement institutions.

Private right of action

A number of provisions were added to both the Company Law and the Securities Law in 2005 which authorize shareholders to bring legal actions for damages if their lawful rights and interests are infringed. On paper, protection for minority shareholders seems to be fine, but legal enforcement remains a serious problem. The local courts are very inefficient and reluctant to hear corporate governance or securities-related claims involving listed companies, although some of the rights of action were explicit as early as 1994 (when the Company Law was established) and the Supreme People's Court have allowed the lower courts to take a limited class of claims arising from false statements by listed companies.[4] Moreover, US-style class actions characterized with an "opt-out" approach are not permitted in China.[5] Although supported by many

2 They examined laws governing investor protection, the quality of their enforcement and ownership concentration in 49 countries. See Raphael LaPorta, Florencio Lopez-de-Silanes, Andrei Shleifer and Robert W. Vishny (LLSV), "Law and finance," *Journal of Political Economy*, Vol. 106, No. 6 (1998), pp. 1113–55. Following the LLSV methodology, for old company law provisions applying to listed companies China's shareholder rights scored 3 (out of 6). After the revision, the score is 4. With the old score, China was below the English-origin average (4) but above the German-origin average (2.33) and French-origin average (2.33), and would have ranked "average" among all LLSV countries (developed and developing); with the new score, China is now doing as well as the average of English-origin jurisdictions, and is in the top part of the LLSV country list.

3 Shen Yifeng, Xiao Ming and Huang Juanjuan, "Investor protection and corporation cost of equity," *Economic Review* (2003). The corporate cost of equity tends to decrease as investor protection gets tighter. Shen Yifeng, Xu Nianhang, Yang Yi, "Test on the law protection of minority investors in different stages." This study supported the main ideas of LLSV from a very different viewpoint.

4 Circular of the Supreme People's Court Concerning Issues Relating to Acceptance of Civil Tort Suits Filed Due to False Representation on the Securities Market (*Zuigao renmin fayuan guanyu shouli zhengquan shichang yin xujia chenshu yinfa de minshi qinquan jiufen anjian youguan wenti de tongzhi*) (issued on 15 January 2002); 2003 SPC False Representation Provisions of the Supreme People's Court Concerning the Acceptance and Trial of Civil Compensation Securities Suits Involving False Representation (*Zuigao renmin fayuan guanyu shenli zhengquan shichang yin xujia chenshu yinfa de minshi peichang anjian de ruogan guiding*) (issued on 9 January 2003).

5 Section 23 of US Federal Rules of Civil Procedure gives shareholders a right to "opt out" of a related-class action, but failure to do so indicates consent to be members of the class, and also to the jurisdiction of the court. Under the arrangement, the apathy of shareholders to "opt out" will probably make the plaintiff class very strong. The "representative suits" (*daibiaoren susong*) provision of China's 1991 Civil Procedure Law provides for an "opt in" approach, which clearly reduces the effectiveness of

voices,[6] class action still seems unfeasible in the foreseeable future. Finally, since there is an absence of key institutions such as the contingent fee and award of attorneys' fees in multi-party litigations, private litigation seems unable to play the role of "private attorney general" in the enforcement of laws.[7]

CSRC administrative proceedings

Improving corporate governance of listed companies has always been an ambition of the China Securities Regulatory Commission (CSRC). Nevertheless, the agency is hampered in several ways. First, the laws do not officially provide CSRC with specific powers to regulate the internal control or governance of those companies. Secondly, as a government agency that must both enforce rules regarding disclosure and regulate merits of the investment quality of the public issuers, the CSRC is limited by its personnel resources to enforce the law.[8]

Disciplinary action by self-regulatory bodies

China's two national stock exchanges are joining the war against irregularities in the securities market, but it is doubtful that they have been given enough effective and appropriate authority to achieve a breakthrough. They may administer private reprimands and public censures, but these are not likely to be effective against determined offenders. For more pressing measures, they may discontinue or suspend the listing of a company. However, even if the exchanges are willing to act, such a move is more detrimental to innocent shareholders than to the guilty controllers who have abused the company assets or resources. The exchanges may declare an offender to be unsuitable for membership of the board of directors or board of supervisors. They may also advise the company to dismiss its secretary of the board of directors.[9] However, they have seldom deployed these sanctions.

---

footnote continued

the class action device. Moreover, "class action is not applicable to securities related actions"; see section 4, 2002 Circular. Drafters of this Circular claimed that the time was not ripe for class actions in China and that such an innovation would not have a legal basis under Chinese law. See Li Guoguang and Gu Wei, "Zhengquan shichang xujia chenshu minshi peichang zhidu" ("The civil liability system for securities market nisrepresentations"), *Falü chubanshe* (2003).

6 Supporters of securities-related class action include the chairman of CSRC, CEO of Shenzhen Securities Exchange and many commentators.

7 Recognizing the role of "private attorney general," legislators can confer standing on private persons, not simply to recover compensation for specific victims but also "to vindicate the public interest." The class action and the contingent fee are the key institutions of the "private attorney general" institution. However, under the Lawyer Service Fee Regulatory Rule (*Lushi fuwu shoufei guanli banfa*, April 2006) promulgated by the State Development and Reform Commission and the Justice Ministry, the contingent fee is not permitted in multi-party litigations (*quntixing susong*). See John C. Coffee Jr., "Rescuing the private attorney general: why the model of the lawyer as bounty hunter is not working," *Maryland Law Review* (1983), pp. 215–88.

8 D.C. Clarke, "Corporate governance in China: an overview," *China Economic Review*, No. 14, pp. 494–507.

9 E.g. sections 17.3, 3.2.4 of Listing Rules of Shanghai Stock Exchange and Shenzhen Stock Exchange (2006).

Alternative Solutions To Domestic Enforcement Regimes

The importance of solving the enforcement problem has led scholars to draft a range of partial alternative solutions to formal domestic regimes. For example, Bernard Black and Reinier Kraakman devised a "self-enforcing" corporate legal framework for Russia, which was specifically designed to minimize resort to legal authority.[10] John Coffee has emphasized the role of cross-listings on foreign stock exchanges as a mechanism by which firms in weak enforcement regimes can bond themselves to "good" corporate law. Listing on a developed foreign stock exchange imposes higher disclosure requirements and a more stringent regulatory environment.[11] Milhaupt maintained that non-profit organizations (NPOs) have emerged as perhaps the most important corporate law enforcement agents in Korea, Taiwan, and Japan; their actions may be another partial solution to the problem of weak investor protection and corporate law enforcement.[12] Evidence of all these models can be found in China's corporate governance practice.

The "self-enforcing" corporate law

Especially when the regulation of related-party transactions is concerned, China's legislators have based the Company Law (at least partly) on the self-enforcing model. As the regulator of China's securities market, CSRC has also been exploring ways to construct a self-enforcing corporate governance model for listed companies. In 1997, 2000 and 2001, CSRC promulgated a series of important rules to strengthen the law governing shareholders' meetings and introduced the independent director system.[13] The agency has also been trying to seek help from the financial intermediaries – especially "sponsors" (*baojianren* 保荐人) and financial consultants (*caiwu guwen* 财务顾问) – to act as "watchdogs" of the market.

Whether the self-enforcing model of corporate law or corporate governance can play a major role in overcoming China's enforcement problem remains to be seen. But as Black and Kraakman recognized, such a model cannot cover all the legal provisions needed to address liabilities and their formal enforcement.[14] The

10 Bernard Black and Reinier Kraakman, "A self-enforcing model of corporate law," *Harvard Law Review*, No. 109 (1996), p. 1911.

11 See John C. Coffee Jr., "Racing towards the top? The impact of cross-listings and stock market competition on international corporate governance," *Columbia Law Review*, No. 102 (2002), p. 1757.

12 Curtis J. Milhaupt, "Nonprofit organizations as investor protection: economic theory and evidence from East Asia," *Yale Journal of International Law*, No. 29 (2004), p. 169.

13 See especially the Guidelines for the Articles of Association of Listed Companies (*Shangshi gongsi zhangcheng zhiyin*), issued on 16 December 1997, revised on 16 March 2006; Regulatory Opinions for General Meetings of Listed Companies (*Shangshi gongsi gudongdahui guifan yijian*), issued on 18 May 2000, revised on 16 March 2006; and Guidance Opinion on the Establishment of an Independent Director System in Listed Companies (*Guanyu zai shangshi gongsi jianli duli dongshi zhidu de zhidao yijian*), issued on 16 August 2001.

14 Black and Kraakman, "A self-enforcing model of corporate law" ("We can only reduce, not wholly avoid, the need for official enforcement"). See also Bernard S. Black, "The legal and institutional preconditions for strong securities markets," *UCLA Law Review*, No. 48 (2001), p. 781 ("Effective regulators, prosecutors, and courts are the most important institutions that control information asymmetry, which is critical for developing strong public stock markets").

key point is, since company laws and securities regulations are inherently "incomplete," ambiguous provisions and gaps will have to be explained or filled in by a regulator or court. Otherwise, corporate governance failures may occur. Furthermore, plagued by the so-called "collective action problem," general meetings of shareholders may be too weak to provide real protection for members. Finally, the supporters of a self-enforcing model may simply overrate the effectiveness of such laws in an emerging market with very weak judicial enforcement, market constraints and soft reputation institutions.

Cross listing

Recently, some of the local well-known companies listed in the American, British, Hong Kong and Singapore markets have faced class action lawsuits filed in the United States against them.[15] Certain officers and directors were even sentenced to prison for misappropriating funds and fraud in connection with share option grants. But it remains a question whether the corporate governance in mainland China can achieve global convergence through encouraging local companies to go to list in the United States or other developed markets. There are various reasons for this. First, until recently, few companies were permitted to list their shares on overseas markets. At the end of April 2006, there were only 129 cross-listed companies in China, of which 109 were issued and listed shares in Hong Kong, and only around 20 in the United States, Britain and other markets.[16] The influence of those companies' governance practices on their local counterparts may be limited. Secondly, as there are very limited channels for domestic citizens to invest their money in foreign markets, and the national exchanges in China are not fully open to foreign capital, real competition among local and foreign stock exchanges have not yet begun. Thus the harmonization of exchanges would be deferred. Finally, cross-border supervision of cross-listed companies needs efficient co-operation among regulators and even courts from different jurisdictions. Lack of co-operation could bring about a failure of enforcement.[17]

Cross-listing may help to improve corporate governance in some local companies, but as Bernard Black points out, for those firms that have "escaped"

15 E.g. Chinalife, Chinadotcom, NetEase.

16 According to a senior officer of CSRC, see the Bank of China May Issues and Lists H Plus A Shares (*Zhonghang keneng caiyong H+A de xingshi shangshi*), *Beijing Modern Business*, 9 May 2006. By comparison, to the end of 1996, there were 416 foreign listings on NASDAQ, 305 on the New York Stock Exchange and 63 on the American Stock Exchange, a total of 784, and this number continued to grow rapidly. See Amir N. Licht, "Regulatory arbitrage for real: international securities regulation in a world interacting securities markets," *Virginia Journal of International Law*, No. 38 (1998), pp. 563, 566.

17 E.g. more and more finance scandals are revealed in mainland China's companies listed in Hong Kong, but the Hong Kong regulators and courts cannot deal with them if the companies' assets and even the key personnel are on the mainland. See "Haiyu shijian kaowen kuajing jianguan nanti" ("The Haiyu event tortures cross-border supervision"), *Shanghai Securities*, 2 August 2006.

their weak home country institutions through foreign listings, without the help of local enforcement and institutions such escape is only partial.[18]

Embryos of NPOs?

It is widely known that China does not have a tradition of active non-profit organizations,[19] but a group of activist lawyers have recently organized themselves as a "justice claiming team" to help aggrieved investors claim compensation after a notorious accounting scandal was exposed.[20] This team could be the embryo of a "justice claiming" NPO in the future. The function of such NPOs may also be executed by a government-sponsored "securities investor protection fund" and a "securities investor protection fund limited liability company," which are in charge of the financing, management and usage of funds.[21]

Conclusion

China's corporate governance has made great advances in the past ten years, during which increased awareness of investor protection has changed into significant policy issues. The most important statutes related to corporate governance, such as the Company Law, Securities Law and Criminal Law, have been revised to meet the increasing demand for protection. Research has shown that improved legal provisions can contribute to the performance of companies and welfare of shareholders. However, plagued by enforcement problems, some good legal provisions still fall short of fulfilling the demand for better governance. The functional substitutes for good local law and enforcement regimes, including "self-enforcing" corporate law models, cross-listings on foreign stock exchanges and non-profit organizations acting as corporate law enforcement agents, will all help to ease the chronic illnesses of the securities market. Notwithstanding these developments, corporate governance and institutions at the heart of a good national investor protection system, though not transplantable or easily created,[22] will still need to be patiently constructed.

18 "A company's reputation is strongly affected by the reputations of other firms in the same country. And reputation unsupported by local enforcement and other institutions isn't nearly as valuable as the same reputation buttressed by those institutions." See Black, "The legal and institutional preconditions for strong securities markets," p. 822.

19 Political, legal and operational constraints hinder non-governmental organizations development in the PRC. See C. David Lee, "Legal reform in China: a role for nongovernmental organizations," *Yale Journal of International Law*, No. 25 (2000), pp. 363, 419–30.

20 "Kelong an lushi weiquantuan: jinkuai sheli touzizhe baohu xiehui" ("Justice claiming team for compensation from Kelon and Deloitte's false statement: the establishment of investor protection association is urgent"), *China Securities*, 24 July 2006.

21 These comprise funds contributed by the securities companies and other funds raised. According to section 7 of the Measures for the Management of Securities Investor Protection Funds (*Zhengquan touzizhe baohu jijin guanli banfa*), issued by the CSRC, Ministry of Finance and People's Bank of China on 30 June 2006, such funds can only be used to compensate the creditors of a securities company when it goes into bankruptcy, is closed or taken over by the government. The "securities investor protection fund limited liability company" was registered on 30 August 2006.

22 Black, "The legal and institutional preconditions for strong securities markets," p. 822.

Finally, I cite Feinerman's evaluation of China's corporate governance, adding a few of my own words: "Much has been accomplished in establishing the basic features of corporate governance; however, there is still much to do"... especially when the effectiveness of enforcement is concerned.

China's Courts: Restricted Reform

Benjamin L. Liebman

ABSTRACT China's courts have in recent years engaged in significant reforms designed to raise the quality of their work. Yet such top-down reforms have been largely technical and are not designed to alter courts' power. Courts have also encountered new challenges, including rising populist pressures, which may undermine their authority. The most important changes in China's courts have come from the ground up: local courts have engaged in significant innovation, and horizontal interaction among judges is facilitating the development of professional identity. Recent developments have largely avoided two central questions facing China's courts: why have courts been permitted to develop even limited new roles, and what additional roles, if any, may they play within the Chinese political system?

Recent developments in China's courts reflect a paradox largely avoided in literature on the subject. Changes to courts' formal authority have been limited, courts still struggle to address basic impediments to serving as fair adjudicators, and they continue to be subject to Communist Party oversight. They have also confronted new challenges, in particular pressure from media reports and popular protests. At the same time, however, the party-state has permitted, and at times encouraged, both significant bottom-up development of the courts and their expanded use as fora for the airing of rights-based grievances, including administrative litigation, class actions and a small number of discrimination claims filed directly under the Constitution. Some courts have engaged in significant innovation. Judges are better qualified than in the past, and are increasingly looking to other courts and judges, rather than Party superiors, in deciding novel or difficult cases. As a result, courts are increasingly coming into conflict with other state institutions, growing numbers of well-educated judges are developing professional identities, and popular attention to both the problems and the potential roles of the courts appears higher than ever before.

The current and potential future role of China's courts has received wide attention. Discussions in both China and the West, however, have largely avoided two central questions. First, why has the party-state permitted the courts to develop even limited new roles? Secondly, can courts play an effective role in a non-democratic governmental system? This article surveys recent developments in China's courts with a view to beginning to answer these questions. The focus is on civil and administrative litigation, where reforms have been more significant than in the criminal justice system.

© The China Quarterly, 2007 doi:10.1017/S0305741007001610

Reformed Courts?

Caseloads

Are Chinese courts playing fundamentally different roles in society from those played in the recent past? There is no clear benchmark for evaluating changes in their position within the party-state. As Donald Clarke has noted, "perhaps Chinese courts are not designed to do, and should not do, the things Western courts do."[1] Courts are one of a number of state bureaucracies with the power to resolve disputes, and lack significant oversight powers over other state actors. Despite these differences, Chinese judges and academic commentators have in recent years looked to Western models of courts and judging in evaluating developments in China's courts.[2]

Reports have noted that Chinese courts are handling more cases than at any time in the past, with some claiming that China is facing a "litigation explosion."[3] The courts reported hearing 8.1 million cases in 2006,[4] more than triple the number heard in 1986. Yet such comparisons overstate the growth of litigation in China: as Table 1 shows, caseloads have grown only modestly, if at all, since 1999. The total number of cases heard in 2006 was only 2 per cent higher than in 2005, and the total number of first instance cases actually decreased by 2 per cent between 1996 and 2006. Similarly, the total number of first instance civil cases decreased in four years between 1999 and 2006; the total number of administrative cases likewise decreased in four of those years.[5] Lower court judges have confirmed in interviews that caseloads have either declined or grown only modestly over the past five years.[6] The modest increases are striking when set against the backdrop of China's rapid economic growth and widespread reports of a surge of civil disturbances in China. Judges attribute the declines to lack of confidence in the courts, in particular to the difficulties

1 Donald Clarke, "Empirical research into the Chinese judicial system," in Erik Jensen and Thomas Heller (eds.), *Beyond Common Knowledge: Empirical Approaches to the Rule of Law* (Stanford: Stanford University Press 2003), pp. 164–92.

2 For example, see Liao Weihua, "Fayuan zuzhi fa jiang chutai zhuanjia jianyi jiang renmin fayuan gaiming fayuan" ("Court organization law will come out, experts suggests changing people's courts into courts"), 4 December 2004, Nanfang Chuang, available from http://www.southcn.com/news/china/zgkx/200412040062.htm. Although noting that any reforms must accord with China's "national conditions," the Supreme People's Court (SPC) has acknowledged the need to look overseas in designing court reforms. SPC, "Renmin fayuan dierge wunian gaige gangyao (2004–2008)" ("The second five-year reform plan of the people's courts (2004–2008)"), 26 October 2005, available from http://www.law-lib.com/law/law_view.asp?id=120832.

3 "Beijing susong shuliang baozhashi zengzhang, qunian 76% anjian weineng jiean" ("The number of cases in Beijing increases explosively, the percentage of not closed cases increased by 76% last year"), *Fazhi wanbao* (*Beijing Legal Times*), 27 April 2005, available from http://news.xinhuanet.com/legal/2005-04/27/content_2884636.htm.

4 Xiao Yang, "Zuigao Renmin Fayuan gongzuo baogao (2007)" ("SPC work report (2007)"), 14 March 2007, available from http://www.chinacourt.org/public/detail.php?id=239089.

5 For analysis of the decline in caseloads, see Xin He, "The recent decline in economic caseloads in Chinese courts: exploration of a surprising puzzle," *The China Quarterly*, No. 190 (2007), pp. 352–74.

6 Interviews. Much of the information in this article is based on interviews with more than 200 judges, lawyers and academics. Interviews were conducted in Beijing, Shanghai, Guangdong, Jiangxi, Hubei, Jilin, Sichuan and Shaanxi between 2003 and 2007.

successful litigants face in enforcing decisions, and to private parties' preference for informal methods of dispute resolution.[7]

Nevertheless, the long-term trend appears to reflect a modest increase in the use of the courts, and that a greater range of cases and cases of greater complexity are being brought. Litigants are also increasingly challenging first instance decisions: appeals have grown at a much faster rate than first instance cases, with appeals nearly doubling between 1995 and 2006. The increase in appeals suggests that litigants may be both more familiar with legal procedures, and perhaps more confident that higher courts will issue decisions that differ from those of lower courts.

The modest growth in litigation in recent years suggests that courts are not necessarily playing a greater role relative to other institutions. As Table 1 and Figure 1 show, the increase in court caseloads coincided with a decline in the total number of disputes resolved through People's Mediation Committees until 2004.[8] Compared to other institutions engaged in dispute resolution, however, the modest rise in the total number of court cases appears less significant. Disputes and complaints of all types have increased in China in recent years, and thus any increase in court caseloads may simply be part of the more general increase in both disputes and grievances. For example, far more grievances are raised through the letters and visits system than through the courts.[9] Commercial arbitration cases, including both domestic and international disputes, increased by more than 20 per cent annually from 2004 to 2006.[10] Labour arbitration cases more than quintupled between 1996 and 2004.[11] The fact that the number of disputes and complaints raised in other institutions has continued to rise suggests that the decrease in the growth of litigation has not resulted from increased clarity of legal norms.

Top-down reform

The modest growth in caseloads does appear to reflect a conscious decision by party-state leaders to strengthen the courts' ability to resolve an increasing number and range of disputes.[12] But the party-state has also emphasized

7 Interviews.

8 The number of disputes resolved through People's Mediation Committees grew in 2005, the first increase in more than a decade. The increase probably reflects renewed state emphasis on mediation as part of efforts to construct a "harmonious society."

9 Although the total number of complaints raised is not made public, the system handles an enormous volume of grievances each year. Carl F. Minzner, "Xinfang: an alternative to the formal Chinese legal system," *Stanford Journal of International Law*, Vol. 42, No. 1 (2006), pp. 103–79.

10 Wen Jie, "2006 Niandu quanguo zhongcai anjian shouli shuju jianxi" ("Brief analysis of arbitration cases decided nationally in 2006"), China-arbitration.com, 15 March 2007, available from http://www.china-arbitration.com/readArticle.do?id=ff80818111440b34011153d7086a0046.

11 Ministry of Labour and Social Security, "Zhongguo laodong tongji nianjian (2005)" ("Yearbook of China labour statistics (2005)"), pp. 523–24, available from http://www.molss.gov.cn/images/2006-11/16/27110316153762520791.pdf.

12 For example, see Jiang Zemin, Report to the 15th National Congress of the Communist Party of China, 12 September 1997 (discussing judicial reform), available from http://dcdj.ccp.org.cn/old/ReadNews.asp?NewsID=3395.

Table 1: **Number of Cases (First Instance and Appeals) Closed Nationwide, 1994–2006**

Year	1994	1995	1996	1997	1998	1999	2000	2001	2002	2003	2004	2005	2006
1st criminal	480,914	496,082	616,676	440,577	480,374	539,335	560,111	623,792	628,549	634,953	644,248	683,997	701,379
1st civil[a]	3,427,614	3,986,099	4,588,958	4,720,341	4,816,275	5,060,611	4,733,886	4,616,472	4,393,306	4,416,168	4,303,744	4,360,184	4,382,407
1st admin.	34,567	51,370	79,537	88,542	98,390	98,759	86,614	95,984	84,943	88,050	92,192	95,707	95,052
All 1st inst.	3,943,095	4,533,551	5,285,171	5,249,460	5,395,039	5,698,705	5,380,611	5,336,248	5,106,798	5,139,171	5,040,184	5,139,888	5,178,838
2nd criminal	52,579	53,942	67,087	64,548	70,767	78,803	86,619	98,157	89,440	96,797	96,204	96,776	94,092
2nd civil	179,687	208,263	243,510	263,664	294,219	339,929	363,522	377,672	357,821	370,770	377,052	392,191	406,381
2nd admin	7,672	9,536	11,365	12,684	14,220	18,072	19,404	22,149	27,649	25,045	27,273	29,176	29,054
All 2nd	239,938	271,741	321,962	340,896	379,206	436,804	469,545	497,978	474,910	492,612	500,529	518,143	529,527
Letters and visits to courts[b]	5,847,948	6,361,495	6,960,162	7,131,469	9,351,928	10,691,048	9,394,358	9,148,816	3,656,102	3,973,357	4,220,222	3,995,244	Not yet available
Mediation by people's mediation committees	6,123,729	6,028,481	5,802,230	5,543,166	5,267,194	5,188,646	5,030,619	4,860,695	4,636,139	4,492,157	4,414,233	4,486,825	Not yet available

Notes:

[a]Prior to 2002 Chinese courts had separate divisions for handling civil and economic cases; they were merged in 2002. The figures for 1994 to 2001 thus include both civil and economic cases.

[b]"Letters and visits" refers to complaints about cases received in writing or in person by courts; for a discussion of the letters and visits system, see below. Complaints about the courts to letters and visits offices at other Party or state institutions are not included in this figure.

Sources:

1994–2005: *Zhongguo falü nianjian* (*China Law Yearbook*) 1995–2006. 2006: 2007 SPC Work Report (for first instance data); Supreme People's Court, *2006 nian quanguo fayuan shenli zhixing anjian qingkuang* (*Details of Cases Tried and Enforced Nationwide in 2006*), available at http://www.dffy.com/sifashijian/ziliao/200703/20070314163527.htm (for data on second instance cases).

Figure 1: **First Instance Cases, Mediation by People's Mediation Committees, and Court Letters and Visits, 1994–2006**

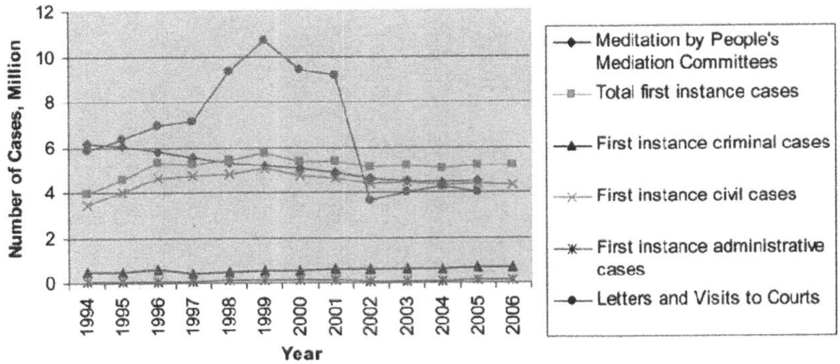

Figure 2: **Second Instance Cases (Appeals), 1994–2006**

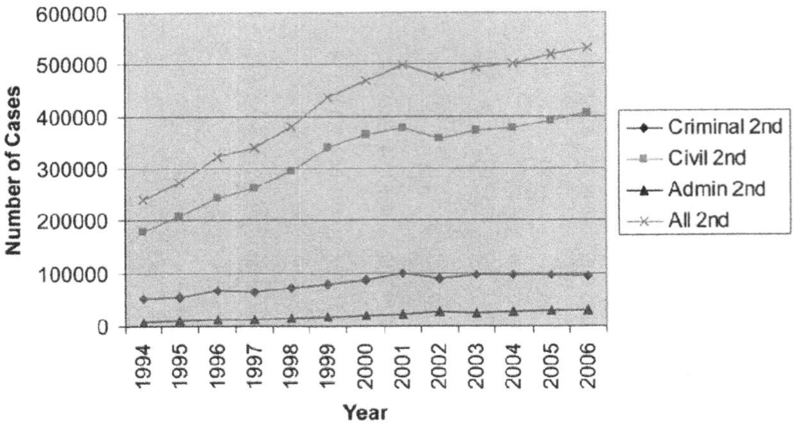

reforming other dispute resolution institutions – including the letters and visits system, mediation, arbitration and administrative review. These moves suggest that the party-state is focused on the need to resolve disputes and grievances, and thus preserve social stability. But they do not necessarily reflect an increased role for the courts in comparison with other institutions.

Court reform has, however, received enormous attention over the past decade. China commenced its project of court reform when it began reconstruction of its legal system in 1978. The role of the courts received increased attention in the late 1990s, as China's leadership renewed efforts to strengthen the legal system. Following the embrace of "rule of law" by the 15th Congress of the Chinese Communist Party in 1997, the Supreme People's Court (SPC) in 1999 issued its first five-year plan for reforming China's courts. This brought increased attention to the need to strengthen the courts. The plan set out 50 goals.[13] In late 2005 the SPC issued a second five-year plan, covering the period from 2004 to 2008, again listing 50 goals.[14]

Both plans address problems in the courts, ranging from judicial training to regularity in court procedures. Such reforms are largely either general and overly abstract, or primarily technical changes designed to address competence and fairness. The goals of the 2005 plan, although similar in number, also appear modest when compared to the 1999 one.[15] The earlier plan embraced some quite significant reforms, including the creation of rules of evidence and the separation within courts of the acceptance of cases from adjudication, and adjudication of cases from enforcement. With one exception – the reform of procedures for capital cases – the 2005 reforms include no major breakthroughs. The 2005 plan does mention the need to address centralizing court appointments, a step towards breaking the link between local authorities, which generally control court appointments, and judges. But it proposes doing so only within "given areas," not nationally. And it raises the topic of centralized financing of courts, but proposes no specific steps towards this goal.

Despite the limited goals of the official plans, courts have undertaken significant reforms designed to strengthen the competence of judges and the professionalism of the court system. Most significantly, the education levels of judges have improved dramatically. Media reports in mid-2005 stated that, for the first time, more than 50 per cent of Chinese judges had university degrees.[16] This marks a sharp increase from 6.9 per cent in 1995. Since 2002, all new judges in China have been required to possess bachelor's degrees. Likewise, in 2002 the Supreme People's Court stated that sitting judges who were below the age of 40 would be required to obtain a degree within five years or lose their jobs. Older judges who lacked a university education would be permitted to stay only if they completed a training course.[17] Many new judges, in particular at higher-level courts in major cities, now possess graduate degrees in law. New judges in China are also now required to pass the national bar exam, which had a pass rate of just 14 per cent in 2005. Those who became judges before 2002, however, are not required to pass the exam. Court presidents – who generally are the most

13 SPC, "Renmin fayuan wunian gaige gangyao" ("The five-year programme for reform of the people's courts"), 20 October 1999, available from http://law.chinalawinfo.com/newlaw2002/SLC/slc.asp?db=chl&gid=23701.

14 "The second five-year reform plan of the people's courts (2004–2008)."

15 Although the plan covers the period 2004–2009, it was not made public until 2005. The delay may reflect internal division regarding its contents.

16 "Woguo faguan he jianchaguan zhengti suzhi tigao benke bili guoban" ("The overall quality of our nation's judges and procurators is raised, more than half are university graduates"), *Renmin ribao* (*People's Daily*), 17 July 2005, available from http://news.xinhuanet.com/legal/2005-07/17/content_3228617.htm. The 50% number probably includes not only graduates of four-year universities, but also those from evening classes, junior colleges, or *da zhuan*, as well as correspondence courses. These degrees are not necessarily in law.

17 "Wenping shangqu budengyu shuiping tigao, faguan peixun buneng zhi benzhe wenping qu" ("An advanced degree does not equal enhanced ability, judge training should not solely aim at degrees"), *Xinhua wang* (*Xinhua Net*), 11 March 2004, available from http://news3.xinhuanet.com/newscenter/2004-03/11/content_1360136.htm. Obtaining such training, however, appears relatively easy.

powerful figures within courts and who take part in deciding major or sensitive cases – likewise are not required to be judges or to pass the bar exam.[18] The SPC has also taken steps to improve the quality of court decisions. In 2005 it issued a notice stating that opinions should include both accurate descriptions of the facts and evidence, and logical arguments and legal reasoning.[19]

Attention to training judges and to well-reasoned opinions appears to be yielding results. Judges comment that greater competence in the judiciary increases the ability of courts to resist external pressure by relying on legal arguments.[20] In addition, judges say that whereas in the past such intervention might have come either formally, in the form of written instructions, or informally through telephone calls, courts increasingly are swayed only by written instructions. Many such instructions tell courts to "emphasize" a case, or handle a particular case "according to law," rather than dictating outcomes, although even instructions in such form may make clear the desired outcome. It is difficult to assess whether interference in China's courts is increasing or decreasing. Some in China argue that external interference is actually growing, reflecting both falling confidence in the courts and the rise of the importance of popular opinion and social protest as means of influence. But it does appear that courts confronted by such pressures are increasingly likely to try to use legal arguments to resist.

Intervention continues, however, and continues to be a legitimate action by Party officials. Greater political sophistication in the courts may also make direct intervention by officials outside them less necessary, because courts are well aware of the cases most likely to be of concern to Party leaders. Improvements have been greater in routine cases than in politically sensitive ones. But the scope of sensitive cases remains wide and includes not only major criminal or political cases, but also those involving the financial interests of the party-state, powerful individuals or high profile companies, as well as cases involving a large number of plaintiffs and those receiving media coverage.

Other reforms have been less successful. Lack of enforcement of court decisions continues to be a major problem. Difficulties enforcing decisions reflect problems that courts cannot address on their own: local protectionism, continued intervention in cases by party-state officials and administrative departments, an undeveloped credit system, and weak punishment for non-compliance with court orders. In an acknowledgement of the continuing difficulties in enforcement, the Party's Central Political-Legal Committee issued a notice in December 2005 calling for the co-operation of the police and the

18 The failure to reform the appointment system for court presidents continues to serve as a major impediment to strengthening the courts.

19 "Zuigao Renmin Fayuan guanyu zai quanguo fayuan minshi he xingzheng shenpan bumen kaizhan 'Guifan sifa xingwei, cujin sifa gongzheng' zhuanxiang zhenggai huodong de tongzhi" ("Notice of the SPC regarding implementing the 'Standardizing judicial acts, enhancing judicial justice' special alteration and correction movement in the civil and administrative divisions of courts nationwide"), 15 July 2005, available from http://www.findlaw.cn/findlaw/lawdetail.asp?id=94852.

20 Interviews.

procuracy in the enforcement of court judgements and for the establishment of a comprehensive enforcement information system that involves government departments overseeing banks, real estate, vehicles and other sectors.[21] Similarly, repeated official statements regarding the importance of combating corruption in the judiciary suggest that corruption continues to be a major problem, one that reflects the difficulty of strengthening the authority of courts so long as they remain subject to extensive external influence.

Depoliticization?

Courts continue to be subject to Party leadership. Nevertheless, scholars in China have argued that the courts have gradually shifted from primarily serving as political tools in criminal campaigns in the early 1980s to focusing on providing justice in individual cases today.[22] Court rhetoric has changed over the past decade, reflecting a modest attempt by the courts to shift from being a tool for enforcing Party policy to being a neutral forum for dispute resolution. Many judges have replaced their military-style uniforms with robes – a change viewed as a step forward by some commentators who see it as a signal that judges and courts are not simply another branch of the party-state.[23] Likewise, the new education requirements for judges represent a shift away from primary reliance on political backgrounds in selecting members of the judiciary.

Depoliticization – to the degree it has occurred – may be possible precisely because the courts are not a challenge to Party authority. Local Party organizations continue to oversee court appointments, court presidents are often primarily chosen for political reasons, and the overwhelming majority of judges continue to be Party members. Within the Party hierarchy, the President of the Supreme People's Court continues to rank well below the Minister of Public Security, a pattern generally replicated at local level.

Courts' loyalty to the Party was re-emphasized in 2006 with the launching of a new campaign on "socialist rule of law theory" in the courts, procuratorates, justice bureaus and public security bureaus. The campaign began with a speech

21 "Zhongyang Zhengfawei: Dongyuan shehui liliang, qieshi jiejue zhixing nan" ("Central Political-Legal Committee: mobilize the resources of society, conscientiously solve the problem of enforcing judgements"), *Xinhua wang*, 23 January 2006, available from http://news.xinhuanet.com/legal/2006-01/23/content_4090238.htm. One response of courts to problems in enforcement has been renewed stress on mediation to reduce contradictions and conflict in society. The most recent SPC work report stated that 30% of all civil cases were resolved through mediation in 2006, and that 55% of first-instance civil cases were mediated or withdrawn prior to judgement (SPC Work Report 2007). Judges cite two primary reasons for this trend: mediated decisions are more likely to be enforced than adjudicated cases, and they are less likely to result in protests and complaints.

22 Yu Zhong, "Lun Zuigao Renmin Fayuan shiji chengdan de zhengzhi gongneng: yi Zuigao Renmin Fayuan linian 'gongzuo baogao' wei yiju" ("On the actual political function of the SPC: using the annual 'work report' of the SPC as a base"), *Qinghua faxue* (*Tsinghua Legal Studies*), Vol. 7, available from http://law-thinker.com/show.asp?id=2829.

23 "Ganshou sifa zunyan: chuan fapao qiao fachui xingshi beihou de yiyi hezai" ("Feeling the honour of the judiciary: what's the meaning behind the actions of wearing robes and hitting gavels"), *Xinhua wang*, 5 June 2002, available from http://news3.xinhuanet.com/newscenter/2002-06/05/content_425067.htm.

by Luo Gan (罗干), head of the Party's Central Political-Legal Committee, in which he stated that the goals were to guarantee the legal and political system's "political colour" and loyalty to the Party, the nation, the people and the law. The five elements of the campaign were "ruling the country by law," "implementing law for the people," "maintaining fairness and justice," "serving the overall situation" and "following the leadership of the Party."[24] In the speech Luo appeared to be drawing a distinction between "rule of law" and "socialist rule of law," with the latter emphasizing the legal system's obligation to follow Party leadership, and in particular Hu Jintao's theory of a "harmonious society." The SPC instructed all courts nationwide to educate judges in these principles. In a follow-up speech, Cao Jianming (曹建明), vice-president of the Supreme People's Court, linked the campaign to the need to avoid the "negative influence of Western rule of law theory"[25] – an apparent reference to those within and outside China advocating Western-style judicial independence for China.

New Pressures

The recent focus on reinforcing political orthodoxy in the courts reflects the modest reach of top-down court reform. The evolution of Chinese society and governance has also resulted in new challenges for the courts. This section discusses pressures on them that threaten to undermine their already fragile authority.

Media pressure

Over the past decade China's courts have confronted increasingly aggressive and influential media. The media have long been far more powerful actors in the

24 "Luo Gan zai shehui zhuyi fazhi linian yantaoban shang qiangdiao: shenru kanzhan shehui zhuyi fazhi linian jiaoyu, qieshi jiaqiang zhengfa duiwu sixiang zhengzhi jianshe" ("Luo Gan emphasizes in a symposium on socialist rule of law theory: deepen education on socialist rule of law theory, enhance the ideological and political construction among workers in the political-legal system"), *Zhongguo fayuan wang* (*China Court Web*), 14 April 2006, available from http://www.chinacourt.org/public/detail.php?id=201753. In a speech in November 2006, Luo again called for strengthening Party oversight of legal institutions. He also added a more direct critique of those advocating judicial independence and Western-style legal reforms. Luo warned against underestimating the influence of such arguments, in particular arguments that deny the Party's leadership of legal and political institutions, on those working in the political-legal system. He also stated that "hostile forces" were trying to use legal institutions as an entry-point for Westernizing and splitting China. Luo Gan, "Zhengfa jiguan zai goujian hexie shehui zhong danfu zhongda lishi shiming he zhengzhi zeren" ("Political and legal institutions shoulder an important historical mission and political responsibility in the construction of a harmonious society"), *Qiushi* (*Seeking Truth*), No. 3 (2007), available at http://www.qsjournal.com.cn/qs/20070201/GB/qs%5E448%5E0%5E1.htm.

25 "Cao Jiaming zai shehui zhuyi fazhi linian yantaoban shang qiangdiao: renmin fayuan yao laogu shuli shehui zhuyi fazhi linian" ("Cao Jianming emphasizes in the symposium on socialist rule of law theory: the people's courts must steadily establish socialist rule of law theory"), *Zhongguo fayuan wang*, 14 April 2006, available from http://www.chinacourt.org/public/detail.php?id=201755. Cao also spoke of the need to avoid "extreme 'left' thoughts" and the "remnants of feudalism." His speech appeared primarily aimed at placing the courts in line with current Party ideology, and thus perhaps designed to insulate them from criticism for excessive reliance on Western models. But such comments also reflect the SPC's move away from aggressively promoting court reform.

Chinese political system than the courts, serving as both the mouthpiece and the "eyes and ears" of the Party. The growth of commercial media in the 1990s allowed the media to combine their traditional official role with marketized mass appeal. This encompassed expanded coverage of the legal system, including a significant volume of critical reporting on the courts. The internet has facilitated such coverage, with news on major cases spreading rapidly online and courts finding it more difficult to block critical reporting.[26]

The media are playing an important role in exposing injustice and in pressuring courts to behave fairly. At the same time, media coverage reinforces Party oversight of the courts. Media efforts to stir up and claim to represent popular opinion can lead officials to intervene in cases. Judges complain that there is little they can do to resist media pressure, even when media views are inconsistent with substantive or procedural law.

When media and court views diverge, party-state leaders appear to continue to trust the media more than they do the courts. In a system in which intervention in individual cases by Party officials remains legitimate, even the threat of intervention can be sufficient to affect cases. Deference to media views is accentuated by concern for social stability: the fact that a case is attracting significant media and popular attention is often sufficient reason to justify intervention, regardless of the underlying dispute. The media's ability to influence the courts, and to do so by stirring up popular sentiment online, reflects the degree to which assuaging popular demands for justice remains more important than deciding cases according to legal and procedural norms.

Petitions and protests

Courts have also increasingly come under pressure from petitioners and protestors. As Table 1 shows, courts reported handling just under four million letters and visits in 2005. The figure includes only letters and visits to the courts – and thus excludes complaints about the courts raised with other party-state actors or institutions.

Judges say that pressure from letters and visits has increased in recent years and that courts are often under pressure from court and Party superiors to resolve petitioners' grievances. This is the case even when, according to judges, such complaints lack legal merit. In some local courts the annual evaluation of judges' performance and bonuses are based in part on the volume of letters and visits resulting from their cases.[27] Court officials and academics have noted that

26 For analysis of court-media relations, see Benjamin L. Liebman, "Watchdog or demagogue? The media in the Chinese legal system," *Columbia Law Review*, Vol. 105, No. 1 (2005) pp. 1–157.

27 For example, see "Beijing fayuan dui zhongda shesu xinfang an jiang shixing lingdao baoan zhidu" ("Beijing courts will implement a system making court leaders responsible for the resolution of major litigation-related letters and visits"), *Zhongguo xinwen wang* (*China News Net*), 28 July 2005, available from http://news.qq.com/a/20050728/000926.htm.

dealing with petitions and visits is distracting judges from their work handling cases and that courts handle nearly as many petitions as they do cases.[28]

Much press coverage of the issue highlights how letters and visits have led courts to alter incorrect decisions or have assisted in compelling parties to implement court judgements.[29] Judges confirm that some petitions and protests do result in courts re-examining and correcting erroneous cases.[30] Other accounts, however, note that courts have paid petitioners themselves when court decisions fail to provide sufficient funds to petitioners.[31] Commentators have argued that courts are being forced to change decisions to protect social stability and that the letters and visits system is weakening judicial authority.[32] Judges comment that they sometimes alter decisions, pay parties from court funds or pressure losing parties to pay more money than ordered by the court in order to assuage protestors.[33]

Judges know that the more they respond to protests, the more they will encourage similar actions by others. As with media influence, courts' inability to resist popular pressure reflects concern with social stability by party-state officials. Fear that popular discontent may result in unrest encourages officials to respond to such complaints. Given such concerns, persuading protestors to terminate their protests becomes more important than following legal and procedural standards.

Other problems are also undermining efforts to strengthen the judiciary. Courts continue to lack transparency, with decisions generally not publicly available.[34] They have also imposed new restrictions on the media's ability to

28 2004 SPC Work Report; Zuo Weimin and He Yongjun, "Zhengfa chuantong yu sifa lixing: yi Zuigao Fayuan xinfang zhidu wei zhongxin de yanjiu" ("Politics and law, tradition and judicial rationality: research centred on the SPC's letters and visits system"), *Sichuan Daxue xuebao: zheshe ban* (*Journal of Sichuan University: Philosophy and Social Science Edition*), No. 1 (2005), available from http://www.usc.cuhk.edu.hk/wk_wzdetails.asp?id=4523. The SPC's 2007 Work Report did not include figures on the total number of letters and visits raised with the courts, but did note that letters and visits to local courts decreased by 11% in 2006 and that those to the SPC decreased by nearly 5%. The continued declines probably reflect the SPC's instruction that courts at all levels should work to reduce litigation-related letters and visits (SPC Work Report 2007).

29 For example, see "Jiangsu Hebei deng sheng bufen qunzhong yueji xinfang shijian diaocha" ("An investigation of skipping-level letters and visits by masses from Jiangsu, Hebei and other provinces"), *Liaowang xinwen zhoukan* (*Outlook Weekly*), 30 October 2004, available from http://news.xinhuanet.com/newscenter/2004-10/30/content_2156474.htm.

30 Interviews.

31 "Jinhua Zhongyuan zhashi zuohao shesu xinfang gongzuo" ("Jinhua Intermediate Court works hard on litigation-related letters and visits"), 27 December 2005, available from http://www.jhcourt.cn/news/news_detail.asp?id=626 (link no longer valid; copy on file with author). Courts have also created "judicial relief" funds to assist poor litigants who are unable to enforce judgements in their favour. "Zuigao fayuan tan tuidong quanguo fanwei nei jianli zhixing jiuzhu jijin" ("SPC discusses promoting the establishment of an enforcement relief fund nationwide"), Sina.com, 21 January 2007, available at http://news.sina.com.cn/c/2007-01-26/114912148273.shtml.

32 "Woguo xinfang zhidu xianru sichong kunjing mianlin fazhi tiaozhan" ("Our nation's letters and visits system encounters four difficulties, faces challenges from rule of law"), *Xinhua wang*, 30 June 2004, available from http://news.sina.com.cn/c/2004-06-30/12143565398.shtml.

33 Interviews.

34 He Weifang, "Panjueshu shangwang nan zai hechu" ("What's the difficulty in putting court decisions online"), *Fazhi ribao* (*Legal Daily*), 15 December 2005, available from http://law-thinker.com/show.asp?id=3025.

cover court proceedings, in an apparent effort to ensure positive coverage of the courts.[35] Courts are increasingly dealing with difficult or sensitive cases by inaction – refusing to accept cases or leaving them unresolved.[36] In addition, there is growing inequality within the courts, with those in less developed areas struggling to find sufficient qualified personnel as existing judges leave to pursue higher paying jobs as lawyers.

Horizontal Development and Innovation

Despite these problems, significant change is occurring in China's courts. The most important recent developments are coming from lower courts. Three trends are particularly notable.

First, lower courts are increasingly looking to other courts for guidance when they encounter new or difficult legal questions.[37] In the past, courts generally had little option but to consult higher courts. In recent years, however, judges have increasingly looked horizontally, to courts of equal rank outside their jurisdictions, for guidance. They routinely consult the internet to assist them when they encounter new questions, to learn how courts elsewhere have handled similar issues. In particular, judges in less developed areas note that they frequently look to online media reports, case summaries and in some cases decisions posted to court websites to learn how other courts have handled cases.

Such judicial networking, and the development of informal patterns of precedent, may lead to more consistent application of the law. The growth of the internet may also be facilitating the development of professional identity among judges, who increasingly interact online and who appear ever more aware of the challenges similarly situated judges face elsewhere in China.[38] Greater professional identity among judges is unlikely to alter how they decide sensitive cases, but it may assist them as they seek to combat interference from both within and outside the courts. The growth of horizontal relationships suggests that courts may be able to expand their own autonomy by looking to other courts for guidance rather than to party-state officials or court superiors.

Secondly, judicial networks may foster legal innovation. A small number of local courts have engaged in significant legal innovation. Courts in China have long engaged in experimentation, but in recent years some have issued decisions

35 Vivian Wu, "Press quiet on changes to reporting court cases," *South China Morning Post*, 14 September 2006.

36 For one example, see "Guangxi bu shouli 13 lei ruoshi qunti an, sheng gaoyuan cheng you guoqing jueding" ("Guangxi refuses to accept 13 categories of cases relating to disadvantaged people, high court asserts it is decided by the situation of the country"), *Zhongguo qingnian bao* (*China Youth Daily*), 24 August 2004, available from http://news.qq.com/a/20040824/000070.htm. Doing so is understandable: many such cases in practice involve complex or sensitive issues potentially touching on social unrest, and are disputes that courts could not resolve on their own.

37 Benjamin L. Liebman and Timothy Wu, "Chinese network justice," *Chicago Journal of International Law*, Vol. 8, No. 1 (2007).

38 Similar observations have been made regarding the growth of trans-national judicial networks. Anne-Marie Slaughter, *A New World Order* (Princeton: Princeton University Press, 2004), pp. 65–103.

that appear directly to challenge existing legal norms or consciously to break new legal ground. Thus, for example, a court in Henan ruled, in what became known as the *Seed Case*, that a provincial pricing regulation was "spontaneously invalid" because it conflicted with the national Seed Law. The court thus challenged norms that dictate that courts lack the power to invalidate laws or regulations. The case generated a backlash from the provincial people's congress, which ordered the judges responsible to be removed from office. The judges regained their positions after the national media reported on the case.[39]

Likewise, courts in Shanghai, Beijing and Guangzhou have innovated by finding for the media in defamation cases brought by famous persons. The courts have directly or indirectly suggested that famous persons should withstand a higher degree of scrutiny than ordinary persons – despite the absence of any distinction between ordinary and "public persons" in Chinese defamation law.[40] And in a series of cases brought by university students, courts have held that universities may be sued under China's Administrative Litigation Law – despite the widespread presumption that the law did not apply to universities.[41] The cases have been interpreted as efforts by Chinese courts to expand their jurisdiction in administrative litigation, a notable trend given that commentators have argued that courts have been reluctant to undertake administrative cases given the often influential positions of defendants in such cases.[42]

Some judicial innovation is a consequence of the wide discretion Chinese judges have in resolving cases. Unclear legal standards mean that courts must frequently fill gaps. Nevertheless, in some recent cases they have gone further, directly challenging norms, as in the *Seed Case*, or creating legal standards that lack statutory support.

Court experimentation and innovation occurs in politically safe cases, and outcomes are usually consistent with the interests of important party-state actors. Indeed, it may be that innovation is only possible in cases in which outcomes are consistent with powerful interests or there are no strong adverse interests. Thus, for example, the first case to find a public person standard resulted in a judgement in favour of a newspaper that was a subsidiary of the official mouthpiece newspaper of the Shanghai Municipal Communist Party Committee.

39 For a discussion of the case, see Zhao Lei, "Li Huijuan: tiaozhan difang lifa" ("Li Huijuan: challenging local legislation."), 25 July 2004, available at http://www.dffy.com/fayanguancha/fangyuan/200407/20040725162155.htm.

40 Benjamin L. Liebman, "Innovation through intimidation: an empirical account of defamation litigation in China," *Harvard International Law Journal*, Vol. 47, No. 1 (2006), pp. 33–177.

41 For analysis of the cases, see Tom Kellogg, "Campus and the courts: education litigation and judicial protection of rights in China," *Harvard Human Rights Law Journal* (forthcoming 2007).

42 For an example of such arguments, see Li Fujin, "Xingzheng shenpan de kunjing yu chulu" ("The difficulties in and remedies for administrative adjudication"), 19 September 2003, available at http://www.dffy.com/faxuejieti/xz/200311/20031119203349.htm.

The modest reach of judicial innovation in China highlights a key element of court reform. The SPC does from time to time issue judicial interpretations that go beyond the text of laws the National People's Congress has passed, but such interpretations rarely directly challenge the authority of other institutions. When courts do appear to be seeking to expand their authority, including in defamation litigation, the *Seed Case* and some aspects of administrative litigation, such steps have come from lower courts.[43] Significant institutional change is not the direct result of top-down reform.

The third trend is that, although China's courts are not fora for adjudicating public rights, they have become the place for airing a range of grievances.[44] Over the past decade, litigants have brought a widening array of what might be thought of as public grievances into the courts – including class actions, public interest lawsuits on such issues as women's and environmental rights, and constitutional claims.[45] Many such cases are being brought with the assistance of lawyers who are explicitly seeking to use litigation to bring social change; the fact that China now has more than 150,000 lawyers[46] is resulting in greater incentives for them to bring novel cases. Courts have not always been receptive to such claims. The party-state appears increasingly wary of these efforts, and has imposed new restrictions on lawyers and on public interest litigation.[47] But the fact that these claims have been permitted and at times even encouraged is particularly notable given China's political system: the combination of class actions, contingency fees, administrative litigation, constitutional litigation, and cause lawyering is not common in authoritarian systems (or in many systems of any type outside the United States).

Such claims also highlight a characteristic of public litigation and cause lawyering in China: when they succeed it is rarely because of court decisions. The primary goal of many of these lawsuits is to generate public, and in particular media, attention sufficient to compel official action. When change does result, it is more often from the intervention of party-state officials than from a court opinion. Litigants may hope for a binding court decision, but using the courts as a forum for generating public pressure is often equally, if not more, important in cases in which claims succeed. The use of litigation to create public pressure and to compel extra-judicial action is not unique to China, but China may be distinct

43 One exception to this pattern was the Qi Yuling case, in which the SPC in 2001 seemed to suggest that a case could be brought directly under the PRC Constitution. The decision was both opaque and controversial, and no subsequent cases have endorsed or acknowledged the principle.

44 Liebman, "Innovation through intimidation."

45 For example, see Benjamin L. Liebman, "Note, class action litigation in China," *Harvard Law Review*, Vol. 111 (1998), p. 1523.

46 China Law Yearbook 2006, p. 1001.

47 In March 2006 the All-China Lawyers Association issued a notice requiring lawyers handling collective (defined as involving ten or more people) or sensitive disputes to report such representation to, and accept "guidance from," the local lawyers' association and justice bureau, "Zhonghua quanguo lüshi xiehui guanyu lüshi banli quntixing anjian zhidao yijian" ("Guidance notice of the All-China Lawyers Association regarding lawyers' handling of group cases"), 20 March 2006, http://www.dffy.com/faguixiazai/ssf/200606/20060620110110.htm.

in its extreme reliance on extra-judicial responses to major public disputes in the courts.

Restricted Reform?

Recent developments do not suggest fundamental changes in courts' power relative to other state actors. This is not surprising: increasing power is not something courts can do on their own, and central Party leaders have not emphasized strengthening the courts' formal power. Nevertheless, despite the formal limitations on court authority, their future role may be significantly influenced by how they define their own roles and by how litigants use them.

Bottom-up developments may also be resulting in courts that are increasingly in conflict with other party-state and official institutions. This is particularly apparent in court interactions with the media, where courts have responded to media oversight by imposing limits on reporting and filing defamation lawsuits. But courts also appear to be increasingly in conflict with people's congresses and procuratorates, both of which have attempted to strengthen their supervision of the courts, and also with administrative departments.

Explaining new roles

Recognizing the limitations of court reform in China is not meant to trivialize the changes thus far. Indeed, asking why China's courts are not more independent or more powerful may be less important than understanding why they have been permitted to develop as they have. Why have courts been permitted to hear a wider range of grievances and to take even modest steps in the direction of increased authority and autonomy?

Western writings on the roles of courts have largely focused on the question of why a democratic regime would create independent courts.[48] Theories include the desire to make political bargains credible, the usefulness of courts to politicians who wish to shift blame for unpopular policies, courts' roles in keeping administrative bureaucracies in line with government policy, and courts' attraction to political parties that may one day find themselves out of power. Such theories have limited applicability in China, where a non-democratic regime has encouraged development of the courts, and where courts have limited powers over other administrative actors.

Another common explanation for the creation of a functional legal system is that such institutions are necessary for economic development. An interest in economic development has certainly played a role in China's legal reforms. But this explanation appears unsatisfactory, because economic development has progressed despite the absence of a legal system that provides effective

48 The list provided here is not exhaustive. For more detailed analysis, see Matthew C. Stephenson, "'When the devil turns…': the political foundations of independent judicial review," *The Journal of Legal Studies*, Vol. 32 (2003), pp. 61–64.

guarantees of property rights. A desire to conform to international norms may play some role – but also seems a weak explanation for China's recent experiences, in particular the encouragement of class actions and cause lawyering. Three alternative theories are more plausible.

First, courts are one of a number of party-state institutions serving as a safety valve for a widening range of popular complaints. Permitting grievances to be raised through class actions, administrative litigation or even (in a small number of cases) constitutional litigation may be preferable to such complaints not being heard at all – or being raised on the streets. The safety valve function of courts also explains why they may accept but then not decide some difficult cases: the hope may be that once cases are filed, grievances will dissipate over time. The courts are not unique, or even particularly prominent, in this role. The letters and visits system plays a broader, and arguably more significant, function as a safety valve. Courts are thus one of a number of fora for raising grievances, and courts that permit such grievances to be raised act in the interests of social stability.

Concern with social stability also helps explain inconsistent trends in court reform. The party-state has emphasized the role of the courts and has given tremendous attention to courts and law in the media. At the same time, party-state leaders continue to tolerate, and even encourage, a range of official and quasi-official actors to intervene in court decision-making. Concerns with social stability force party-state officials to strive to be even more responsive to public views regarding the courts than might be the case in a democratic system, where the political process provides a mechanism for public grievances to be aired and resolved. The legitimacy of China's leadership depends on its ability both to channel and to contain populism; concerns that popular expressions of outrage may spin out of control encourage rapid intervention in the legal system. The counter-majoritarian function of courts thus may be harder to accept in a non-democratic society, where courts lack authority and public confidence, than in a democracy. This is particularly the case in China, where the rise of social unrest makes officials particularly sensitive to public opinion and where the courts lack a history of being viewed as either authoritative or neutral.

Secondly, the evolving roles of courts, including increasing conflicts with other party-state institutions, reflect the development of institutional competition in the Chinese political system. The central party-state has encouraged a range of official actors – including courts, the media, letters and visits bureaus, the procuratorates, Party discipline authorities, and people's congresses – to play oversight roles, often over each other. Attempts by the courts to expand their autonomy and authority are consistent with similar steps being taken by other actors. This reflects an emerging characteristic of institutional relationships in China, one that appears to be a crucial part of the institutionalization of the party-state that has helped to explain its resilience.[49] The aim appears to be to

49 Andrew J. Nathan, "Authoritarian resilience," *Journal of Democracy*, Vol. 14, No. 1 (2003), pp. 6–17.

encourage a range of official actors to expand their roles in resolving grievances and fighting abuses, and to serve as checks on each other. Some greater transparency is encouraged, but within the limits of Party oversight and primarily by party-state actors. Wrongdoing is addressed, and party-state legitimacy is maintained, without fostering the development of non-state checks on official action. Thus any expansion in court roles or authority may reflect the increased attention to resolving grievances and expanding oversight in the Chinese system in general, not greater authority of the courts. China's leadership is sensitive to the possibility that allowing more prominent roles to non-state actors may undermine central authority. In the legal system, however, allowing a widening range of grievances to be brought by individuals and organizations may also be an effective tool for asserting state control.

Thirdly, bottom-up development of the courts may be a source of judicial power. The ability of judges to network horizontally may lead to greater authority and autonomy of the courts. The trajectory of court development may not be entirely determined by top-down edicts or constitutional structure. Chinese judges themselves are increasingly looking to the roles judges play in other countries as they seek to define their own positions. Likewise, litigants' aspirations for the legal system appear to derive from both rising attention to the role of law and courts and from international norms.

Fairness without independence?

Understanding why the Chinese party-state has permitted even the level of court reform experienced thus far yields insight into a central question facing China's courts: what are the possible limits of court development in a non-democratic society? Many in the West and in China have looked to China's courts in the hope that they may play a transformative role in the Chinese political system. But the more pertinent question may be what role courts can play within the current system. Can they serve as fair adjudicators of private disputes, and as checks on some forms of official action, without political change? And, if they do, will they legitimize Party rule, or will the development of a more professionalized judiciary inevitably lead to courts that challenge Party authority? Recent developments and debates in China have largely avoided this question.[50]

China's effort to create courts that act fairly without challenging single-party rule is not unprecedented. Other single-party states – including Spain under Franco and modern Singapore – have had courts that commentators have viewed as largely fair and independent in their handling of non-sensitive or non-political cases.[51] Parallels may also be drawn with Japanese courts, which

50 One exception is the work of "new-left" scholars such as Pan Wei, who have argued that China can and should establish rule of law without democracy. See, for example, Pan Wei, "Fazhi yu weilai de zhongguo zhengti" ("Rule of law and China's future political system") *Zhanlüe yu guanli* (*Strategy and Management*), No. 5 (1999), at pp 30–36.

51 José J. Toharia, "Judicial independence in an authoritarian regime: the case of contemporary Spain," *Law and Society Review*, Vol. 9, No. 3 (1975), pp. 475–96.

were largely independent both in the late imperial period and also, after democratization, during the long period of Liberal Democratic Party rule.[52] Similarly, research on Egypt has explored why that authoritarian regime has created an independent constitutional court.[53]

Recent Chinese experience does not fit squarely into any of these models. In contrast to Singapore and Japan, for example, the range of cases deemed to be sensitive in China is extraordinarily wide – and includes not only direct challenges to Party authority or major criminal cases but also a wide range of cases attracting public attention, as well as those involving litigants with ties to party-state officials. In contrast to Franco's Spain, where a degree of independence was possible because courts' powers were extremely limited and courts played little role in creating legal values, China's courts have become significant fora for the airing of rights-based grievances. And in contrast to Egypt, where the constitutional court was established and developed to a great extent because of its role in furthering economic development, courts in China have developed into significant fora for the airing of rights-based claims even without serving as effective guarantors of property rights.[54] Moreover, the most significant changes in Chinese courts' roles appear to be coming from lower courts.

Developing the capacity of China's courts to handle routine cases fairly would be a significant accomplishment. Doing so would also be consistent with two of the three explanations offered above for the development of the courts to date: serving as a safety valve for discontent and grievances, and institutionalizing the operation of the party state. But the third explanation, that horizontal and bottom-up development may lead to greater court autonomy, suggests that further development of the courts may also give rise to increased tensions with other party-state actors. As courts continue to develop horizontally, and as judges develop professional identities, it may become increasingly difficult to constrain court development. By encouraging the development of more professional judges, the party-state may also be fostering greater challenges.

Recent developments suggest that courts' ability to serve broader aims may depend on their developing greater authority, either on their own or at the behest of the party-state. Their ability to do so will be shaped by party-state

52 John O. Haley, "The Japanese judiciary: maintaining integrity, autonomy and the public trust," Washington University in St Louis School of Law, Faculty Working Papers Series, Paper No. 05-10-01 (forthcoming in Daniel J. Foote (ed.), *Law in Japan: A Turning Point* (Seattle: University of Washington Press, 2007)). Haley notes a long tradition of judicial independence in Japan stretching back to the 19th century. In contrast, Mark Ramseyer and Eric Rasmusen argue that courts in democratic Japan, although generally independent, have yielded to LDP interests in certain sensitive cases. J. Mark Ramseyer and Eric B. Rasmusen, *Measuring Judicial Independence: The Political Economy of Judging in Japan* (Chicago: University of Chicago Press 2003), pp. 122–23. Haley finds no evidence of such political influence on modern Japanese courts.

53 Tamir Moustafa, "Law versus the state: the judicialization of politics in Egypt," *Law and Social Inquiry*, Vol. 28 (2003), pp. 883–930.

54 In Egypt, as Moustafa describes, the Constitutional Court has developed into a forum for challenging the regime. In China, in contrast, courts have neither challenged single-party rule nor served as fora for those seeking to do so.

policy, but will also reflect their continued bottom-up development. The roles of courts and judges are no longer solely defined by top-down pronouncements. Judges appear to be looking to the roles judges play in other countries as they seek to define their own positions; litigants' aspirations likewise appear to derive both from rising attention to the role of judges and from international norms. Recent attempts to steer judges away from "Western rule of law theories" are a tacit acknowledgment of such trends. Continued bottom-up development may be crucial to courts' serving the Party's interests – but may also promote new challenges. The most significant development regarding China's courts is that their role in Chinese society is increasingly contested.

Commentary on "China's Courts: Restricted Reform"

Shen Kui

Benjamin Liebman has written a good article on a difficult subject. I have only a few comments, divided into three parts. In the first two parts, I consider Liebman's approach to such a historically complicated matter. I think it is appropriate to deal with it by focusing on the central question of whether the role of the courts in China's political system has changed as a result of reform; after an initial discussion, I show that Liebman has actually engaged in a political system analysis to reply to that central question. The third part presents my initial ideas about three different possible tests for evaluating judicial reform. Using these tests, I will look at the question of the sense in which reform could be regarded as "restricted," as Liebman has suggested.

The Central Question and Historically Appropriate Approach

Liebman adopts an extremely useful perspective from which to survey such a complicated reform process. He does not focus directly on the detailed, and mostly technical, contents of every judicial reform policy, nor attempt to describe all the effects of these reforms, which would have made a broad overview virtually impossible. Instead, he moves directly to the central question of whether the reform has resulted in a substantial shift or change in the position or role of the courts.

As a historical methodology, it is a useful approach because any acute and deep insights into a complex history require a main thread around which the related materials can be based, or more accurately renarrated, without getting bogged down in less relevant aspects.[1] Case-by-case evaluation of concrete policies may be a good approach to consider the legitimacy, feasibility and effectiveness of a specific policy or to work out what policy to adopt to achieve a desired goal, and has been effectively used by many Chinese scholars. However, it is much less useful in assessing the long-term prospects and progress of reform as a whole. Raising an appropriate central question is a good tool for helping to grasp a historical theme.

Given that that is the case, it is important to find a suitable central question. For example, simply asking what the effects of judicial reform are provides no clearly defined and agreed-upon external references and would lead to either a

1 History is usually a coherent and continuous picture created by the historian who uses constructive imagination on the available historical data. See R. G. Collinwood, *The Idea of History* (London: Oxford University Press, 1946).

© The China Quarterly, 2007 doi:10.1017/S0305741007001622

mission impossible or a slide into the case-by-case approach. Similarly, asking what effects – if any – judicial reform has had on public confidence in the judiciary does create a suitable reference-oriented framework for evaluation, but is a much narrower question because it could be regarded as a subset of the broader question of the position of the courts within society.

Different from these two sorts of questions, the question that Liebman has chosen not only provides the necessary point of reference – the effect of judicial reform on the political position of the courts – but also has the advantage of being relevant to virtually all reform measures. Questions as diverse as the effect of judicial reforms on judicial independence, openness, fairness, effectiveness, integrity, improved organization of the judiciary, improved judicial quality and public confidence on the judiciary can all be connected to this central question.

Political System Analysis

Liebman does not try to give an answer to his central question solely from the perspective of law. Actually, it is not a legal question but a political one. Liebman's approach is similar to the discipline of political science known as systems theory.[2] This discipline emphasizes the empirical study of actors and interactions among them in a specific political system as a means to understanding the actors' behaviour, position and dynamics. In this view, the behaviour of any actor can be attributed either to the demands of the actor itself or to the demands placed on it from outside forces, or to some mixture of both.

The systems analysis can be seen at various points in the article. For example, in Liebman's view, the modest growth of caseloads may reflect the coexisting and self-contradictory attitude of the Party leadership to the role of courts. On the one hand, the leadership hopes to strengthen the courts' competence to resolve a growing number of disputes. On the other, it does not rely on the judiciary to be the most important body to quell social dissatisfaction and uneasiness.

Certainly, the dynamics of judicial reform also involve the internal demands of the judiciary. However, the fact that the courts are to a large extent subject to the populism-oriented Party leadership means that even internal dynamics are mostly generated by the courts' response to outsiders' demands, and are limited by the demands of outsiders as well. Reform policies, whether on general matters such as legal training or on technical matters such as the evidentiary rules, are regarded by many scholars as efforts to promote the fairness and efficiency of courts, and further to have an indirect positive effect on judicial independence. Nevertheless, even if reformists from within the court system have similar ideas in mind while designing policies, they would rather talk about their goals in

2 Systems theory in political science was first conceived by David Easton. See David Easton, *A System Analysis of Political Life* (New York: Wiley, 1965); *A Framework for Political Analysis*, 2nd ed. (Chicago: University of Chicago Press, 1979).

terms of judicial fairness and efficiency rather than in terms of judicial independence.[3]

This attitude may be a response to the perceived attitudes of the Party leadership and the public. The Party leadership is reluctant to create truly independent institutions that it cannot control, and many people fear that a fully independent judiciary, freed from Party or People's Congress supervision and discipline, would become even more corrupt and less responsive to public needs.[4] This is why Liebman has said that reform has not focused on changing the role or relative power of the courts within the system.

The internal demands of judiciary could also result in some limitations on judicial reform. The presumption that any actor in a political system will take self-interested steps to maintain its existence, as systems theory reveals, can partially explain what Liebman calls "controlled transparency." Since the courts are facing a lack of public confidence, it is no wonder that they try to reduce the number of negative media reports about themselves. And because the media in China are supervised by the propaganda departments of Party organizations, it is easy for the courts to restrict unflattering media coverage, as long as they can convince propaganda officials that negative reports will cause more problems with social stability.

Evaluative Tests and Restricted Reform in What Sense

After raising an appropriate central question and engaging in a political system analysis, Liebman reached a general conclusion that reform of the courts in China has been a case of restricted reform. I agree with the conclusion in the sense that judicial reform has not yet brought about any significant change in the position or role of courts in China's political system. Chinese courts are still heavily influenced by the Party leadership and Party organizations, other state institutions and the local authorities, and by the media and the public. Even though they have become more competent as fair and efficient arbitrators in dealing with ordinary cases, their lack of independence in deciding politically or socially sensitive cases, and the way they take into account many legally irrelevant considerations while deciding cases, demonstrates their real position.

3 For example, the Supreme People's Court Work Report (Zuigao Renmin Fayuan gongzuo baogao) delivered in 1996 mentioned emphatically that courts should exercise judicial power independently in accordance with law under the leadership of Party. Since then, from 1997 to 2006, there were only three SPC Work Reports delivered in 2000, 2002 and 2004, mentioning, but not stressing, the issue of independent exercise of judicial power. In the 2000 Report, the issue was connected with the readjustment of some branches of basic-level courts (*renmin fating*). The issue was connected with the requirement of WTO on the judiciary in the 2002 Report, and with the supervision and guidance of the SPC on the lower-level courts in the 2004 Report. Comparatively, judicial fairness has always been an important issue in annual reports.

4 See e.g. Tang Zhongmin, "'Sifa duli' buneng zhenzheng jiejue sifa bugong he sifa fubai" ("'Judicial independence' cannot veritably resolve the problems of judicial unfairness and judicial corruption"), *Tansuo* (*Probe*), Vol. 1 (2003).

This article has also prompted me to think about another question: what test should be applied to evaluate the achievements of judicial reform in respect of the role or position of the courts? There may be three tests which need to be discussed. The first, adopted by Liebman, could be called the ideal-based test. This takes judicial independence as a necessary aspect of the rule of law in modern democracy and hence evaluates reform of the courts from the perspective of whether it has caused the judiciary to be more independent. It is also a principle generally accepted by most Chinese scholars that courts or judges should make decisions only according to the law without any obvious interference from outside.[5] From the perspective of the ideal-based test, as mentioned above, Liebman's conclusion is unquestionably correct.

The second one could be called the goal-based test, assessing judicial reform in the context of whether it has realized the goals laid out by the policy makers themselves. In China, despite the desire and expectation for judicial independence among many law scholars and students, official documents have never proclaimed this as one of the goals of judicial reform. Instead, as Liebman pointed out, the main goal is limited to improving the efficiency and fairness of the courts. From the perspective of the goal-based test, the conclusion would be that judicial reform has been modestly successful but still restricted. Many reform policies in general have improved courts' ability to be more efficient and fair, but judicial reform is still restricted since there are also many cases in which the courts have not satisfied the expectation of the public to adjudicate well.

These two tests are quite different, but have similarities in that both of them are results-oriented. Comparatively, the third test is to evaluate judicial reform against the background of the long and difficult process of political reform in China. I would like to call it a process-based test.

It must be admitted that the political reform being currently undertaken by the Party leadership and Chinese people is unprecedented in world history, a very big challenge requiring sophisticated wisdom. In particular, the Party leadership must, first, continue with economic reform, maintain economic development, and avoid the stagnation or collapse of the economy, which might cause a decline in the fortunes of many Chinese people and therefore directly threaten the legitimacy of Party governance; secondly, resolve as many complicated social problems as possible and maintain public confidence in the party-state's ruling competence; and thirdly, conduct political reform step by step, meanwhile guarding against the possibility of a political earthquake which might indirectly affect economic development. It is a more difficult mission in reality than on paper to manage these major matters, because they are linked to each other in complex ways and yet need to be faced simultaneously.

5 It is also a principle in China's Constitution. Article 126 states that the people's courts exercise judicial power independently, in accordance with the provisions of the law, and are not subject to interference by any administrative organ, public organization or individual. Many Chinese scholars rely on this article for judicial independence.

Against this background, judicial reform, as part of the process of political reform, has been inevitably very hard and exceedingly slow. There are at least two reasons for a more positive assessment than the one presented by Liebman. On the one hand, the modest success of judicial reform has bred expectation for even more progress: popular attention to both the problems and the potential role of the courts appears to be higher than ever before. In some ways, the fact that the role of courts is increasingly contested may be viewed as one of the great achievements of the reform. On the other hand, since the future image of democratic politics with Chinese characteristics is not very clear, the question raised by Liebman as to what is the appropriate or potential future role of courts in China is still waiting to be explored. Instability is inevitable during a dramatic movement to an unclear future, but this instability may have positive effects for further development. The elites and the common people in China at least have learned a lot from the reform by discussing advantages, as well as limitations, of any possible measure to promote judicial competence and fairness. Such accumulation of knowledge is a necessary beginning for the future construction of a more satisfactory judiciary.

In sum, from the perspective of the process-based test, I would say rather that judicial reform has not been restricted in the past decade.

Principals and Secret Agents: Central versus Local Control Over Policing and Obstacles to "Rule of Law" in China*

Murray Scot Tanner and Eric Green

ABSTRACT This article extends the enduring debate over the balance of central versus local government control to China's cornerstone of state coercive control: the public security (civilian police) system. A recent series of studies argues that during the 1990s central authorities made terrific progress in regaining influence over local officials across a wide variety of issue-areas. This study, by contrast, argues that each policy sector in China has developed its own historical and institutional set of "lessons" that help structure power in that sector. Likewise, the particular issues in each policy sector create unique challenges for "principals" trying to monitor their "agents." Regarding internal security, the historical lessons the Party has derived from past security crises combine with the uniquely difficult challenges of monitoring police activities to create a system in which local Party and government officials have tremendous power over policing. The many institutions intended to help central authorities control, oversee and monitor local policing actually provide weak control and oversight. These obstacles to central leadership create tremendous additional challenges to building rule by law in China.

State Coercion and Central–Local Relations

What is the balance of power among central and local officials, and what is the impact of that balance on state power and policy? Few questions have been more central and enduring in the study of modern Chinese politics. The long-running debate over central–local relations has been reawakened recently by several studies arguing that the wave of decentralization of power that occurred in the 1980s has, in important ways, been reversed since the early 1990s, thus reviving

* The views and analysis expressed in this article are those of the authors and do not necessarily reflect those of Western Michigan University, the RAND Corporation, or RAND's management or corporate clients. After the final changes to this article were made, Dr Tanner accepted a position as Deputy Staff Director of the United States Congressional-Executive Commission on China (CECC) Needless to say, the views in this article also do not necessarily reflect those of the CECC, its staff or membership, or its leadership. The authors are grateful for comments from Donald Clarke, Pitman Potter, Benjamin Liebman, Kenneth Lieberthal and Melanie Manion for comments on earlier versions. Dr Tanner dedicates this article to the late Michel Oksenberg, who inspired his interest in this topic.

 doi:10.1017/S0305741007001634

the Chinese central state's capacity in finance, administration and personnel, monitoring, and coercion.[1]

As Jae Ho Chung has pointed out, there has long been a pronounced and somewhat troubling sectoral bias in the literature on central–local relations. "The predominant majority of studies on China's central–local relations have to date focused on their economic dimensions, and most notably the fiscal aspect (largely on budgetary arrangements and investment controls)."[2] It is especially unfortunate that very little of this research has focused on what Weber and most state theorists have considered the touchstone of state power – legal coercion.[3]

This article attempts to expand our understanding of state power and central–local relationships to include the vital legal-coercive sector – specifically, China's public security system. In so doing, it also attempts to put forward some more general criteria for distinguishing policy issues on which the central government will have an easier or harder time exerting its control. This work draws upon a large body of newly available documentation and interviews to analyse the central–local balance of power over policing and its significance for state coercive power and the rule of law.

Our key conclusion is that notwithstanding recent efforts to strengthen central control over police and build nationwide standards of law enforcement behaviour, powerful historical and institutional factors continue to reinforce the power that local Party officials exercise over police. The result is a relatively decentralized and feudal system of law enforcement and state coercion that constitutes a major obstacle to building rule by law in China. These obstacles, moreover, would still be difficult to overcome even if the current or future central leadership had a higher level of commitment to establishing rule by law than it does.

Multiple Principals and Secretive Agents

As with other state organs, the Chinese Communist Party (CCP) central leadership long ago tried to structure control over public security through an

1 Barry J. Naughton and Dali L. Yang (eds.), *Holding China Together: Diversity and National Integration in the Post-Deng Era* (Cambridge: Cambridge University Press, 2004); See the debate in *The Journal of Democracy*, Vol. 14, No. 1 (2003); also Maria Edin, "State capacity and local agent control in China: CCP cadre management from a township perspective," *The China Quarterly*, No. 173 (2003), pp. 35–52.

2 Jae Ho Chung, "Reappraising central–local relations in Deng's China," in Chien-min Chao and Bruce J. Dickson (eds.), *Remaking the Chinese State: Strategies, Society and Security* (London: Routledge, 2001), p. 52. See also Jae Ho Chung, "Studies of central–provincial relations in the People's Republic of China: a mid-term appraisal," *The China Quarterly*, No. 142 (1995), pp. 487–508.

3 Exceptions include Donald C. Clarke, "The execution of civil judgements in China," *The China Quarterly*, No. 141 (1995), pp. 65–81; Stanley Lubman, *Bird in a Cage: Legal Reform in China After Mao* (Stanford: Stanford University Press, 1999), esp. ch. 9, pp. 250–97; and Karen G. Turner, James V. Feinerman and R. Kent Guy (eds.), *The Limits of the Rule of Law in China* (Seattle: University of Washington Press, 2000); Randall J. Peerenboom, *China's Long March Toward Rule of Law* (Cambridge: Cambridge University Press, 2002); Melanie Manion, *Corruption by Design: Building Clean Government in Mainland China and Hong Kong* (Cambridge, MA: Harvard University Press, 2004); also Murray Scot Tanner, "The institutional lessons of disaster: reorganizing the People's Armed Police after Tiananmen," in James Mulvenon (ed.), *The People's Liberation Army as an Organization* (Washington, DC: RAND, 2002).

interlocking system of vertical-professional control by superior public security organs, and horizontal control by local Party and government organs. The result, however, was not redundant avenues of central control, but rather a "principal–agent" structure in which local police became "agents" formally subject to the leadership of multiple, often competing principals – the two most important being superior-level public security departments, and CCP committees and governments at the same level.[4] This article examines the distribution of power resources and monitoring mechanisms that central and local officials have at their disposal to influence police behaviour, and the incentives these power resources create for police to obey one set of principals at the expense of the other.[5]

Many studies of central–local relations have attempted to draw system-wide generalizations about the balance of central and local power across all or most issue areas. But our study of public security work suggests that, as a general rule, the balance of central–local power is substantially affected by the nature of the policy issues at stake. In the case of public security work, there are at least two major reasons for the powerful impact of policy issue upon the central–local relationship.

First, and probably most importantly, the nature of the challenges that principals face in monitoring compliance by their agents often varies enormously across issue areas. Just as policy process theorists have argued that the process of policymaking can vary with the nature of the political goods at stake, it is also inherently much easier for principals to monitor their subordinates' compliance with certain types of orders than others. A variety of characteristics of the issue involved – tangibility, accessibility, concreteness, quantifiability, the inherent "publicness" – can all either facilitate or complicate monitoring.

It makes sense, therefore, that scholars who research activities that are intrinsically easier to monitor would end up stressing the centre's enduring or revived power. Did a factory really hand over its assigned quota of steel? Was a capital construction project actually built on time? Does a government office exist or not? The answers to all of these are relatively easy to confirm.

Conversely, scholars who focus on activities that are inherently hard for central principals to monitor often find that localities enjoy great autonomy (such as over the total amount of extrabudgetary tax and fee revenues that localities collect). Moreover, as Jean Oi's work clearly illustrates, the ease or difficulty of monitoring can create powerful incentives for local

4 On "principal–agent models" and central–local relations in China, see in particular Jean C. Oi, *Rural China Takes Off: Institutional Foundations of Economic Reform* (Berkeley: University of California Press, 1999), esp. chs. 1, 5 and 6, pp. 1–16, 139–90; more generally, see Terry Moe, "The new economics of organization," *American Journal of Political Science*, Vol. 28, No. 4 (1984), pp. 739–77.

5 For earlier examinations of power resources and incentive structures in central–local relations see Oi, *Rural China Takes Off*, also Huang Yasheng, *Inflation and Investment Controls in China: The Political Economic of Central–Local Relations During the Reform Era* (Cambridge: Cambridge University Press, 1996); Huang Yasheng "Central–local relations in China during the reform era: the economic and institutional dimensions," *World Development* (April 1996), pp. 655–72.

agents – encouraging them to focus their energies on those activities over which they enjoy greatest autonomy, or which principals cannot easily monitor.

State legal coercion and enforcement emphatically falls into the second category. Even in the most open and legalistic societies, the quality of policing and of "law enforcement" are among the most difficult activities for superiors to monitor. This is especially true for principals who are not police officers themselves, or who live outside the locality being monitored. For many reasons, the classic problems of the agent's "information advantage" (that is, agents always know more than their bosses do about their actual level of compliance and quality of work) are enormous for law enforcement work.

First, the goals of policing are often nebulous, hard to quantify and potentially contradictory: "maintain good social order," "establish good working relations with society," "respect the rights of citizens." Since their success is often measured by the absence of crime and disorder, proving that success is difficult in the same way it is hard to "prove" a successful case of deterrence. In China, even highly quantifiable targets, such as "case-cracking rates" can easily be manipulated by tampering with the denominator and failing to open formal case files on hard-to-solve cases.

Secondly, since policing requires a large, irreducible and easily justifiable realm of secrecy, police are permitted far greater confidentiality over their activities, information, files, budgets, manpower levels and allocations than nearly all other bureaucracies. This secrecy is typically compounded by "compartmentalization" of information on a "need to know" basis.

Thirdly, most police work is carried out at great distance from direct supervisors. Authorities must entrust agents with tremendous discretion to respond quickly, flexibly, and often with deadly force or violence. Consequently, principals must rely heavily on selecting reliable personnel and subjecting them to intensive training rather than direct monitoring.

Finally, because of their coercive power over witnesses and evidence, police enjoy an almost unrivalled capacity to suppress or cover-up the very information their principals require to monitor their activities. An obvious example is the infamous and well-known device of an officer removing his or her wristwatch before beating a suspect to avoid leaving detectable marks that would facilitate an official inquiry into torture charges.

Given these obstacles, there should be little wonder that Terry Moe, a seminal theorist of principal–agent theory, singled out policing as the quintessential example of an administrative activity in which monitoring is extremely difficult, the risks of "adverse personnel selection" of agents are very high, and therefore, government subcontracting of the service to private agencies is particularly ill-advised.

The second major reason for the powerful impact of policy issue upon the central–local relationship is that the power structures in different policy sectors are, in part, shaped by different historical-institutional "lessons" hammered out through political struggles unique to that sector. Battles within the Party over how to evaluate its past victories and failures produce issue-specific institutional "lessons" about policies and power structures in those realms ("crisis learning" is an example). The "lessons of history" have taught the Party that for certain issues, certain types of power allocations lead to better policy outcomes, while other power allocations may risk disaster. The Great Leap Forward catastrophe, for example, clearly had an enduring impact on the structure of agriculture, while the scarring wars in Korea and Vietnam (1979) contributed greatly to the People's Liberation Army's (PLA) long-term trend towards professionalization, modernization and centralization. In other policy sectors, however, the "lessons" of these three crises do not loom as large. Conversely, CCP industrial policy experts do not invoke the Party's tragic 1931 policy failures in the Jiangxi Soviet. But the Party's internal security experts do. Thus, official perceptions of certain key historical incidents in internal security work still cast a long institutional shadow. In a sector with genuine "life or death" consequences, such lessons can be uniquely powerful.

The competition between higher-level police specialists and generalist local Party officials for control over local police is shaped by these issue-specific factors as well as by system-wide trends. The historical-institutional lessons of early security crises helped set in place a highly decentralized power structure. The unique nature of police work helps shape the relative effectiveness of the CCP's classic tools of central control.

This article focuses on these two important factors in this central–local competition: the impact of institutional history on the central–local balance of power over the police; and the central–local balance of control over key power resources and systems that can influence local police. These include policy leadership, organizational and personnel power, financial controls, and avenues of oversight and monitoring.

For decades, the official leadership system in Chinese communist public security work has been summed up in two awkward phrases: "unified leadership with management divided by levels" (*tongyi lingdao, fenxi guanli* 统一领导, 分级管理) and "combining vertical and local leadership, with local leadership as the main part" (*tiaokuai jiehe, yi huai wei zhu* 条块结合, 以块为主). The formal system, whose roots date back to the 1930s, in theory grants superior-level public security organs "unified leadership" over "professional" police matters. But it also grants local CCP committees and governments the primary leadership over public security organs and personnel. As this article will demonstrate, the systems of organizational, personnel and financial power over policing create much more powerful incentives for local police units to obey their local Party and government "principals" than their superior public security "principals" or the central leadership. Moreover, the classic institutional counterweights to the agency problems of localism and "moral hazard" – oversight and monitoring systems – are especially difficult to employ with respect to policing work, and in China they are largely structured so that they do more to strengthen local Party control than professional police or central control.[6]

This central–local distribution of power over police work has enormous consequences for several aspects of state power and policy, in particular the maintenance of social order, problems of "predatory" policing, and prospects for the gradual construction of "rule of law." The relatively weak controls and monitoring devices available to central principals suggest that instead of the emergence of any nationally uniform pattern of coercive controls and law enforcement, we should expect a variety of local patterns shaped in part by specific local interests, power balances, economic resources and state–society relations. Many of these patterns will be fundamentally at odds both with Beijing's near-term security goals and with the long-term emergence of "rule of law" – especially if "rule of law" is conceived in classic Weberian terms of legal professionalism and relatively equitable, fair and universalistic enforcement of rules across jurisdictions or among citizens.

We do not, however, contend that decentralization has created an entirely "zero-sum" relationship between the centre and localities.[7] Quite the contrary, one of the most powerful forces favouring the continued survival of the CCP regime is the common interest Party leaders at all levels still appear to feel in maintaining single-party political control, suppressing dissident and labour organizations, and keeping crime rates tolerably low. But this research makes clear that in important ways, the legal and security interests of the centre, provinces and localities are far from identical. And in a classic case of the collective impact of individual actions, local Party leaders, while pursuing their own security interests, frequently order police actions that inadvertently undermine the centre's strategies for refurbishing regime legitimacy and maintaining social control.

In the past 15 years numerous public security officials and analysts at all levels have criticized this highly localized policing system for undermining many of Beijing's security policies. In particular, they charge that excessive decentralization undermines police professionalization by creating powerful institutional incentives for local police abuses, corruption, predation and "protectionism." More reform-oriented officials and scholars criticize this localism as a major obstacle to establishing rule of law.

With the classical tools of Leninist control over the police overwhelmingly in local Party hands, Party advocates of either greater central control or greater "rule of law" find themselves in a dilemma. Facing powerful local resistance,

6 Oi discusses the problems of "moral hazard" and monitoring compliance in *Rural China Takes Off*, pp. 139–41, 152–53; on the irreducible challenges of directly monitoring police work, see Murray Scot Tanner, "Will the state bring *you* back in? Policing and democratization," *Comparative Politics* (October 2000), pp. 101–23; and Paul Chevigny, *The Edge of the Knife: Police Violence in the Americas* (New York: The New Press, 1995).

7 For critiques of the "zero sum" assumptions in much literature on central–local relations, see Jae Ho Chung, "Studies of central–provincial relations"; Linda Chenlan Li, *Center and Provinces: China 1978–1993* (Oxford: Clarendon Press, 1998), esp. pp. 30–35, 296–98; Oi, *Rural China Takes Off*, p. 142.

their only choices may be to accept local Party control and all that these dangerous incentives imply for the Party's future, or risk trying to strengthen *non-Party* oversight and monitoring institutions and information networks, perhaps even making common cause with social forces that could further erode one-party control over society.

Historical-Institutional Lessons: The Origins of "Yi Kuai Wei Zhu"

The origins of local Party committee control over internal security lie in classic "crisis learning" – a major, self-inflicted security crisis the Party faced in the late 1930s that caused it to reject USSR-style security work. Public security historians now freely concede that during the early 1930s, the Chinese Soviet governments in Jiangxi made a massive mistake by setting up State Political Security Bureaus (guojia zhengzhi baowei ju 国家政治保卫局, SPSB) that simply "copied" the highly centralized, independent and secretive system of Stalin's GPU (later the NKVD and the KGB). These historians lay much of the blame for the widespread, self-destructive intra-Party purges of this period on the SPSB's "vertical leadership" system (*chuizhi lingdao* 垂直领导) and their independence to penetrate and purge Party and Red Army units. While more objective historians should look on this official interpretation with scepticism, it still remains a powerful historical-institutional "lesson" for contemporary security work. After the pivotal Zunyi meeting, the SPSBs were criticized and dismantled, and by 1939 the Party established new *Party* (not *state*) internal security organs under the leadership of territorial Party committees – the equally infamous Social Affairs Departments (shehui bu 社会部, SAD).[8] The SADs participated in the massive Yanan purge campaigns of the early 1940s, but official historiography has excused local Party secretaries and their unprofessional, mass-based "anti-spy campaigns" for these abuses. Instead, the purges were blamed largely on the machinations of Mao's SAD chief, Kang Sheng, and the SADs, which allegedly became "divorced from real Party leadership" – a charge even more deserving of scepticism. Thus, the institutional "lesson" was officially preserved, and police historians laud local Party control over security as a "unique characteristic" of China's system, not practised in the other socialist countries that were more heavily influenced by Stalin's Soviet Union.[9]

The CCP's attainment of state power compelled a controversial reconsideration of police–Party relations, and beginning in October 1949 the Party's Social Affairs Departments were converted into state "public security" organs. But despite reported Soviet pressure for the CCP to resume emulating Soviet security work, the principles of local Party control – *tongyi lingdao, fenji guanli* and *tiaokuai jiehe yikuai weizhu* – were quickly affirmed. Mao dramatically

8 On this period see Murray Scot Tanner "Who wields the knife? An institutional history of Chinese Communist police and intelligence organs, 1927–1950," draft ms.

9 *Zhongguo tese gongan zhi yanjiu* (*Studies in China's Special Public Security*) (Beijing: Qunzhong chubanshe, 1996), pp. 55–56.

reinforced this rule in 1950, when he criticized the new minister of public security Luo Ruiqing for reporting to Premier Zhou Enlai – but not to the Party Chairman – on counterrevolutionary suppression work. Very soon thereafter, Mao issued the most famous organizational directive in Chinese security work: insisting that "security work must especially emphasize Party leadership ... and *in reality* accept direct leadership by Party committees."[10] Since this directive, the general principle of "Party leadership over security" has been exclusively equated with just one organizational form – local Party committee leadership over the police.[11] If we contrast this police structure with the PLA, the importance of sectorally-specific institutional histories becomes apparent. In the PLA, the Party's role as "principal" ("the Party must control the gun") has nevertheless long been regarded as entirely compatible with standard military style "vertical" leadership forms.

Key institutional levers of police control were decentralized to local Party committees throughout the 1950s. Through a series of reorganizations, formal control over police personnel quotas (*bianzhi*) was decentralized, first to public security officials in the six great administrative regions in 1952, with local Party committees gaining joint control over police political officers in their area.[12] Between 1953 and 1955, the central Ministry of Public Security (MPS) and the CCP Organization Department granted local Party committees authority to manage leading public security cadres at the same level – essentially the same basic system that endures today.[13]

Public security and finance departments jostled repeatedly over control of public security budgets, reorganizing the system five times between 1949 and 1958. By late 1954 Luo Ruiqing persuaded Chen Yun and other central leaders to grant the MPS nationwide "vertical management" over "special" or "professional expenditures," which the Ministry of Finance turned over to the MPS for direct disbursement. But local governments frequently comingled these "special funds" with regular police administrative budgets, forcing police to use them for ordinary needs. One longstanding MPS financial official indicates that by about 1956, many local public security bureau (PSB) chiefs felt it would be

10 Mao's directive was a comment on the report of the 1950 Economic Security Work Conference. See *Luo Ruiqing dajiang san ci danan bu side* (*General Luo Ruiqing: Thrice Endangered but Undying*) (Beijing: Zhonggong dangshi chubanshe, 1994), pp. 123–24.

11 On the Mao-era system, see MPS Political and Personnel Depts (ed.), *Gongan renshi guanli* (*Public Security Personnel Management*) (*GARSGL*) (Beijing: Qunzhong chubanshe, 1997), esp. ch. 3, pp. 42–75; *Zhongguo renmin gongan shigao* (*A Draft History of Chinese People's Public Security*) (Beijing: Jingguan jiaoyu chubanshe, 1997), esp. pp. 186–255; Xu Xinyuan, "Woguo gongan jiguan he renmin jingcha zuzhi jigou lishi yange" ("The historical evolution of our country's public security and people's police organizational structure"), *Gongan yanjiu* (*Studies in Public Security*) (*GAYJ*), No. 3 (1999), pp. 91–94; Liu Jiying "Gongan yewu jingfei baozhang jizhi jianshe huigu yu sikao" ("Reminiscences and reflections on constructing the system to guarantee public security professional expenditures"), *GAYJ*, No. 2 (1999), pp. 56–58; Feng Shuangping in MPS Political Department and Personnel Bureau (ed.), *Gongan duiwu zhengguihua jianshe lilun yu shijian* (*Theory and Practice of Building Standardization in the Public Security Corps*) (*GDZJLS*) (Beijing: Zhongguo renmin gongan daxue chubanshe, 1998), pp. 80–91; also the sources cited in Tanner, "Who wields the knife?"

12 *GARSGL*, p. 14; Liu Jiying, "Reminiscences and reflections," p. 56.

13 *GARSGL*, pp. 342–46.

less of a hassle to have all their funds – professional and administrative – coming from local governments.[14]

Public security leadership, personnel and funding underwent wholesale decentralization during the Great Leap Forward. After mid-1958, although the MPS remained officially "responsible" for security work nationwide, local Party committees became the main leaders of security work in their areas. Local personnel allotment committees exercised unified management over police personnel quotas, with local PSBs merely "assisting" them. "Professional" finances were decentralized from the MPS to provincial officials, and administrative funding remained under local control.

It appears that after the Great Leap, however, public security control was less fully and less quickly recentralized than economic and other policy sectors. Not until 1965 was control over personnel quotas recentralized, and then only to the provincial level. Beijing tried, however, to insulate police personnel numbers from bureaucratic competition with other departments by ordering provinces to list police quotas separately (*danlie* 单列) from other personnel quotas.[15] Despite repeated efforts by the MPS and Ministry of Finance to recentralize or insulate police funding, the basic system of same-level government funding has remained in place until the present.[16]

The destruction of central control was completed during the Cultural Revolution, when the central MPS was taken over and virtually closed down, and its bureaucratic links to lower-level PSBs were severed almost completely for several years. A slow recovery began in 1971, but even as late as 1978 the centre could do little more than "encourage" local finance departments to support their public security units better – especially the many local police stations (*paichu suo* 派出所) that were destroyed by riots or taken over by local officials.[17]

Many Party and security officials interpret the abuses of the Cultural Revolution as proof of the lessons of Party control over the police. Although much of the system was closed down, Kang Sheng and others were able to employ selected security officials in the MPS and Central Investigation Department to persecute their rivals. A key aspect of the normalization of Party life after the Cultural Revolution was a reaffirmation of the principle that the "organs of dictatorship" should not be employed within the Party itself, and buffers to protect Party leaders from most police investigations were re-established.

By the advent of the reform era, the institutional principle of local Party committee leadership of public security had acquired considerable historical weight. Still, despite this seemingly inviolable norm, many police officials have clearly felt the desire to strengthen "vertical" police leadership and professional independence, and this remains a contentious issue. For three decades Peng

14 Liu Jiying "Reminiscences and reflections," pp. 56–57.
15 *GARSGL*, p. 66.
16 Liu Jiying "Reminiscences and reflections" p. 57.
17 *Ibid.*

Zhen, the senior Party official most responsible for political-legal work, repeatedly inveighed against efforts to revive vertical leadership.[18] At various times Luo Ruiqing, Hua Guofeng, Kang Sheng, Wang Dongxing and other senior security officials have all been charged with trying to emulate the KGB's organizational independence. Since the early 1980s, persistent calls for greater "militarization," "professionalization," "standardization" and "unification" of the public security corps have clearly reflected this desire.[19] Unquestionably, an enduring cleavage persists between defenders of the historical lesson of the need for absolute local Party leadership over public security and police critics of excessive localism.

Present-Day Central–Local Influence Over Public Security

The central and local principals can employ four types of power resources to create incentives for police to obey their directives: control over formal policy authority, personnel and organizational systems, financial and budgetary resources, and oversight and monitoring mechanisms.

Influence over formal policy decisions

Although the MPS formally exercises "unified leadership" over nationwide public security work, local Party committees enjoy substantial authority to interpret and implement policy in their regions. This includes responsibility for ensuring correct implementation of the Party's "line," "direction" and policies. They have authority to decide "important policy questions," draft public security legislation, make strategic police deployments and manage local security "incidents." This last one is important. Although much control over People's Armed Police (PAP) anti-riot units was transferred from public security units to the PLA during the early to mid-1990s, local Party committees and governments nevertheless retain authority to "activate," "employ" and lead the PAP units in their regions.[20] Among the Party committees' most important powers is

18 See Peng Zhen, *Lun xin Zhongguo de zhengfa gongzuo* (Beijing: Zhongyang wenxian chubanshe, 1991), pp. 11–12, 100–01, 144–45, 242, 390; and former Minister of Public Security Tao Siju's memorial essay in *Mianhuai Peng Zhen* (*Remembering Peng Zhen*) (Beijing: Zhongyang wenxian chubanshe, 1998), pp. 90–91.

19 On historical efforts at "unification" and "militarization" see Feng Shuangping, *Theory and Practice of Building Standardization*.

20 Control over PAP units was changed by the 3 March 1995 joint State Council-Central Military Commission "Decision on adjusting the leadership structure of the Chinese People's Armed Police forces." See Murray Scot Tanner, "The institutional lessons of disaster: reorganizing the People's Armed Police after Tiananmen," in James Mulvenon (ed.), *The People's Liberation Army as an Organization* (Washington, DC: RAND, 2002). See also Xu Yongqing, "Xin shiqi wujing budui jianshe de zhongyao zhidao sixiang" ("The important guiding thought on building the People's Armed Police forces during the new era"), *Qiushi*, No. 20 (1997), pp. 35–36; *Xiandai wujing suzhi* (*On the Quality of the Contemporary PAP*) (Beijing: Qunzhong chubanshe, 1996), p. 3; Du Shuyun, "Zhongguo tese de wuzhuang jingcha budui" ("Armed police forces with Chinese special characteristics"), in Chinese Police Study Society (ed.), *Lun Zhongguo tese de gongan* (Beijing: Qunzhong chubanshe, 1997), pp. 121–29.

authority to resolve disagreements among the various local political-legal departments, including the justice departments, courts, procurators and even the more independent state security organs.[21]

Influence over organizational structure and personnel

Control over organizational structure and personnel has several aspects: control over the internal structure of subordinate PSBs, overall personnel quotas, specific hiring plans, individual hiring decisions and management of leading cadres.[22] The MPS officially "directs" the system's overall structural development, sets overall personnel allotments and "rationalizes" relations among public security offices nationwide. Although official MPS manuals like to play up the rationality and central control of this system, many official sources suggest it is more formal than real.

Some Western analysts contend that control over institutional structure is an important source of central control.[23] The MPS has promulgated many regulations regarding the internal structure of lower-level public security organs,[24] although these do grant localities considerable flexibility to establish specialized organs to meet particular local security problems, such as anti-drug, anti-smuggling, or special religious and minority affairs offices. Within the broad parameters set by the MPS, the authority to establish or reorganize new bureaucratic units is moderately decentralized, using a "two level" (*geji* 隔级 or *liangji* 两级) system. Under this system, "the organ that is directly superior to the organ that wants to establish, change or merge a significant new organ is responsible for seeking approval from the leading organ one level up."[25] In other words, PSBs below the provincial level that want to establish or reorganize any major sub-organs are supposed to obtain approval from their direct superiors and the next level up – including both the public security departments and people's government and sometimes Party committees. Thus, county PSBs that wish to establish major new offices (*ke* 科 or *gu* 股 rank) must obtain approval from both the prefectural/municipal and the provincial levels.[26] But the authority to establish lower-ranking new offices, institutions and enterprises can often be granted by Party and government organs at the same level.[27]

Still, many public security sources complain that local PSBs, especially at the county level, frequently ignore these regulations and establish unauthorized internal offices. The resulting increase in administrative personnel exacerbates

21 *Studies in China's Special Public Security*, pp. 58–61. Significantly, this last point suggests that state security departments, which are more centralized and independent that public security departments, must also sometimes bow to local Party committees.

22 *GARSGL*, pp. 42–75.

23 Huang Yasheng, "Central–local relations in China during the reform era."

24 Essential offices include political departments, criminal investigation, social order management and political security departments.

25 *GARSGL*, p. 56.

26 *Ibid.* pp. 59–61. The source unfortunately provides no concrete examples below the central level.

27 *Ibid.*

the shortage of quality police personnel "on the street" where they are most needed.[28]

Police, unlike the military, are considered state administrative personnel. But China has many categories of "police" personnel under the control of many different units and levels, and the overwhelming majority are not under direct control of the MPS. A large and growing number are not even under the public security system.

Official MPS descriptions of the personnel quota approval process are somewhat self-contradictory and ambiguous. The centre (specifically, the MPS and the Central Personnel Quota Committee) reportedly checks and sets the overall personnel quotas and deployment plans for each level of the system, and then these plans are sent down and managed level by level. But when a local PSB requests an increase in personnel, for a new or existing department, these requests are handled by government personnel departments at the same level.

Even within the public security system, many personnel fall outside these quotas and are difficult for the MPS to control. Excluded are many "non-administrative" personnel attached to public security institutions and enterprises, as well as the MPS's border management, fire fighting and bodyguards bureaus, which have long been part of the PAP military service personnel quota.[29] Some local governments have responded to reform-era police shortages by adding special "local quotas" and temporary "contract system police" hired outside government quotas. Many major enterprises and institutions have established their own "public security organs" outside government personnel quotas, as well as employing security service company guards (who are part of the authorized staffing level (*bianzhi* 编制) of the units they serve). Finally, public security quotas also exclude massive numbers of citizen security volunteers in neighbourhood residents' committees, joint protective teams and security protective committees.[30]

In recent years central authorities have tried to use their influence over the *bianzhi* to shift police personnel resources into areas of desperate need. Between 1986 and 1995 the centre authorized a special nationwide increase of 44,000 traffic police.[31] Another priority has been strengthening elite, well-armed, quick response forces, including anti-drug units, "special police," and mobile "patrol police." In April 1990, the MPS authorized an increase of 27,000 public security anti-riot forces in several "keypoint" major cities. Many cities apparently did not heed this central directive, however, and Beijing once again called on large cities to strengthen public security anti-riot units in January 2001. Only

28 *Ibid.* pp. 45–48, 54–57; Zhu Chunlin in *GDZJLS*, p. 12.

29 The PAP has been under the State Council military *bianzhi* since well before the PAP's post-Tiananmen militarization. See the 1988 MPS internal organization plan in *ZRGGFQ*, pp. 1447–50; also Tanner, "Reorganizing the PAP after Tiananmen."

30 Yan Junxing, *Jingcha yewu quanshu*, pp. 99–100; *GARSGL*, pp. 57–59, 62–68.

31 *GARSGL*, pp. 64–65, 68.

in 2005 was there evidence that these units were being manned in large numbers.[32]

Despite the many ways in which local officials can and do skirt centrally imposed limits in the personnel quota system, influence over the total *bianzhi* may actually be one of the centre's stronger control devices. For example, despite the tremendous differences among provincial PSBs in their per capita personnel, the centre has been able to concentrate forces in those key cities (most notably Beijing and Shanghai) whose stability is crucial to the party-state's internal security strategy.

Public security departments must get approval for specific hiring plans for their regular police officers and lower-level cadres. This approval system is formally structured to share power between local officials and superior-level public security offices. The central MPS apparently has little control over these plans, and the power of upper-level security officials only extends one level downward. According to current regulations, the hiring plans of provincial-level PSBs are drawn up by these bureaus and approved by the governments at the same level. County-level PSBs, for example, must obtain approval from their municipal PSB as well as the county government.[33] Although county level PSBs have no formal authority to hire people's police directly (this is supposed to be done at the municipal level), public security sources indicate that this rule is widely disobeyed.[34]

Despite its weak control over local hiring plans, the MPS has tried to use its guidance authority to improve the professional quality of police officers, and prevent the hiring of untrained and under-qualified personnel. A particularly thorny political problem has been the pressure on local political-legal departments to hire demobilized PLA personnel.

Another source of concern has been the hiring of unemployed "social youth" and other untrained personnel as "contract police." Beginning in 1984 the MPS authorized local PSBs to use local funds to hire largely untrained and non-professional (non civil service) contract police as a temporary stopgap in rapidly growing and severely under-policed regions. By 1990 the number of contract police had ballooned to well over 100,000 nationwide (one-tenth of the total national force). The MPS sees these contract officers as a major discipline problem, and believes that under the growing body of civil service and people's

32 Note that these are Public Security anti-riot forces and not PAP forces. See "China: Beijing strengthens security responsiveness," *Oxford Analytica*, 6 September 2005; "Gonganbu guanyu zai zhongdian chengshi zujian gongan fangbaodui de tongzhi" ("MPS notice on organizing public security anti-riot brigades in keypoint cities"), 24 April 1990, in *ZRGGFQ*, pp. 1453–54; Beijing Xinhua (English), 27 January 2001; Erik Eckholm, "Chinese order cities to bolster riot police forces," *New York Times*, 30 January 2001, p. 4.

33 *GARSGL*, pp. 105–07. The 15 August 1984 MPS/MLP regulations "Guanyu xishou renmin jingcha de guiding" may be found in *ZRGGFQ*, pp. 1443–44.

34 See the articles by MPS vice-minister Zhu Chunlin and Zhang Zhaoduan in *GDZJLS*, pp. 23, 61–70; Chen Shaoji, "Yifa jiaqiang gongan duiwu jianshe weihu zhengzhi he shehui changqi wending," in *Renmin jingchafa lilun yu shijian lunwen xuan* (*Collected Essays on Theory and Practice of the People's Police Law*) (Beijing: Qunzhong chubanshe, 1996), p. 3.

police laws, there is no "legal basis" for them to perform law enforcement work. They are also frequent culprits in police abuse and torture cases. Finally, in defiance of MPS directives, many rural governments have paid for these officers through all sorts of special fees and exactions from peasants. After years of trying to ease out contract officers, in 1996 the MPS conceded that more than 37,000 were still employed, and many regions continued to defy MPS orders by hiring them under different titles. More recent sources still cite them as a periodic problem.[35]

Central public security leaders would prefer recruiting from police training programmes, and regard the continued employment of ex-servicemen and contract police as significant obstacles to police professionalization. A 1996 MPS–Ministry of Personnel joint directive instructed local departments to meet their personnel quotas mainly through properly tested professional "civil service" channels, recruited from police training programmes. Demobilized soldiers and "social youth" were only to be used as "supplementary" hiring pools.[36] But the MPS's admission of local resistance to getting rid of contract officers underscores the limitations on central power to enforce compliance.

Despite the special sensitivity of public security work, central *nomenklatura* controls over the appointment, removal, promotion and transfer of leading cadres do not extend any deeper for public security departments than they do for other state administrative organs.[37] As noted above, since the 1950s local Party committees have dominated management of leading security cadres. Formally, superior public security organs one level up are only authorized to "assist" local Party and government officials by making "suggestions" about cadre decisions that local leaders are supposed to "consider." In cases of "major disagreements in principle," the decision may be referred to higher levels, but the final decision still goes to the superior-level territorial Party committee, not the public security organ.

It might be argued that the centre could use its appointment influence over provincial public security officials by rotating security chiefs among the provinces in the manner that senior PLA officers and provincial Party secretaries are rotated. But the available evidence indicates that this rarely

35 "Gonganbu guanyu zuohao qingtui hetong minjing shouwei gongzuo de tongzhi" ("MPS notice on doing a good job of work on withdrawing contract police officers") (5 February 1996), in *ZRGGFQ* (1995–97), pp. 988–89.

36 *GARSGL*, p. 105. For the original MPS/Ministry of Personnel regulations see *ZRGGFQ* (1995–97), pp. 1008–09.

37 According to John P. Burns' sources, the central *nomenklatura* in public security is virtually the same as for other state ministries and commissions. The list of public security cadres "managed" by the centre includes the minister, vice-ministers, the head of the political department, the MPS Party core group secretary, deputy secretaries and members, and the head of the Party group's discipline inspection group. Public security cadres "reporting" to the Party centre include all MPS bureau chiefs, deputy chiefs, bureau-level investigators, researchers, auditors, discipline inspection group heads, department heads, deputy department heads, and all provincial-level public security bureau chiefs and deputy chiefs. The only difference between MPS and other ministries is that public security departments have political departments. See Burns (ed.), *The Chinese Communist Party's Nomenklatura* System (Armonk, NY: M.E. Sharpe, Inc., 1989), esp. pp. 122–36.

happens, and nearly all those provincial public security chiefs on whom we have information have spent virtually their entire careers in the same province.[38] A 2001 Hong Kong report claims that provincial leaders may have begun experimenting with rotating county and municipal-level PSB chiefs within the province in response to a wave of local police corruption cases, but available data do not suggest this is yet a widespread practice.[39]

Influence over budgetary and financial resources

Since at least the late 1950s, the bulk of public security budgets have been paid from the coffers of local governments at the same level.[40] The central and provincial governments provide local security departments with some supplemental funding, primarily for investigating "large and major cases" and some special equipment. But officials report these are "not a large percentage" of police funding. Complete data are not available either nationwide or for individual provinces. But in 1996 one unnamed provincial-level government spent 40 million yuan on public security and only received an additional one million yuan from central-level public security organs. Within the various provinces, moreover, funding formulas differ; some large and medium cities are more centralized than other, geographically more dispersed regions. Beijing and a number of smaller cities divide financial responsibilities, with the city government paying some "professional" expenditures, and lower levels meeting "administrative" costs, including salaries.[41]

Control over the substantial sources of revenue that local public security departments can generate – both legitimate and illegitimate – is a key aspect of this localized budgetary system that creates powerful behavioural incentives for police and local officials. Among the major sources of revenue controlled by police are many forms of licensing and fines, notably those related to "social order management" and "traffic management." Official figures on "social

38 As a very rough test of this hypothesis, we examined background information on all the identifiable provincial-level public security chiefs in the online database China Vitae (http//chinavitae.com, accessed October 2006) and in *Who's Who in China: Current Leaders* (1992 and 1994 editions) (Beijing: Foreign Languages Press, 1992, 1994). Of the approximately 25 current and former provincial PSB chiefs on whom we found data, only two had not apparently spent their entire career in the same province.

39 Hong Kong *Ming pao* (internet version) 11 June 2001, *FBIS Daily Report*, 11 June 2001.

40 On the expanded sources of revenue under local control since the early 1980s, see Oi, *Rural China Takes Off*, esp. pp. 17–57.

41 "Cong Guangdong de shijian kan shehuizhuyi shichang jingji tiaojianxia gongan gongzuo xin tese" ("Using Guangdong's experience to look at the new characteristics of public security work under the conditions of a socialist market economy"), and "Lun shehuizhuyi shichang jingji tiaojian xia jianchi fahui xianxing de gongan lingdao guanli tizhi de tese" ("Continuing to give full play to the special characteristics of the existing public security leadership and management system under the conditions of the socialist market economy"), both in Chinese Police Study Society, *Lun Zhongguo tese de gongan*, esp. pp. 162–63, 370–73; Xiao Yong, "Wanshan shoudu gongan jingfei baozhang jizhi de sikao" ("Reflections on perfecting the capital's public security expenditure guarantee system"), *Renmin gongan bao*, 15 August 1998, p. 4; Xing Xin, "Guanyu wanshan shoudu gongan jingfei baozhang jizhi de sikao" ("Reflections on perfecting the capital's public security expenditure guarantee system"), *GA YJ*, No. 5 (1998), pp. 35–37; Liu Jiying, "Gongan yewu jingfei baozhang jizhi jianshe huigu yu sikao" ("Reminiscences and reflections on constructing the system to guarantee public security expenditures"), *GA YJ*, No. 2 (1999), pp. 56–58; see also *GA YJ*, No. 3 (1997), p. 56.

order"-related revenue are not available. Traffic management includes vehicle inspections, drivers' licences, driver training, fines from traffic violations and so on. While it is unclear what percentage of total public security revenue and expenditure these funds account for, the level is clearly substantial. In 1997 the officially reported traffic management revenue nationwide totalled over 13.5 billion yuan, making it a significant, if not enormous, revenue source.[42] However, over half this official figure came from inspections, licences and driver training, and very little from traffic fines, suggesting these may be systematically underreported. To put this figure in perspective, if it were divided by 32 provincial-level units, it would equal approximately 422 million yuan per province, or more than ten times the total annual public security expenditure reported by the provincial government noted in the preceding paragraph.

As the volume of traffic has exploded in recent years, control over these funds has become a major object of struggle between financial and public security departments at a variety of local levels. According to an MPS traffic official, traffic management funds are shared according to two formulae. Although the revenues from vehicle inspections, drivers' licences and driver training are considered "administrative" fees, they are in general handled in the same way as "within budget" local revenues: they are passed up level-by-level and shared by the PSBs and finance departments at the local, prefectural/municipal and provincial levels according to (unspecified) fixed amounts.[43] Apparently little or none of this money makes it to the central government. The revenues from traffic fines, however, are handled more like "extrabudgetary revenues"; they are primarily retained by local-level PSBs and finance departments. In recent years provincial and local finance departments have moved aggressively to try to secure prompt control over these funds.[44]

These revenue handling rules give local governments and their police departments a powerful incentive to engage in predatory fine collection and maximize their share of those revenues that are retained locally, while devoting somewhat less attention to collecting revenues that must be shared with upper levels. This would mean, for example, collecting as many fines as possible from people and units that are not powerful in local politics and not essential to local economic growth (for example, by maximizing traffic fines on out-of-area travellers).[45]

Beginning in the early 1980s, when the balance of financial power shifted towards the localities, public security dependence upon local funding became a major object of criticism, even among security officials who generally support

42 Our judgement is based on data in Oi, *Rural China Takes Off*, figs. 2–4, pp. 40–44.

43 *Ibid.* pp. 38–47.

44 "Feishui gaige zhong gongan jiaotong guanli jingfei baozhang wenti de yanjiu" ("Research on the problems of guaranteeing public security traffic management finances amidst the reform of funding and taxation"), *GAYJ*, No. 6 (1998), pp. 81–83.

45 Guo Yu and Li Guoqiang, "Jingcha quanli lanyong de yuanyin fenxi ji qu kongzhi" ("An analysis of the reasons for the abuse of police authority and its control"), *Jilin gongan gaodeng zhuanke xuexiao xuebao*, No. 1 (2005), p. 71. This line of analysis is inspired by Oi, *Rural China Takes Off*.

local Party leadership.[46] Many officials and analysts charge that local governments often show little understanding of police budgetary needs and are slow to fund necessary expenditures for increased personnel, equipment, communications and other professional needs. Their fundamental objection is that police funding levels are now principally a function of local levels of economic development and political support for security, rather than actual social order conditions. Long-term stable funding is replaced by a last-minute system of "one problem, one request; one problem, one approval." In impoverished areas, "funds for handling cases, for cadres and police housing and medical care are all hard to come by."[47] A 1998 report by the MPS planning and finance office suggests that local payouts of only 70 per cent of real expenditure is a common figure nationwide, with 50 per cent not unusual. This has often produced vast gaps among jurisdictions in police personnel numbers, salaries, arms, equipment and other expenditures.[48]

Influence over oversight and monitoring mechanisms

Oversight and monitoring mechanisms are a key weapon for central principals to overcome the advantage local principals and agents have in knowing how faithfully central policies are being implemented. Like most other state administrative departments, China's public security organs are at least formally subject to a remarkably large number of oversight systems. These include public security internal oversight organs (including the "legality" offices (*fazhi* 法制), auditing (*shenji* 审计), the masses letters and visits offices, and the relatively new oversight police (*ducha jingcha* 督察警察) organs); Party-based external oversight organs (including Party organization and discipline inspection); the state-based external oversight organs (including the procuracy, the courts and administrative supervision); and increasingly the official press, especially the political-legal press.

46 See MPS Equipment and Financial Bureau (ed.), *Gongan houbu baozhang gongzuo yanjiu* (Beijing: Zhongguo renmin gongan daxue chubanshe, 2003), pp. 4–7.

47 Wang Mingxin, *Gongan zhandouli lun* (*On Public Security Fighting Strength*) (Beijing: Jingguan jiaoyu chubanshe, 1993), pp. 98–99; Liu Jiying, "Reminiscences and reflections," p. 58; Lan Rongzeng, "Shenhua gongan gaige, jianli gongan gongzuo xin jizhi" ("Deepen public security reform, establish new structures for public security work"), *GAYJ*, No. 5 (1997), p. 61; Zhou Yuanxi, "Qiantan gongan duiwu buzhengzhifeng de zhuyao yuanyin ji duice ("A cursory discussion of improper practices in the public security corp, reasons for them, and countermeasures"), *GAYJ*, No. 4 (1991), pp. 7–9; Fu Hongjie, *GAYJ*, No. 1 (1996), pp. 31–32.

48 Wang Mingxin, *On Public Security Fighting Strength*, p. 101; Zhao Dabin (MPS finance and planning bureau director), "Zhuazhu jiou, yifa yanjiu zhiding gongan jiguan jingwu baozhang gongzuo de zhengce yu guihua" ("Seize the opportunity, research and establish work to guarantee public security organs and police work policies and plans according to law") in *Renmin jingchafa lilun yu yanjiu shijian lunwen xuan* (*Selected Essays on the Theory and Practice of the People's Police Law*) (Beijing: Qunzhong chubanshe, 1996), pp. 34–39; Sun Xiaodong, "Qianlun gongan duiwu zhengguihua jianshe de chengjiu yu cunzai de zhuyao wenti yu duice" ("A superficial discussion of achievements in constructing public security regularization, problems that exist, and policies for dealing with them"), *GDZJLS*, p. 44; Shang Wu (Hubei PSB political department), "Gongan gongzuo de kunjing yu gaige chuyi" ("The predicament of public security work and modest proposals for reform"), *GDZJLS*, pp. 95–96; Liu Jiying, "Guanyu zai shehuizhuyi chuji jieduan gaohao gongan jingfei baozhang bongzuo de sikao" ("Reflections on doing a good job of guaranteeing public security finances during the initial stage of socialism"), *GAYJ*, No. 3 (1998), pp. 43–45.

Recent studies have generally not painted a picture of active, aggressive, honest monitors. Melanie Manion's careful and detailed study of China's anti-corruption institutions – the CCP discipline inspection organs, the procuracy and the state supervision departments – demonstrates how the Party's obstinate insistence on "policing its own" has prevented the rise of a self-generating, self-sustaining system to fight corruption. Instead, these systems tend to be dominated by local leaders, and show a marked bias toward secretive, "in-house" investigations, low rates of cases being handed over to the formal legal system and relatively weak punishments.[49]

Central monitoring of public security is further undermined by the fact that internal police oversight organs tend to be dominated by the local PSBs within which they are contained, while Party- and state-based external oversight organs tend to strengthen the control of local Party officials over public security. Incentives for these local departments to report faithfully to the centre are not strong. This section briefly reviews some major oversight organs, although space limitations prohibit an analysis of procuratorial, court or press oversight of policing.

First, within the political departments of all public security units at and above the county level (and all PAP *zongdui* 総隊) are discipline inspection (DI) units. When these units were re-established after the Cultural Revolution, they were initially led by the Party organs within each PSB. From 1983 to at least 1994 they were changed into directly deputized (*paichu* 派出) units of the local Party committee's discipline inspection commission. These units now reportedly fall under "dual leadership" with local Party committee DI organs providing the main leadership while the host public security unit provides "guidance."[50] Their government counterparts, the supervision departments, were merged with the Party DI units in the MPS and most local PSBs after July 1992 as part of a post-Tiananmen rollback of "separating Party and government."[51]

According to rules promulgated by MPS Party officials in 1992, violations of Party and state discipline by public security and PAP officials are handled primarily by local Party organization, discipline inspection and state supervision departments at the same level. Superior level public security units play a subsidiary role, and are consulted and/or must agree to punishments determined in cases involving higher-ranking officials.[52]

49 Manion, *Corruption by Design*, pp. 145–54.

50 See Yun Shiying (MPS DI group head), "Yikao dangwei lingdao, fahui zhineng zuoyong, nuli zuohao gongan jijian gongzuo," in CCP Central Discipline Inspection Commission General Office (ed.), *Zenyang gaohao dangfeng dangji he lianzheng jianshe* (*How to Do a Good Job of Building Party Style, Party Discipline and Clean Government*) (Beijing: Zhongguo fazhi chubanshe, 1991), pp. 266–75; Yan Li *et al.*, *Zhongguo gongan yewu quanshu*, pp. 67–68; *Gongan shi zhishi wenda* (*Questions and Answers About Public Security History*) (*GASZSWD*) (Beijing: Qunzhong chubanshe, 1994), p. 129.

51 *GASZSWD*, p. 129.

52 Quan Jun and Yu Yong, *Gongan jijian jiancha* (*Public Security Discipline Inspection and Oversight*), pp. 37–38; "Gonganbu jiwei, jianchaju guanyu chachu weiji anjian fengong de guiding [shixing]" ("MPS discipline inspection committee, supervision bureau regulations the division of labour in investigating and handling cases of violating discipline [for trial implementation]"), in *Zhifa shouce* (*Law Enforcement Handbook*), Vol. 14 (1992) (Beijing: Qunzhong chubanshe, 1993), pp. 602–05.

Secondly, auditing departments monitor how public security units handle the wide variety of financial streams and fees under their control, including administrative, professional, educational and research, and capital construction finances, and foreign exchange, extrabudgetary, fine and confiscation, and traffic control funds.[53] Leadership over auditing departments in public security units is not entirely clear, but it appears that largely for reasons of police secrecy, they are dominated by the local public security organs within which they are established. Thus, the auditing organs in the public security system seem to provide the central state with significantly less independent monitoring control than they do vis-à-vis other state administrative units.

In 1984, the State Auditing Administration established directly deputized offices within the MPS, and by 1986 similar offices were established in provincial and municipal PSBs with jurisdiction over all PSBs in their territory. County-level PSBs now have either auditing organs or specialized auditing personnel to oversee their subordinate organs. But public security auditing references stress the "special nature" of auditing work in their system, noting that "public security auditing work" is "internal oversight" rather than "external oversight," and these departments are "far less independent" from their host units than are state auditing organs in other administrative departments. A 2004 internal volume on police auditing work notes that public security officials within these departments not only directly lead the auditing work, they also exercise administrative leadership and management over the auditing departments. PSB auditing offices are also supposed to accept the "professional guidance and oversight" of state auditing departments and report to them in addition to their public security superiors. In part, this independence is driven by police secrecy concerns, and was clearly affirmed in a January 1990 State Auditing Administration order granting public security organs the authority to self-audit the budgets of their most secret programmes and operations.[54]

Many security officials feel that under existing oversight systems, "upper level public security organs lack effective mechanisms to constrain lower-level public security organs." They protest that local officials' influence over DI, state supervision and auditing units hampers upper-level investigations of improprieties and has even "turned some local public security units into the guards of local protectionism."[55]

Thus in 1997 the third major new internal system – the oversight police – was established to strengthen the legal and professional oversight capacity of higher level police organs. Their principal focus is on law enforcement procedure and

53 See Oi, *Rural China Takes Off*, pp. 144–57 on the importance of auditing departments in monitoring local finances.

54 Guo Ying, *Gongan shenji* (*Public Security Auditing*) (Beijing: Zhongguo renmin gongan daxue chubanshe, 2004), esp. pp. 2–11; see also *GASZSWD*, p. 129; Sun Mingshan *et al.*, *Xin shiqi gongan zhengzhi gongzuo shouce* (*Handbook on Public Security Political Work During the Current Period*) (*XSGZGS*) (Beijing: Qunzhong chubanshe), pp 288–99.

55 *Gongan jiguan ducha tiaoli shiyong zhinan* (*Guide to Using the Regulations on Public Security Oversight Organs*) (*GJDTSZ*) (Beijing: Zhongguo renmin gongan daxue chubanshe, 1997), p. 50.

discipline, especially monitoring crime scene investigation, though official sources concede that their function overlaps significantly with other oversight organs. Some scholars have compared them to Internal Affairs Departments in American police departments, and one oversight officer has characterized his unit to one of the authors as "the police within the police."

To strengthen vertical leadership, oversight organs are responsible for monitoring police behaviour at their own geographical level and one level down. Likewise, they fall under the dual leadership of their own department and the oversight organ one level up. Although formally this might tend to counterbalance local control, cadres in oversight organs are still principally managed by local Party offices, just like other security cadres.

Writing almost a decade after the establishment of these units, however, a Jilin provincial security analyst painted a discouraging picture of their performance, suggesting that local control over budgets and personnel was overwhelming official efforts to institutionalize more vertical leadership in these units:

> Although the existing oversight police structure also has all sorts of regulations making these units responsible to upper-level oversight police organs, still, in the establishment of organs, the deployment of personnel, organizational and personnel relationships, and various other aspects, they still "take local leadership as the main element (*yi kuai wei zhu*)."[56]

This analyst goes on to charge that the system of local leadership makes it difficult for oversight police units to carry out effective monitoring of police several levels down the system, and encourages them to focus on average police cadres and not leading police cadres. Until this system is more centralized and vertical, he concludes, the oversight police system will never develop the necessary level of institutional independence.[57]

Thus, many officials express frustration that, notwithstanding a matrix of supervisory and oversight organs within the public security system, upper levels lack the independent, reliable information sources they need to monitor and enforce discipline. Some authors have made increasingly bold suggestions that public security organs borrow stronger oversight systems from foreign police forces in order to break down what in other systems is commonly called the "blue wall of silence." These include holding all members of a PSB leadership group "corporately responsible" for serious violations of law and discipline that the unit fails to detect and punish, or instituting a form of the "secret report officer" system that Chinese police scholars believe was pivotal in attacking corruption in the New York City Police Department.[58]

56 Chen Shaokui, "Guanyu woguo jingwu ducha gongzuo de jidian sikao" ("A few points of reflection on our country's police affairs oversight work"), *Senlin gongan* (*Forestry Public Security*), No. 3 (2005), pp. 9–11.

57 *Ibid.* p. 10.

58 On such proposals, see Sun Xiaodong, "A superficial discussion," p. 47.

The Impact of Decentralized Policing on State Power and Rule of Law

Obstacles to professionalization

Most public security leaders see "professionalization" and "regularization" of the public security corps as essential to accomplishing more sophisticated social control strategies in China's increasingly restive and mobile society. The more reformist police and legal scholars agree, but also see professionalization as a key intermediate goal on the path to building the "rule of law." Force professionalization requires great improvements in police skills, discipline and legal norms. Organizationally, it also requires moving away from China's traditionally high reliance upon untrained citizen security activists and entrusting enforcement chores to state employees with professional law enforcement training. Such a transition requires police to be allowed to train a professional corps of sufficient size and quality to handle law enforcement tasks quickly, effectively, legally and with greatly reduced violence.

Many sources insist that local control over personnel and budgets has exacerbated several structural problems in the police corps, most notably very low ratios of full-time professional police to citizens and a highly uneven distribution of those personnel. According to official sources, in 2005 China's total public security forces at all levels numbered 1,700,000 persons, equivalent to just 13 officers for every 10,000 citizens.[59] Analysts frequently protest that China's police/citizen ratio lags far behind not only developed urban societies such as Japan and South Korea but even other large developing Asian societies such as India, Pakistan and Thailand.[60] Within China, ratios vary greatly across provinces and municipalities. The ratios fall off dramatically at lower levels and especially in rural areas. In the mid-1990s, even some relatively wealthy agricultural counties averaged a mere 2.5 officers per 10,000 citizens.[61]

Taking into account that more than one-fourth of police officers are assigned to various enterprise, transport and forestry duties,[62] and persistent complaints that far too many are assigned to "desk" jobs, it becomes clear that the police's "street presence" in many areas of China is slight. In response, the MPS is pushing for departments to aim to place 85 per cent of their personnel on street duty by 2008.[63]

59 Total public security police and cadres rose from 658,000 in 1982 to 870,000 in 1995 to 1.4 million by 2006, reflecting several waves of personnel increases from 1986. Data from Jia Chunwang's speech in *GDZJLS*, p. 7, MPS Political Department Personnel Bureau (ed.), *GARSGL* (*Public Security Personnel Management*) (Beijing, Qunzhong chubanshe, 1997), pp. 67–68. This total apparently does not include PAP border guards, fire-prevention and guards (*jingwei*) personnel. See "Gonganbu zhineng peishu neishe jigou he renyuan bianzhi fang'an," in MPS, *Zhifa shouce*, Vol. 16, Part 1, pp. 432–39.

60 *GARSGL*, pp. 67–68.

61 Fu Hongjie, *GAYJ*, No. 1 (1996), p. 31.

62 In 1993, of 923,000 officers more than 270,000 were assigned to these specialized duties. MPS Public Security Research Institute (ed.), *Qicao renmin gongan jingchafa cankao ziliao xiexuan* (*Selected Reference Materials for Drafting the People's Police Law*) (Beijing: Qunzhong chubanshe, 1997), pp. 3–4.

63 "2008 yi xian shi zhan jingli daoda 85%" ("Fill out police strength on the first line to 85% by 2008"), http://www.chinalegalnews.com.cn/legaltimes/20060220/0601.htm.

Many security experts believe that one serious consequence of low police–citizen ratios is that they force local PSBs and other institutions to rely heavily upon non-professional law enforcement personnel, including citizen activists and "semi-police."[64] There are entirely separate non-public security police units under banking, industrial/commercial, taxation, civil affairs, posts and telecommunications, electrical power, hydropower, agricultural, mining, oil field, factory, hospital, public transport and other departments and units.[65] Most factories, hotels and other economic units now also employ guards from semi-private security companies (*bao'an gongsi*) who receive a couple of weeks' training from local public security units, but thereafter are controlled and paid entirely by their new work units.[66] The proliferation of these undertrained and weakly disciplined new security officers (many of whom illegally purchase genuine public security uniforms and regalia to enhance their image) present new obstacles to dealing with the problems of torture and abuse. A 1997 study by the Supreme People's Procuratorate indicated that enterprises' security officials may now have supplanted public security officers as the foremost perpetrators of illegal detention crimes in China.[67]

Police sources also protest that local Party control has caused security departments to lose control over their "entrances" (hiring), "exits" (retirement and dismissal) and "elevators" (promotions and demotions). Local leaders direct their PSBs to hire cronies who are unqualified for police work, while police training academy graduates are unable to find jobs. A 2005 report by Gansu PSB officials protested that during their hiring campaigns, even though superior levels insisted that all new hires pass appropriate police tests, many local officials signed forms overriding the directives and ordering the hiring of unqualified applicants.[68] In 1998 the Hubei provincial PSB investigated 988 police hired by various county-level PSBs since 1994, and discovered that more than half did not meet minimum hiring standards. In one county PSB, of 133 recent hires, 85 failed to meet standards, and 41 of these had hiring recommendations signed by senior county Party and government officials in their personnel dossiers.[69]

64 Guizhou Provincial PSB chief Jiang Yanhu, for example, contends that the major problem is low personnel "quality" rather than low raw numbers or per capita ratios. See *Collected Essays on Theory and Practice of the People's Police Law*, pp. 19–20.

65 See, for example, Hubei Deputy Public Security Chief Ai Hanjin's complaints in *GA YJ*, No. 1 (1993), p. 2.

66 Information gathered by one of the authors from conversations with over three dozen Chinese security guards, 1995–2005.

67 Zhang Zhijie, *Feifa jujin zui* (*The Crime of Illegal Detention*) (Beijing: People's Procuracy Press, 1997), pp. 20–22, 30–33. This volume indicates that many illegal detentions are committed by factory, enterprise and mine security officials detaining, torturing and/or killing employees and others on suspicion that they have stolen enterprise property.

68 Gansu Provincial Public Security Bureau Political Department Study Group, "Gongan duiwu zhengguihua jianshe de nandian ji jiejue tujing" ("Problems in building standardization in the public security corps and paths to their solution"), *Gongan yanjiu*, No. 2 (2005), pp. 33–38.

69 Shang Wu, "The predicament of public security work and modest proposals for reform," p. 93; see also *Renmin gongan bao*, 6 August 1998, p. 1.

Since social order is a major item in the political evaluation (*zhengji*) of local Party officials, many have pressured local security officials to alter reports on social order to improve their reputations. Dating all the way back to the 1983 Anti-Crime Campaign, police statistical experts have criticized this pressure to misreport social order conditions. Pressure becomes even greater during anti-crime campaigns, when local Party leaders are held personally responsible for improving crime rates.[70]

Obstacles to intelligence-sharing

Police analysts have also argued that local Party dominance over law enforcement creates powerful incentives for local police departments to neglect their responsibilities to share crime-related data and intelligence with other jurisdictions. As cross-jurisdictional organized crime increases, experts in counter-narcotics policing in particular have attacked many local departments for only collecting intelligence that is germane to specific local cases, and not even developing independent, comprehensive law enforcement intelligence departments for their own localities. Information sharing within single public security departments is sometimes very weak (between, for example, the economic crime investigation and the regular criminal investigation offices). The MPS has attempted to overcome this problem through greater use of nationwide computer networks, and through the formation of special offices, such as its Counter-Narcotics Bureau, with nationwide mandates to facilitate intelligence sharing. But a 2005 article reports that relatively few provincial and municipal PSBs followed the MPS's lead and authorized their counter-narcotics offices to encourage effective intelligence sharing among local PSBs within their province.[71]

Legality and non-police duties: "collecting debts, beating dogs, and tying tubes"

Public security leaders have repeatedly attacked some local officials for treating the police as their "personal all-purpose tool of dictatorship" and ordering them to undertake numerous improper duties. MPS commentators contend that the use of police coercion for such officially banned tasks as collecting grain from farmers, forcing farmers off their land, enforcing birth control regulations, detaining businesspeople in contract disputes or attacking local residents who complain about such abuses has become a major issue in the increasing wave of

70 Li Maolin, *GAYJ*, No. 1 (1993), p. 3; see also Fu Hongjie, *GAYJ*, No. 1 (1996), pp. 32–33. On local Party pressure to misreport statistics, see Murray Scot Tanner, "State coercion and the balance of awe: the 1983–86 'stern blows' anti-crime campaign," *The China Journal*, July 2000.

71 Zhen Yonghong and Li Boyang, "Lun xibu diqu de jindu qingbao xiezuo" ("On counter-narcotics intelligence co-operation in China's western regions"), *Guizhou jingguan zhiye xueyuan xuebao*, No. 1 (2005), pp. 81–84, esp. p. 82; also Yang Xijun, "Lun jindu qingbao fuwu" ("On service in counter-narcotics intelligence"), *Shanghai gongan gaodeng zhuanke xuexiao xuebao*, February 2005, pp. 66–69, esp. p. 67.

protests since the mid-1990s. As one commentator noted in 2004, because of the system of *tiaokuai jiehe yikuai weizhu* for leadership management and budgetary guarantees, "public security organs have no choice but to 'follow orders' from local Party secretaries."[72] In 1992, one police scholar who is otherwise sympathetic to local control surveyed 75 county PSBs and found that on average 10–15 per cent of their work was taken up by non-police duties ordered by local officials.[73] As one local official pointed out, many security officials increasingly resent that these demands for them to "collect debts, beat dogs and tie-off tubes" are destroying relations between local police and citizens.[74] Although several recent documents have officially forbidden such use of security forces, and explicitly authorized local police leaders to defy local leadership and decline such tasks, the incentives for police officers to obey are often overwhelming. Police sources claim that as Party demands for "absolute leadership" over security have increased in recent years, many local officials have wielded the charge of "disobeying the Party" as a club to threaten unwilling police.[75]

Local financing and police predation

Central security officials have attacked local financing of security for creating powerful incentives for a wide range of police abuses and predatory practices. Legal media blame weak local government funding and low police salaries for widespread police "moonlighting" running karaoke bars, brothels and other jobs dramatically at odds with their legal duties. Central leaders have demanded that the police, like the military, stop "eating impure grain" (*chi zaliang* 吃杂粮) and live exclusively off of "the emperor's grain" (*chi huangliang* 吃皇粮). In 2004 Ma Yongmei, a commentator for *Public Security Internal Reference*, stated that "when 'the Emperor's grain' is inadequate … it can get so bad that basic-level people's police have no choice but to use 'violating discipline' as a substitute financial guarantee, severely undermining police–citizen relations."[76]

Equally disturbing to police officials have been allegations that local governments are increasingly demanding that public security units use fines, confiscations and fees to cover very large percentages of their own regular administrative budgets and to generate government revenues.[77] Data on such

72 Ma Yongmei, "Dangqian yingxiang jingmin guanxi yisu tanxi" ("An analysis of current factors influencing police-mass relations"), *Gongan yanjiu*, No. 8 (2004), pp. 53–56, esp. p. 54. This pattern has been widely discussed in the literature, see David Shambaugh (ed.), *Is China Unstable? Assessing the Factors* (Washington, DC: Sigur Center for Asian Studies, 1998), esp. the essay by Thomas Bernstein; also Elizabeth J. Perry and Mark Selden (eds.), *Chinese Society: Change, Conflict, and Resistence* (London: Routledge, 2000), esp. the essays by Perry and Selden, Lee, Pei, and Zweig.

73 Wang Mingxin, *On Public Security Fighting Strength*, p. 99.

74 This vivid quote is from Shang Wu, "The predicament of public security work and modest proposals for reform," p. 94.

75 Fu Hongjie, *GAYJ*, No. 1 (1996), pp. 32–33.

76 Ma Yongmei, "An analysis of current factors influencing police-mass relations," pp. 53–56, esp. p. 54; Sun Xiaodong, "A superficial discussion," p. 43.

77 "Using Guangdong's experience to look at the new characteristics of public security work" and "Continuing to give full play to the special characteristics of the existing public security leadership and management," esp. pp. 162–63, 370–73.

abuses are of course unavailable, but even senior MPS finance bureau officials note that "many prefectural and county public security organs nationwide rely on income from fines and confiscations, outside assistance, administrative income, and running economic entities to generate about 50 per cent of their budgets." One senior security analyst recounts the story of a county public security official who submitted his annual budgetary request to the local finance department, and was only granted 40 per cent of his request. "You are the police. You have special powers. You can fine people!" was the proposed solution to the funding shortfall.[78] Many PSBs have responded by using funds generated from traffic and social order management cases to defray the costs of "unprofitable" criminal investigations or by "substituting fines for punishment" to generate revenue.[79]

The centre's apparent powerlessness to control this problem is amply demonstrated by the endless string of demands for an end to such practices. In traffic management alone, for example, the MPS together with other departments issued at least seven nationwide documents demanding an end to "three arbitrary abuses" (arbitrarily charging fees, exacting fines and setting up traffic checkpoints) in just 18 months from May 1995 and November 1996.[80] Yet in subsequent directives and speeches, senior officials bluntly conceded that these problems are as bad as ever.[81]

Conclusions: Assessing the Central–Local Balance and its Impact

Local police in China are "agents" formally subordinate to a variety of central, police and local party-state "principals." An examination of the balance of "power resources" indicates that the centre certainly does have important sources of influence. Its major levers are over general policy directives and laws, the appointment of provincial Party secretaries, the organizational structure of provincial PSBs, and overall personnel quotas. But the widespread local disobedience to central directives cited here demonstrates that these resources do not translate into detailed, effective control over local police behaviour. The powers in the hands of local party-state leaders – leadership authority, hiring of regular officers, leading cadre management, finance and budgeting, and setting salaries – still loom much larger. They create powerful incentives for local public

78 Security scholar, interview, 1998.

79 Zhao Dabin, "Zhuazhu jiou, yifa yanjiu zhiding gongan jiguan jingwu baozhang gongzuo de zhengce yu guihua" ("Seize the opportunity, according to law research and set policies and plans for work to guarantee public security organs' police work"), in MPS, *Renmin jingcha fa lilun yu shijian lunwenxuan* (*Essays on Theory and Practice of the People's Police Law*) (Beijing: Qunzhong chubanshe, 1996), p. 37; also Liu Jiying, *GA YJ*, No. 3 (1998), p. 44; and Shang Wu, "The predicament of public security work and modest proposals for reform," p. 96.

80 These documents, whose titles are too long to list here, are all in *ZRGGFQ* (1995–97), pp. 676–84, 1059–61, 1723–25.

81 See the directive of the State Council, the MPS and several other offices on the "san luan" issued on 6 February 2005, Ministry of Supervision website, www.mos.gov.cn/Template/article/display0.jsp?mid=20050205009965; See also Wei Jianxing, *Renmin ribao*, 16 May 1998, p. 1.

security officials to obey their local Party "principals" more than either their superior public security "principals" or the Party centre. Finally, the variety of legal, administrative, discipline inspection and auditing oversight systems that are supposed to help strengthen central monitoring and access to information for the most part actually end up reinforcing control by local Party committees and PSBs.

Our conclusion is that in this cornerstone sector of state power – legal coercion – the levers of central control over provinces and localities are relatively weak, and very shallow in their reach. If central and provincial-level authorities want to monitor compliance in a particular locality, they must enlist the active support of local Party leaders, and must often pay significant information and transaction costs by dispatching inspection teams or political-legal press reporters, or hoping that "letters from the masses" will reach them.

To strengthen their monitoring capacity, upper-level officials might benefit from making greater use of the emerging institutions that allow officials to tap into and mobilize information sources and political pressure from local citizens who know first hand about many of the failings of law enforcement officials. These institutions include village elections, administrative lawsuits, an increasingly open and investigatory press, and of course the internet. All of these have periodically strengthened the centre's access to information that is needed to monitor police officials in at least some areas. In recent years, for example, internet users have transformed the cases of police shooting demonstrators in Dongzhou, Guangdong, and of Sun Zhigang (a Guangdong student who was killed in police administrative detention) into nationwide "focusing incidents" to spread popular knowledge of law enforcement problems. But during the past three years, the Party leadership has, if anything, backed away from building up such hard-to-dominate institutions rather than making a serious effort to mobilize them to strengthen the centre's monitoring capacity.

Impact on social order and rule of law: Pinkertons of the local state?

Local Party and public security officials face many powerful incentives and opportunities to undermine both central government goals for police professionalization and social control, and long-term prospects for building "rule of law." In particular, police sources have highlighted obstacles to police professionalization as well as local leaders' abuse of police to enforce illegal and predatory policies, which are a major source of local resentment, protests and riots. These include coercive grain collection, land confiscations, tax and fee shakedowns, improper "enforcement" of contracts, family planning, "local protectionism" and revenge against those who complain about such abuses. The incentives form a major obstacle to building the rule of law in China. This point is independent of any assessment of the centre's real commitment to building a state that is legally accountable.

We suspect that decentralized power over public security is not likely to result in the emergence of any nationally uniform pattern of coercive controls and law enforcement. Rather, we expect a variety of local patterns to emerge that are shaped in part by local power balances, leadership commitment to legality, social networks, economic resources and so on.[82] Many localities will probably produce patterns that are fundamentally at odds with the long-term emergence of "rule of law" – especially if "rule of law" is conceived classically in terms of legal professionalism and institutional independence, limits to arbitrariness, or universalistic enforcement of rules across regions or among citizens. It may be that in some large, relatively prosperous cities with high education levels, extensive financial resources to devote to professional police forces and relatively strong "pro-law" professional groups there will be "pockets" of relative legality. However, in localities where a small, tight elite of Party leaders and entrepreneurs collaborate to dominate both state and economy, there are increasing signs that the police (and semi-private "security companies") are emerging as the repressive, anti-labour "Pinkertons" of "local state corporatism." Finally, some still more menacing patterns could emerge, as they did when Yunnan's Pingyuan county was taken over by drug lords in the early 1990s, or more recently in coastal Fujian, where extreme poverty apparently contributed to local police becoming bodyguards for the local government-protected trade in drugs and illegal emigrants. The role local Shanxi and Hunan police played in protecting slave labour brick kilns there recently is an even more chilling example. Any of these latter cases make the prospects for growth of the "rule of law" appear bleak indeed.

82 On locally variant patterns of state–society relations, see Elizabeth J. Perry, "Trends in the study of Chinese politics: state–society relations," *The China Quarterly*, No. 139 (1994), pp. 704–13.

The Police and the Rule of Law: Commentary on "Principals and Secret Agents"

He Weifang

Among Chinese political scientists and legal scholars, indeed within the Chinese academic world as a whole, research into the police is to a great degree marginalized. As the media have become more active, and in particular as internet media have arisen, it has become easier for some incidents of police infringements of human rights to attract nationwide attention. But there has been very little discussion of the relationship between these incidents and the police management system, or the division of police management power between the central and local governments and its ultimate influence on the construction of society in China under the rule of law.

The article by Scot Tanner and Eric Green analyses China's police management system from the angle of the division of power between the central and local governments. The authors describe the historical evolution of the relationship between the Chinese Communist Party (CCP) and the police and show the basic features of the current system. In particular, they show how the centre attempts to control local police through its powers over policy-setting, personnel and organization, and finance and budgeting, as well as through its system of monitoring and control, and the difficulties it encounters in doing so. They also show the influence this system has on the behaviour of the police. Their conclusion is highly instructive to observers of China's progress towards the rule of law: although this system provides a certain space for diverse models of promoting social order and building the rule of law in different localities, it constitutes a major obstacle to the achievement of the Weberian conception of the rule of law.

As an insider, I would like to add some supplementary comments to the penetrating article by Tanner and Green. My first point concerns the special reliance on the police of China's current political structure and system. In any place, the police are an important force in the maintenance of social order. But the Chinese political system places a special reliance on them: they often become an important force in the maintenance of the CCP's monopoly on state power and in the suppression of any resistance to this system. This is the oath taken by the Chinese police:

> I swear that I desire to be a people's policeman; that I will be loyal to the Chinese Communist Party, the motherland, the people and the law; that I will obey the law, follow orders, take direction, strictly observe discipline, keep secrets and carry out the law fairly; that I will be honest and incorruptible, not fear difficulties and not fear sacrifice; and that I will wholeheartedly serve the people and firmly uphold the interests of the state and the people. I wish to dedicate myself to the noble calling of people's public security and to struggle hard to realize my oath.

 doi:10.1017/S0305741007001646

The political role of the police acts as a double-edged sword. After obtaining loyalty, a political party can only give the police more free discretionary power and political influence, and this threatens the goal of the rule-of-law society that the CCP wishes to promote.

Therefore, it could be said that from the time the CCP emerged as an influential political force, the head of the police or the secret police has often had a prestigious political position. In a continuation of this tradition, the 16th Party Congress in 2002 confirmed the position of Zhou Yongkang as a member of the Politburo, member of the Central Committee's secretariat, and standing deputy secretary of the political-legal committee; at the same time, he is the minister of public security, and in fact is one of the chief leaders in command of the whole judicial and police system (*sifa he gong'an xitong* 司法和公安系统). Virtually all localities follow this example: the head of the public security bureau is generally at the same time a member of the standing committee of the Party committee or the secretary of the political-legal committee. This leads to the universal phenomenon of police power being higher than judicial power.

In the process of law implementation as well as in court proceedings, the police enjoy a great deal of supra-legal discretionary power – for example, in the way they can restrict the personal liberty or property of citizens, and especially in their powers respecting the much-criticized over-term detentions and re-education through labour. In investigating and bringing to court criminal cases, the superior strength of the public security departments over the procuratorate and the courts is clear to see. Some procedural law specialists use a homely metaphor to describe the relationship of the three: the police make the food, the procuratorate serves it and the court eats it. The latter can only eat the food that has been supplied by others. We can imagine what kind of pressures a court will face when citizens bring a suit against the police. In fact, this superiority of police power over judicial power is in my view a greater obstacle to the construction of a rule-of-law society in China than the confused division of police management power between the central and local governments.

Therefore, the second supplementary question I wish to address is whether judicial power can bring a new equilibrium to the resolution of the police problem both at the level of central–local relations and at the level of the construction of the rule of law as a whole. The principles of *tongyi lingdao, fenji guanli* (统一领导,分级管理 unified leadership, with management at different levels) and *tiao kuai jiehe, yi kuai wei zhu* (条块结合,以块为主 integration of vertical and horizontal leadership, with horizontal leadership as primary) were applied to the administration of the procuratorates and the courts in a way somewhat resembling their application in the public security system. It is worth noting that when China imported the Soviet procuratorial system in the 1950s it made changes in two key areas. First, it did not accept the principle of general supervisory power (一般监督权 *yiban jiandu quan*), instead limiting the supervisory jurisdiction of the procuratorate to what is commonly called the "political-legal system" (政法系统 *zheng-fa xitong*). Secondly, it changed the

Soviet system of vertical leadership to one of "vertical and horizontal integration" (条块结合 *tiao kuai jiehe*). The reason for these changes is not very clear; it may be related to China's lack of the tradition of the unique Russian-Soviet procuratorial system. In short, because of the similar administrative model, virtually all the shortcomings found by Tanner and Green in the police system can be found in the judicial system as well. Moreover, in view of the importance of judicial independence, when such shortcomings occur in the judicial system they are especially pernicious.

Judicial reform over the past nearly 20 years has more and more touched on these systemic failings. The importance for dispute resolution of the judicial system's maintaining the most basic level of independence is common knowledge. In addition, an independent judiciary is itself an important element in adjusting central–local relations. In both unitary and federal states, court jurisdictional arrangements can allow the dynamic adjustment of central–local relations or – from the standpoint of the centre – allow the centre to exercise a certain supervision and control over local government through the judiciary. But for two reasons, this type of control is impossible to achieve in China.

The first reason is that of institutional arrangements. Although the Constitution stipulates that courts shall be free of interference from administrative powers, because finances and personnel are all controlled by the People's Congress and administrative power at the same level, in handling cases touching on local interests courts have difficulty escaping from the influence of governmental power. Moreover, local administrative chiefs almost all serve concurrently as deputy secretaries of the local Party committee. Therefore, it is simple and straightforward to order courts around through the channel of Party leadership. In addition, as shown above, viewed from the standpoint of the structure of a political party's power, the head of the public security department occupies a stronger position than his court or procuratorate counterparts. In this way, not only the police but also the courts have become Pinkertonized. How can a judiciary like this exercise effective supervision and constraint over police power?

The second reason is that of path dependency in the governance techniques of the Party and the state. There has been excessive reliance on the Party system, the military, the police and the media, and reliance on the judiciary has been not more than secondary. Thus, it has been difficult to summon the determination and find effective measures to carry out reform of the various shortcomings in the administrative structure of courts and procuratorates. In recent years, the highest authorities have been very concerned about the local protectionism and danger to the market economy brought on by local control over the judiciary. But because they do not dare to adopt radical reform measures, they can resort only to ineffective education campaigns. For example, a little over a year ago there was a nationwide "socialist rule-of-law concept education" campaign, of which an important element was stress on "serving the overall interest" and obeying the "leadership of the Party." But the orders of local Party committees also serve the leadership of the Party, and so judicial organs can only be like public security departments and be primarily obedient to the local Party leadership. This is because even if this kind of obedience is erroneous, if higher levels want to pursue responsibility, then at the very least the Party committee and administrative power at the same level will provide protection and conceal relevant information. But if one defies the will of the local Party or government, that is enough to bring on immediate punishment and retribution.

This brings us naturally to the last question about which I wish to add supplementary remarks: that of the freedom of the press. Tanner and Green noted the informational advantage enjoyed by an agent and analysed the difficulty of obtaining information about the police and their activities. In China, this kind of informational advantage is especially obvious because there is no freedom of the press. Because of the reliance of the party-state on the public security forces, negative reports in the realm of public security in the official media (in China, "official media" means all traditional media) have always been strictly controlled. This has led to local public security departments or police becoming ever more able to do just as they please, and has exacerbated the difficulty of central control. Even though the rise of internet media has changed this closed situation to a certain extent, it is difficult at present to say where things will go in the future.

Transforming Family Law in Post-Deng China: Marriage, Divorce and Reproduction*

Michael Palmer

ABSTRACT This article considers the principal changes in family law in the People's Republic of China during the post-Deng period. The developments that have occurred during the period of review have been notable for their pace and their contribution to a growing legal sophistication in China's corpus of family law. They expand on a series of major reforms in family law documented in my earlier *China Quarterly* article. Overall, it is in the area of divorce that the most dramatic changes have taken place in family law over the past decade.

This article examines the continuing evolution of family law in the People's Republic of China (PRC). Since the publication in 1995 of an earlier *China Quarterly* article on post-Mao Chinese family law,[1] the legal framework for family life has been reformed in order, inter alia, to deal with problems encountered with the regulatory system built up in the 1980s and early 1990s, and to respond to changes taking place in Chinese society. Two legislative developments are highly significant. First, the Marriage Law was revised in 2001,[2] and greater judicial attention then given to its implementation, especially

* I thank participants in the conference on "Developments in Chinese Law: the Past Ten Years" for their helpful comments on the draft version of this article. Responsibility for any remaining errors is mine alone.

1 Michael Palmer, "The re-emergence of family law in post-Mao China: marriage, divorce and reproduction," in Stanley Lubman (guest ed.), "Law in China Under Reform," *The China Quarterly*, No. 141 (1995), pp. 110–34; republished in Stanley B. Lubman (ed.) *China's Legal Reforms* (Oxford: Oxford University Press, 1996), pp. 110–34.

2 For details see, for example, Ma Yinan, *Hunyin jiating fa xinlun* (*New Discussions on Marriage and Family Law*) (Beijing: Beijing daxue chubanshe, 2002); Liu Shuqiang (ed.), *Zhonghua renmin gongheguo hunyin fa tiaowen jieshi* (*Explanation of the Articles in the Marriage Law of the People's Republic of China*) (Chengdu: Sichuan renmin chubanshe, 2001); Yang Xueming and Qu Zhi, *Xin "hunyin fa" redian jujiao* (*Focus on Controversial Issues in the new Marriage Law*) (Shenyang: Liaoning huabao chubanshe, 2001); Ma Yuan (ed.), *Xin hunyin fa ji sifa jishi shiyong zhinan* (*Practical Guidance on the New Marriage Law and Judicial Interpretations [on Marriage Law]*) (Beijing: Renmin fayuan chubanshe, 2002); Ma Yuan (ed.), *Xin hunyin fa: anli pingxi* (*The New Marriage Law: Case Analysis*) (Beijing: Renmin fayuan chubanshe, 2002). Within family law circles in China, the debate on the reform of the Marriage Law amendments is regarded as a significant step forward in public participation in the process of law reform. Nevertheless, a number of the more radical suggestions made were rejected and the extent to which the debate was truly free and open must be doubted, given party-state control of the media.

 doi:10.1017/S0305741007001658

in relation to divorce.[3] These changes were followed in 2003 by a further revision of the rules governing marriage (and divorce) registration.[4] Secondly, a synthesizing, national code of family planning was finally introduced, also in 2001,[5] and then extended in 2002 by State Council Measures on the Administration of Social Upbringing Charges.[6] Other notable developments include the 1998 revision of the Adoption Law[7] and the continuing evolution of a corpus of social protection law (*shehui baozhang fa* 社会保障法) including in particular the introduction of a law protecting the rights and interests of the elderly in 1996 and a revision of the 1992 Women's Protection Law in 2005.[8] A number of the changes mentioned above and considered in greater detail below are also related to shifting policies and practices regarding the role of various forms of dispute process – especially "mediation" (*tiaojie* 调解) – in Chinese social life in general and intra-familial disputes in particular.

Three specific aspects of family law are focused on: marriage, divorce and reproduction. These are the core of PRC "family law." This focus does not accord exactly, however, with the "official" view in China, which regards rules and issues of family planning as largely falling outside family law, so that, for example, even compendia of rules on family law matters intended for judicial practice omit direct reference to legislation relating to reproduction and associated issues.[9] The present article and its predecessor, however, both assume that planned births and population policies and rules are so critical for

3 That is, the 2001 "Zuigao renmin fayuan guanyu shiyong 'Zonghua renmin gongheguo hunyin fa' ruogan wenti de jieshi [1]" ("Interpretation of the Supreme People's Court on several problems concerning the application of the Marriage Law of the PRC [1]"), promulgated and in force 24 December 2001, and the 2003 "Zuigao renmin fayuan guanyu shiyong 'Zonghua renmin gongheguo hunyin fa' ruogan wenti de jieshi (2)" ("Interpretation of the Supreme People's Court on several problems concerning the application of the Marriage Law of the PRC [2]") promulgated 25 December 2003 and in force 1 April 2004 in *Hunyin fa peitao guiding* (*A Complete Set of Rules on the Marriage Law*) (Beijing: Zhongguo fazhi chubanshe, 2006) at pp. 14–18 and pp. 18–22 respectively. See also Zuigao renmin fayuan minshi shenpan diyi ting (First Civil Trial Chamber of the Supreme People's Court) (ed.), *Hunyin fa sifa jieshi ji xiangguan falü guifan* (*Judicial Interpretations of the Marriage Law and Relevant Legal Provisions*) (Beijing: Renmin fayuan chubanshe, 2001); Huang Songyou (ed.), *Hunyin fa sifa jieshi (2) de lijie yu shiyong* (*Understanding and Applying The Second Judicial Interpretation of the Marriage Law*) (Beijing: Renmin fayuan chubanshe).

4 Marriage Registration Regulations (Hunyin dengji tiaoli), promulgated by the State Council, 8 August 2003 and in force 1 October 2003, in *A Complete Set of Rules on the Marriage Law*, pp. 42–48.

5 "Zonghua renmin gongheguo renkou yu jihua shengyu fa," promulgated 29 December 2001 and in force 1 September 2002, in *Renkou yu jihua shengyu fa ji qi peitao guiding* (*The Population and Birth Planning Law and a Complete Set of its Rules*) (Beijing, Zhongguo fazhi chubanshe, 2003) at pp. 1–9.

6 "Shehui fuyang zhengshou guanli banfa," in *ibid.* at pp. 135–37.

7 "Zhonghua renmin gongheguo shouyang fa," revised and in force 4 November 1998, in *A Complete Set of Rules on the Marriage Law*, pp. 23–27.

8 See Michael Palmer, "Protecting the rights and interests of the elderly: developments in the family law of the People's Republic of China, 1996–8," in A. Bainham (ed.), *The International Survey of Family Law: 1999* (Dordrecht: Kluwer (for The International Society on Family Law), 1999), pp. 95–107, and Michael Palmer, "On China's slow boat to women's rights: revisions to the Women's Protection Law, 2005," in P. W. Chan (ed.), special issue of *International Journal of Human Rights* on "Equality in the Asia Pacific," Vol. 11, Nos. 1 and 2 (2007), pp. 151–77.

9 See, for example, China Legal System Press, *Hunyin jiating ban'an changyong shouce* (*An Everyday Handbook for Handling Cases of Marriage and Family*) (Beijing: Zhongguo fazhi chubanshe, 2006), and Huang Songyou (ed.-in-chief), *Hunyin jiating sifa jieshi shili shijie* (*Marriage and Family: Explanation of Judicial Interpretations and Concrete Cases*) (Beijing: Renmin fayuan chubanshe, 2006).

family life in contemporary China that their inclusion is essential. The current study therefore examines developments in this area, as well as in another and related mode of reproduction and recruitment to the family, namely adoption. It thus considers the nature and significance of the legal changes that have taken place in these four dimensions of family law since 1995. While highly important changes have occurred in all four areas, it is probably in the law of divorce that the most significant developments have occurred.

The Reforms of 2001

The socio-political contexts within which the two most significant statutory developments since 1995 took place offer a strong contrast. On the one hand, much publicity proceeded and accompanied the revision in 2001 of the Marriage Law (*hunyin fa* 婚姻法) 1980, with often heated debate among those doing the revision, and also a considerable degree of openly expressed controversy over some of the key issues.[10] These included the nature of marriage, the notion of a "relative" (*qinqi* 亲戚), and various aspects of divorce including the grounds for divorce, property and custody rights, compensation for morally blameworthy conduct leading to divorce, and the appropriate responses to domestic violence. Within these discussions, it was possible to discern shifting ideas about appropriate boundaries between the public sphere and private life – in particular, the appropriateness of state intervention in family matters. On the other hand, remarkably little fanfare surrounded the promulgation of the Population and Birth Planning Law (*renkou yu jihua shengyu fa* 人口与计划生育法) later the same year. In formal, legal terms this is perhaps best explained by reference to the different legislative tracks that the two developments were apparently assigned. Although both legislative advances were promulgated by the Standing Committee of the National People's Congress, the Marriage Law revisions took place within a procedural framework clearly informed by some of the reforms encouraging openness and greater public consultation introduced by the 2000 Law on Legislation. In contrast, the family planning code involved a much more restricted approach, with virtually no public deliberation. This lack of openness reflected the politically-sensitive nature of population control, and such conservatism should be borne in mind, for example, when making judgements about the significance of family law in post-Deng China for an emerging civil society.

Marriage

As indicated in the earlier *China Quarterly* article, in the PRC marriages are concluded in law by registration, not by celebration. The legal requirement of

10 For an admirable analysis of key aspects of the reform of the Marriage Law in 2001 see William Alford and Yuanyuan Shen, "Have you eaten, have you divorced? Debating the meaning of freedom in marriage in China," in William C. Kirby (ed.), *Realms of Freedom in Modern China*, Vol. 15, "Making of modern freedom" series (Stanford, CA: Stanford University Press, 2004).

registration must be fulfilled, but in practice is often ignored by couples and their families, who consider celebration of marriage in traditional style more important.[11] This has resulted in various difficulties including, in particular, official treatment of unregistered unions and enforcement of family planning rules.

The system of compulsory marriage registration remains in place today, but during the past few years attempts have been made to respond to pressures of legal practice and social change, and to give greater recognition to the view that marriage is a private process. Changes were introduced by, first, the 2001 revision to Chapter 2 of the Marriage Law; secondly, by two Interpretations from the Supreme People's Court on the revised Marriage Law in 2001 and 2003 respectively; thirdly, by the 2003 revision of the rules on the processes of marriage and divorce registration in which a new meaning for "marriage registration" is promoted (symbolically indicated by discarding the term "administration" from the rules' title)[12]; and finally, the 2005 revision of the Women's Protection Law.[13]

As a result, modifications have been made to the legal conditions of capacity for marriage. Reflecting medical advances in China, leprosy is no longer explicitly characterized as a condition rendering a person unfit for marriage.[14] In addition, difficulties in identifying and dealing with invalidity of marriage are addressed by provisions in the revised Marriage Law at Articles 10 and 12. In particular, a marriage is characterized as void (*hunyin wuxiao* 婚姻无效) *ab initio* if the minimum legal ages of marriage have not been attained (albeit with rectification possible if the union has not been registered: see below), one of the intending spouses is already married, or the proposed marriage falls within the prohibited degrees.

Unregistered "marriages" between parties in which at least one of the intending spouses is underage have been a widespread problem in post-Mao China, reflecting not only continued adherence to traditional ideals that regard marriage as a matter of celebration rather than registration but also social pressures for early wedlock in order to commence reproduction. The authorities' response has been increasingly to impose strict requirements of registration and to limit judicial recognition of unregistered unions as "de facto marriages" (*shishi hunyin* 事实婚姻). However, this restrictive approach, closely associated with family planning policy, was criticized during the debates on revision of the Marriage Law, and was in particular considered to be inimical to the interests of rural women. As result, the revised Marriage Law permits retrospective registration: "in the absence of marriage registration, the man and the woman

11 Palmer, "The re-emergence of family law in post-Mao China," at p. 118.

12 Marriage Registration Regulations, 2003 replacing the Regulations on the Administration of Marriage Registration, 1994. See further below, n. 19.

13 That is, "Zhonghua renmin gongheguo funü quanyi baozhang fa" ("The Law on the Protection of Rights and Interests of Women of the People's Republic of China"), revised and in force 25 August 2005, in *A Complete Set of Rules on the Marriage Law*, pp. 28–36.

14 Marriage Law of the People's Republic of China 1980, as revised 2001, at Article 7.

should (*yingdang* 应当) go through registration procedures."[15] The 2003 revised Marriage Registration Regulations provide at Article 8 for a process of "remedial marriage registration" (*buban jiehun dengji* 补办结婚登记) for unregistered unions. In addition, the courts have the jurisdiction to deal with cases of void marriage, and their decisions in such cases are then filed with the relevant marriage registration organs (Article 16). The revised Marriage Law itself affords little scope for retrospectively legitimating a union as in many cases the problem is that the parties commenced their union when one partner (or both) was underage.[16] In order to deal with this problem, the 2001 Interpretation at Article 4 allows for recognition of unregistered relationship in which one party (or both) was underage: the union may be characterized as one of lawful marriage from the moment when the parties attain the age of capacity to marry. Moreover, when a couple in an unregistered relationship seek divorce, then the relationship may be characterized as de facto marriage if both parties satisfied the substantive conditions for marriage prior to promulgation of the Regulations on the Administration of Marriage Registration on 1 February 1994. In cases in which one or both parties only attained the age of capacity to marry subsequent to that date, the couple must register their union before any matrimonial proceedings may commence (Article 5).[17] Nevertheless, the above developments indicate an important shift in official policy on unregistered unions. Hitherto, the trajectory of change had been increasingly to regard unregistered unions an unlawful cohabitation (*feifa tongju* 非法同居). There is now some relaxation in this approach, reflecting official acknowledgement of the predominance in numerous areas of the countryside of customary celebration over legal registration in the conclusion of marriage.

In the process of declaring a marriage void, significantly greater attention is also given to procedural issues. Thus, Article 10 of the revised Marriage Law not only gives the spouses themselves but also confers on "persons with an interest" (*li-hai guanxi de ren* 利害关系的人) the right to apply for a declaration of void marriage in cases of bigamy. Such interested persons include not only close relatives but also "grassroots" organs. Moreover, in considering the validity of a marriage following an application under Article 10 of the revised Marriage Law, mediation may be used by the court only in respect of distribution of property and custody of children: the decision on the substantive validity of the "marriage" itself must be made by adjudication. In addition, the 2003 Interpretation provides that an application for a declaration of void marriage, once started, may not be retracted. The court must declare the marriage void if it finds merit in the application (Articles 2 and 3). If there are concurrent suits for a

15 At Article 8.

16 Article 10 provides that a "marriage" remains invalid if the parties fall short of the minimum legal ages of marriage, and a void marriage is invalid from its inception (Article 12).

17 Article 6 provides that the same principles also apply where one party dies and the other claims succession rights in the estate of the deceased.

declaration of void marriage and for divorce, the former is given prior consideration by the court (Article 7).

A third significant area of development concerns forced marriage (*xiepo hunyin* 胁迫婚姻). The revised Marriage Law introduces new provisions (in Article 11) that empower a party coerced into marriage to seek abrogation of the marital relationship within one year either from the date of marriage registration or of securing their freedom. Only the coerced party in a marriage may make such an application, according to the 2001 Interpretation at Article 10, which characterizes such "marriages" as unions in which one party compels the other "to enter into marriage against her or his will by threatening the intimidated party or close relatives of that party with harm to life, health, reputation, property and so on." This is clearly an important step in strengthening women's rights, although the time limit of one year is rather short for a woman thus coerced to adjust to her new situation and to decide on whether to remain in the forced marriage.

Perhaps indicative of the relatively widespread nature of forced marriage, the 2003 revised Marriage Registration Regulations allow marriage registration organs as well as courts to handle applications from those pressed into marriage against their will (Article 9). The petitioner submits the appropriate documentation to a registration official who then considers the facts of the case. If there is sufficient evidence of coercion, and problems concerning child maintenance, property and debts are revolved, the registrar rescinds the marriage and declares the marriage certificate invalid (Article 9). It would seem, however, that no procedures are yet in place for dealing with customary unions that have been entered into by force.[18]

Fourthly, the revised Marriage Law attempts to deal with growing problems in the "monogamous" nature of marriage. In particular, there has been the re-appearance in southern China of the phenomenon of taking concubines (*bao'er nai* 包二奶). This reflects, inter alia, enhanced wealth in the southern China countryside and the continued popular belief in the importance of maintaining patrilineal descent lines (an importance that continues to be indirectly acknowledged officially in family planning regulations, as shown below). In the debates surrounding the revision in 2001 of the Marriage Law, the All-China's Women's Federation pushed hard to make the taking of concubines into a national moral panic, and in this atmosphere some critics of the practice of concubinage argued that the revised Marriage Law should make it a criminal offence. Such arguments were rejected on the ground that the Marriage Law is essentially civil law, and to criminalize concubinage would be to overextend public interest in private matters. However, the General Principles section of the revised marriage code now provides that "cohabitation of a married person with

18 The detailed rules on the property division dimensions of void and voidable marriages are not considered here, for reasons of space. Suffice it to note that the 2003 Interpretation at Article 1 guarantees cohabiting parties the right to bring suit if disputes arise over division of property and custody of children.

any third party shall be prohibited" (Article 3, para. 2), and concubinage is also made a ground for divorce. Nevertheless, concubinage does not in itself constitute a crime and the 2003 Interpretation also sets limits on the public response to it: in ordinary cases of cohabitation, the courts may not order the cohabitants to cease living together, and it seems that a man and his concubine in a stable relationship will not be required to terminate their cohabitation unless a complaint is made to the court (Article 1).

A fifth notable change is in the procedures for marriage registration. As noted above, the change in name from Regulations on the Administration of Marriage Registration (*hunyin dengji guanli tiaoli* 婚姻登记管理条例), promulgated in 1994, to Marriage Registration Regulations (*hunyin dengji tiaoli* 婚姻登记条例) in 2003 reflected official acceptance of the view that hitherto there has been excessive state interference in married life.[19] The more liberal procedures may also be seen as a response to the declining importance of state-owned enterprises as institutions of social control. The amendments were also a product of a change in official thinking on the "private international law" dimensions of marriage registration, as the 2003 reforms create a unified system in which the parties are not only Chinese citizens but also "compatriots" in Hong Kong, Macau and Taiwan, and foreign parties, thereby ending the hitherto separate regimes for these categories (Article 5). The revised Regulations introduce two further changes. First, the marrying parties must now themselves demonstrate that they have the capacity to marry – assuring the registrar that they are not already married to others nor close consanguines, and so on. Prior to this change, this responsibility was often assumed by work units. Secondly, the policy increasingly imposed in the 1990s requiring intending spouses to undergo pre-marital medical check ups – expressed in robust terms in Article 9 and 10 of the 1994 Regulations – has been abandoned. In part, this reflects the fact that the examination scheme has not worked well. It also reflects an official recognition that marriage and reproduction are not quite the same thing. Thus, although the 2003 Regulations no longer require pre-marital medical check-ups, the revised Women's Protection Law of 2005 at Article 51 contains a new provision on pregnancy health care systems that suggests that women will still be encouraged to undergo pre-marital medical check-ups, and certainly prior to attempting pregnancy.

Finally, the revised Marriage Law also attempts to deal with the somewhat paradoxical situation that while parental interference in marriage has declined in post-Mao China, the obstruction of parental marriage by adult children – anxious, for example, about the adverse impact of an intended re-marriage on their inheritance rights – has been on the increase.[20] As a result, the revised Marriage Law contains a new provision at Article 30 which forbids children

19 See, for example, Yang Dawen and Long Yifei, *Hunyin jiating faxue* (*Marriage and Family Law*) (Beijing, Zhongguo renmin daxue chubanshe, 2006), pp. 116–19; the full text of the revised regulations is provided at pp. 330–33.

20 See Palmer, "Protecting the rights and interests of the elderly."

from blocking the remarriage of a parent.[21] Moreover, and consistent with welfare policies that continue to define the family as an important unit of care and welfare for the elderly, the same Article stipulates that the remarriage of a parent does not release the children from their obligation to support (*shanyang* 赡养) their parents. This confirms Article 19 of the Elderly Persons Law 1996, which also safeguards the right of the elderly to divide and distribute their own property (*geren caichan* 个人财产) as they see fit, free from any obstruction from their children or other relatives, including attempts by such kinsfolk to secure the property by force.

Divorce

The issue of divorce has also been subject to very significant legal change over the past decade. The statistical evidence points to a considerable increase in the divorce rate during the post-Mao period as a whole – from an initial figure of 3 per cent to 20 per cent in some areas by the late 1990s.[22] This is the result of a number of different causes, but several stand out as especially important: a relaxation in the grounds for divorce in contested applications,[23] a reduced willingness on the part of young people to endure unhappy marriages in China's increasingly open and economically developed society, and the emergence of a more professional and younger judiciary. Freedom of divorce, especially for women, appears at long last to be becoming a reality in socialist China.

Nevertheless, the 2001 revisions to the Marriage Law continue to reflect a moralistic and judgemental approach to contested divorce. This approach infused the 1989 Supreme People's Court Opinions on divorce,[24] and the 2001 revisions have now put in place a system that deals more effectively with issues of fault and compensation for blameworthy conduct. In particular, compensation may be sought by a "party without fault" (*wu guocuo fang* 无过错方) if matrimonial breakdown results from bigamy, cohabitation with a third party, domestic violence, or maltreatment and desertion.[25] Another highly significant

21 See also Article 18 of the 1996 Law on the Protection of Rights and Interests of the Elderly, which provides: "freedom of marriage of the elderly is protected by law. Children and other relatives may not interfere in the divorce, remarriage or married life of the elderly. The obligations to provide support … does not alter with a change in the marital relations of the elderly person." Zhonghua renmin gongheguo laonianren quanyi baozhang fa, in Guowuyuan fazhi bangongshe (Office of the Legislative Affairs Office of the State Council) (ed.), *Xinpian Zhonghua renmin gongheguo changyong falü fagui quanshu* (*Newly Complied Compendium of Frequently Used Laws and Regulations of the People's Republic of China*) (Beijing, Zhongguo fazhi chubanshe, 1999) pp. 1700–05.

22 Michael Palmer, "Marriage reform and population control: changing family law in contemporary China," in A. Bainham (ed.), *The International Survey of Family Law: 2005* (Bristol: Jordan Publishing (for The International Society on Family Law), 1997), pp. 173–201, at p.185.

23 See Michael Palmer, "The People's Republic of China: more rules but less law," in M. Freeman (ed.), *Annual Survey of Family Law: 1989*, Vol. 13 (London: The International Society on Family Law, 1991), pp. 325–42, at pp. 333–36.

24 *Ibid.*

25 These provisions, contained in Article 46, have been elaborated in the 2001 Interpretation, which provides that a court may not disallow a divorce application if the petitioner is to some extent also blameworthy (Article 23), and by the 2003 Interpretation, which stipulates at Article 27 that when marriage registration organs are dealing with cases of divorce by mutual consent, it is still possible for one party to seek compensation for the matrimonial misconduct of the other spouse.

development has been a growth in concern with the issue of domestic violence (*jiating baoli* 家庭暴力). Economic restructuring, international pressure (in particular from CEDAW)[26] and an increased tendency for husbands to take revenge against an unfaithful spouse[27] are among the factors which encouraged the introduction, at Article 43 of the revised Marriage Law, of new provisions which attempt to provide better protection for women victims. Moreover, the 2001 Interpretation offers a definition of domestic violence for the first time in national law, and includes within that definition beating, tying-up, maiming and restricting personal freedom (for example by the use of force) such that mental or physical harm results. Maltreatment, however, must be "persistent" and "frequent" before it can be characterized as domestic violence. Another significant limitation is that, according to Article 3 of the 2001 Interpretation, a victim of domestic violence may not bring suit under Article 4 of the revised Marriage Law, even though that Article encourages mutual respect and assistance between family members.

Women suffering from domestic violence continue to be encouraged to seek intervention from their local people's mediation committee, which is expected to persuade the husband to cease his misconduct. However, in more serious cases the local public security bureau is also expected to intervene and, at the victim's request, may impose administrative sanctions on the husband. In addition, a wife who has suffered domestic violence may bring a private prosecution (*zisu* 自诉), and both the public security bureau and the procuracy are expected to assist her.

This shift in the policy and regulatory framework for dealing with domestic violence is significant. Although the processes of mediation and administration sanctioning continue to be emphasized, domestic violence is now characterized as not only a private dispute but also a matter of public concern, and therefore also the concern of criminal law and judicially imposed punishment. As in the debates on concubinage, the public–private divide is shifting in order better to protect women.

Matrimonial estate

The regulatory framework governing domestic property relations was put under increasing stress in the 1990s as a result of China's rapid economic development and social change. The forms and value of domestic property have expanded significantly, and property dealings between spouses and third parties grown considerably. Accordingly, the ownership, contents and value of matrimonial

26 See "Patriarchy, privacy and protection: slowly conceptualizing domestic violence in Chinese law," in Natalia Iu. Erpyleva, Jane Henderson and M. Butler (eds.), *Forging a Common Legal Destiny: Liber Amicorum in Honour of Professor W. E. Butler* (London & New York: Wildy, Simmonds and Hill, 2005), pp. 786–812.

27 Yang Xueming and Qu Zhi, *Xin "hunyin fa" redian jujiao* (*Focus on the Controversial Issues in the New Marriage Law*) (Shenyang: Liaoning huabao chubanshe, 2001), pp. 212–61.

assets have become more complicated, often making difficult the task of dividing the estate upon divorce.[28]

One probable result of this increasing complexity is that negotiation between the parties for securing division of the matrimonial estate is the preferred form of decision-making. While a negotiated outcome should be lawful, and not contravene the interests of third parties, serious power imbalances will nevertheless often affect the decision-making process. There is a real danger that the rights and interests of divorcing wives are insufficiently safeguarded. Some protection is offered by Article 47 of the revised Marriage Law, which provides that a party who is discovered to have concealed or alienated the property, or to have created false debts, will receive, inter alia, a smaller share of the matrimonial estate (Article 47).

The changing circumstances also stimulated vigorous debate on a number of key issues: for example, should the intellectual property rights of one spouse be included in the matrimonial estate to be divided at divorce, or excluded on the basis that this will be an incentive for originality and creativity? The revisions to the 2001 Law are a compromise, with earnings from intellectual property rights characterized as joint spousal property, but the ownership of the property rights themselves remaining under the individual ownership of the inventive spouse. These provisions are now contained in Article 17 of the revised Law, and that and the following Article together with the relevant sections of the two judicial interpretations of the Marriage Law now offer a significantly reformed system. Thus, the 2003 Interpretation now provides explicit rules on the often difficult

28 Custody is not considered to require new regulation so that the provisions in the Marriage Law and the 1993 "Zuigao renmin fayuan guanyu renmin fayuan shenli lihun anjian chuli zinü fuyang wenti de ruogan juti yijian" ("Several concrete opinions of the Supreme People's Court on the problems of bringing up children in divorce cases handled by the Supreme People's Court"), 3 November 1993 remain the main source of rules. The fundamental principle is found in Article 36 of the revised Marriage Law (Article 29 in the old version of the 1980 Law) which provides that after divorce ordinarily the mother is awarded custody of a child that is still being breast-fed (in the 1993 Opinions the wording is a child who is under two years of age). For older children, custody is a matter of agreement between the two parties. However, if they are unable to reach an agreement and a dispute arises, the court is expected to award custody on the basis of the child's interests, the circumstances of the divorcing spouses, and in cases in which the child is ten years old or above, the wishes of the child (Article 36 of the revised Marriage Law, and Articles 3 and 5 of the 1993 Opinions). The 1993 Opinions at Article 3 envisage a range of circumstances in which custody might be awarded to the father rather than the mother. Although neither the revived Marriage Law nor the 1993 Opinions deal with the issue of access for non-custodial parents, the Opinions do allow for joint custody (Article 6). Child support payments for children up to the age of 18 are a function of the child's needs, the financial circumstances of the parents and local cost of living, but ordinarily will not exceed 30% of a parent's fixed income (Article 7). For a more detailed analysis of custody provisions at divorce see Michael Palmer, "Women to the fore: developments in the family law of the PRC," in A. Bainham (ed.), *Annual Survey of Family Law: 1994* (Dordrecht: Kluwer (for The International Society on Family Law), 1996), pp. 155–79. Suffice it to say that court awards of custody to women continue to suffer from problems of enforcement, especially in rural areas. The revised Law at Article 38 does, however, confirm the rights of non-custodial parents to visit their children. These are in the first instance a matter of negotiation between the parents and only if they are unable to agree should a court make an order. If visitation by a non-custodial parent leads to a decline in the wellbeing (include mental health) of a child, then the court may order a cessation of the visits until such time as the child's wellbeing is restored.

issue of betrothal gifts,[29] allowing for their return in matrimonial proceedings where the spouses failed to register their marriage or to cohabit after marriage registration, or where the donor has experienced financial difficulties as a result of his generous gift.[30] In Article 18 of the 2001 revised Law and Article 11 of the 2003 Interpretation, significantly clearer guidance is given to judges faced with the sometimes difficult task of separating out individual and matrimonial property. Very importantly, from the point of view of gender equality, the matrimonial estate includes investment income, endowment insurance and other property and benefits acquired during the marriage. Similarly, Article 13 of the 2003 Interpretation provides that any demobilization fee or similar payment made to a spouse leaving the People's Liberation Army is characterized as joint spousal property, to be divided equally at divorce.

Another problematic area of matrimonial property relations arises from the fact that increasingly the estate involves property that is in part external to the family in that it relates to business dealings, debt, and equity and partnerships. Take, for example, the case of a partnership in which one of the divorcing spouses is a partner. Article 17 of the 2003 Interpretation stipulates that the other spouse may join the partnership if all the other partners agree. If such consent is not forthcoming, one of several solutions is permitted, including purchase or return of the divorcing spouse's share, followed by a partitioning of the proceeds between the wife and husband. To take another example, in the case of a family debt, should repayment be made by the party who originally borrowed the sum, or should it be repaid by both parties from their mutual property? The 2003 Interpretation offers a variety of answers, depending on the circumstances under which a debt was incurred and used. Thus, a debt incurred by one spouse prior to marriage remains a personal debt unless it has been "spent on family living during the marriage" (*yongyu hunhou jiating gongtong shenghuo* 用于婚后家庭共同生活) (Article 23) whereas a debt incurred during the course of the marriage is presumed to be the joint liability of the spouses unless otherwise agreed, with the spouse against whom a joint debt has been enforced able to recover the money from the other spouse by an agreement at divorce or a court order (2003 Interpretation, Article 23; 1980 Marriage Law [as revised 2001], Article 31).

The development of privately owned housing, too, requires new rules for apportioning rights in the matrimonial home. Reflecting the shift from housing provided by the work unit to private ownership, Article 19 of the 2003 Interpretation provides that a home rented by one spouse before marriage but

29 For earlier discussions of the difficulties that the people's courts have faced in resolving betrothal gift disputes, see Michael Palmer, "The People's Republic of China: problems of marriage and divorce," in M. Freeman (ed.), *Annual Survey of Family Law: 1987*, Vol. 11 (London: The International Society on Family Law, 1988), pp. 57–79, at pp. 65–66, and Michael Palmer, "Caring for young and old: developments in the family law of the People's Republic of China," in A. Bainham (ed.), *The International Survey of Family Law: 2000* (Bristol: Jordan Publishing (for The International Society on Family Law), 2000), pp. 95–107, at p. 100.

30 See Section 10, paragraph 1 of the 2003 Interpretation.

purchased by the couple post-marriage is characterized as joint property even if registered in the name of only one spouse. If there is a dispute between the parties on ownership or the value of the matrimonial home, a negotiated agreement is the preferred outcome, and the people's court is not allowed to make a decision on ownership. If the property is not sold and the proceeds divided (Article 20), the court may award occupation to one of the spouses based on actual circumstances of the case (*yingdang genju shiji qingkuang panjue you dangshiren shiyong* 应当根据实际情况判决由当事人使用) (Article 21). The lack of detail and precision in these rules seems unlikely to assist the position of the divorcing wife, although some protection may be offered in the characterization in Article 22 of parents' contribution to the purchase price of matrimonial property as a personal donation to their own child. With respect to work unit housing, Article 42 of the revised Marriage Law is confirmed by Article 27 of the 2001 Supreme People's Court Interpretation as encouraging a husband whose work unit has provided accommodation for a married couple to assist in continuing to provide such accommodation for the use of his erstwhile wife. Again, the lack of a firm requirement for such help is not likely to safeguard the position of the wife in these circumstances.

Reproducing – Population Control

Although one of the most important ways in which the state has intruded into Chinese family life in the post-Mao period has been through restrictions placed on reproduction and family size,[31] it was not until the turn of the century that a full, national-level code of birth control was introduced. In 2000 the Central Committee of the CCP and the State Council issued a joint Decision on Strengthening Population and Family Planning Work,[32] and late in the following year the Law on Population and Birth Planning was promulgated. This provides a general framework within which the more detailed provincial regulations on family planning may now operate. It continues to reflect an approach that sees population control as a demographic problem, to be dealt with by bureaucratic regulation, rather than an issue of reproductive rights. The Law has since been supplemented by, in particular, the State Council's 2002

31 For excellent analyses of the tensions between the state and the family, especially as manifested in the countryside, and of the conflicts between the official ideal of a "socialist family" and continued adherence to the values of the patriarchal family see the work of Tyrene White, including "Two kinds of production: the evolution of China's family planning policy in the 1980s," *Population and Development Review*, Vol. 20, Supplement: "The new politics of population: conflict and consensus in family planning," 1994, pp. 137–58, "Domination, resistance and accommodation in China's one-child campaign," in Elizabeth J. Perry and Mark Seldon (eds.), *Chinese Society: Change, Conflict and Resistance* (London & New York: Routledge, 2000) and the splendid *China's Longest Campaign: Birth Planning in the People's Republic 1949–2005* (Ithaca, NY : Cornell University Press, 2006). Also see the insightful study by Susan Greenhalgh and Edwin A. Winkler, *Governing China's Population: From Leninist to Neoliberal Biopoltics* (Stanford, CA: Stanford University Press, 2005).

32 "Zhonggong zhongyang, guowuyuan 'guanyu jiaqiang renkou yu jihua shengyu gongzuo wending dai shengyu shuiping de jueding'," issued 2 March 2000, at http://www.chinapop.gov.cn/rkzh/rk/wxzl/t20040326_2869.htm.

Measures on the Administration of the Upbringing Charge, as well as some revisions to the provincial regulations.

Article 2 of the 2001 Law declares that birth planning is a fundamental policy of the state, and re-affirms the commitment to both the quantitative and eugenics aspects of population control. In recognition of the manner in which the population control programme has persistently affected women negatively, the 2001 Law stipulates that population and birth planning work should be supplemented by efforts to enhance women's educational and employment opportunities, health and social status. In addition, Article 22 prohibits maltreatment of both daughters and women who give birth to daughters or who are infertile. Family planning workers are obliged to observe the law in performing their duties, to respect citizens' rights and interests, and to enforce the law in a civilized manner (*wenming zhifa* 文明执法). Birth targets remain a central feature of the system, according to Articles 9 to 12 of the 2001 Law, with all levels of government – from the State Council down to neighbourhood and township government, assisted by local urban residents' and villagers' committees – being given responsibility for meeting such targets. Local regulations too sustain the target system: "a target management responsibility system (*mubiao guanli zeren zhi* 目标管理责任制) is implemented in population and birth planning work. A people's government at a higher level assigns population and birth planning responsibilities to lower level people's governments, and examines, rewards and punishes the lower entities" according to their success in implementing such responsibilities (Article 11, Beijing Municipal Regulations on Population and Birth Planning, 2003).[33]

Chapter 3, "Regulating reproduction" (*shengyu tiaojie* 生育调节), structures the way in which this system affects individual families. It continues to be assumed that reproduction only takes place within marriage,[34] and therefore requires "husbands and wives" to practise family planning (Article 17) by using contraceptives, accepting the advice of birth planning services and terminating "unwanted pregnancies" (非意愿妊娠 *fei yiyuan renshen*) (Article 20). Late marriage and late childbirth are encouraged, and ethnic minorities are also required to practise birth planning (Article 18). Nevertheless, Article 17 also concedes that "citizens have the right of childbearing (*shengyu*

33 "Beijing shi renkou yu jihua shengyu tiaoli" ("Beijing municipal regulations on population and birth planning"), at http://www.bjfc.gov.cn/Article/Detail.asp?UNID=6485, adopted 18 July 2003 and in force 1 September 2003. Since the introduction of the 2001 Law, many of the provincial regulations on family planning have been amended, and the 2003 Beijing Regulations are used here as an illustration of the new generation of such rules.

34 "Waishengbu 'guanyu xiuding renlei buzhu shengzhi jishu yu renlei jingziku xiangguan jishu guifan jiben biaozhun, he lunli yuanze de tongzhi'" ("Notice of the Ministry of Health 'Regarding the revision of the relevant technical parameters, basic standards and ethical principles related to IVF technology and sperm banks'") (available at http://www.moh.gov.cn/newshtml/3215.htm) at Section 4, Articles 5 and 13 bans surrogacy, thereby overruling a radical provision introduced by the Local People's Congress of Jilin which allowed surrogacy and therefore birth outside marriage. "Jilin sheng renkou yu jihua shengyu tiaoli" ("Regulations of Jilin province on population and birth planning") adopted 27 September 2002 and in force 1 November 2002, available at http://www.chinalaw.gov.cn/jsp/contentpub/browser/contentpro.jsp?contentid=co32938550-7.

生育)"[35] and Article 18 confirms that while the basic rule is that each married couple may bear only one child, there are certain circumstances in which a second is permitted. These conditions, which are detailed in local-level rules, typically include the birth of a first child who has developed a non-hereditary disability that will make it difficult to perform productive labour later in life, the fact that both husband and wife are themselves single children, a misdiagnosis of barrenness in the wife combined with a passage of more than five years after the adoption of a child, a remarrying husband and wife who have between them only one child, and so on.[36]

Chapters 4 and 5 of the 2001 Law codify the schemes of incentives and penalties that evolved in the 1980s for the purpose of promoting good conduct in family planning matters. In Chapter 4, Article 25 allows couples who marry and give birth at a relatively late age to enjoy, inter alia, the bonus of an extended wedding holiday and longer childbirth leave. Article 26 stipulates that benefits may be conferred on individuals who undergo abortion and sterilization, as well as special protection afforded working women during pregnancy, childbirth and breast feeding. In addition, couples willing to make a public pledge to use birth control and to limit themselves to one child are entitled to receive their "Honour Certificate for the Parents of a Single Child" (*dusheng zinü fumu guangrong zheng* 独生子女父母光荣证) and the benefits this may bring. Such rewards will vary from area to area but typically include monthly subventions, privileged housing provision, access to health service without charge, reduced school fees and so on. More generally, Article 24 promises the development of pension and similar welfare schemes in order to encourage couples to think of the state rather than a large family as a source of support in old age. On the other hand, Chapter 5 provides for punishment of those who break the official rules of the family planning game: perhaps most importantly, there is the Social Compensation Fee (*shehui fuyang fei* 社会抚养费), regarded as reimbursement to society for the additional load imposed on it by a couple bearing a child outside the plan. Failure to pay such charges on time gives rise to additional charges, and if necessary these may be enforced through the people's courts (Article 41). In addition, those employed by the state who bear a child outside the plan will also incur administrative or disciplinary punishments (Article 42). An unanticipated consequence of the system of heavy fines, however, is that those outside the state sector who are able to afford the charges increasingly see such payments as merely an additional cost necessarily incurred for the sake of having a family of

35 This has given rise to worries within China that Article 17 may be relied on as a defence against accusations of rape within marriage.

36 Ordinarily, the couple will also have to wait four years after the birth of their first child before a second child application will be permitted: see Article 17 of the Beijing Municipal Regulations. Article 17(6) allows a couple to apply for a second child where the husband is a rural resident and he is the only one of several brothers who is able to procreate. In these circumstances he is likely to allow any son born as the second child to be adopted by his brother in the classic form of *jiantiao* or "double ancestral hall" adoption, which is aimed specifically at continuing a patriline that would otherwise become extinct.

the size that they want.[37] Perhaps in an effort to counteract this tendency, the 2002 Measures provide that the level of charges may vary in accordance with local living standards (Article 3). Other punishments include return of a single-child certificate and the benefits is has conferred (see, for example, the Beijing Regulations, Article 39), and sanctions against state officials and others who produce false certificates, take bribes, overcharge and otherwise conduct themselves in an unlawful manner that undermines the system (2001 Law, Articles 36–39). Those subjected to punishment under the Measures may seek relief through either administrative review or an administrative suit (Article 9).[38]

Three additional problems that receive attention in the 2001 Population and Birth Planning Law are eugenics, migrants and gender. Thus, the Law confirms the Mother and Child Health Care Law's concern with eugenics. At Article 11 it states that its purposes include not only the protection of the health of mothers and children but also the enhancement of the quality of China's population (*renkou suzhi* 人口素质). The 2003 Beijing Regulations, too, at Article 2 maintain the goal of improvement of "population quality," and both the national Law and local regulations support the system of gynaecological clinics that is strongly linked with China eugenics policies (2001 Law, Articles 30–34, and Beijing Regulations, Articles 28–32). The problem of evasion of birth limitation rules by China's migrant workers[39] is addressed in Article 14 of the 2001 Law. This provides that ensuring migrant workers' compliance with the family planning restrictions is a task for not only their place of household registration but also their current place of residence, and that it is the authorities in the current location that bear the principal administrative responsibility. The Beijing Regulations stipulate that a special duty for managing population and birth planning work among migrant workers is borne by the public security organs.

With respect to gender issues, in addition to the problem of domestic violence, a continuing general difficulty is the disproportionate responsibility placed on women for shouldering the burdens of the population control system. The post-2000 revisions to birth planning law do little to change this situation other than by the general provisions noted above, although the greater role in the legislative process that is envisaged for the All-China Women's Federation by the 2005 revisions to the Women's Protection Law may also improve the position longer

37 The ability of some families to afford an extra child does, of course, have eugenics dimensions: in effect, it allows economically more successful urban residents to enjoy larger families, and this is something that has been considered in the past as a way of helping China to develop a "higher-quality" population. See Michael Palmer, "Protecting the health of mothers and their children? Developments in the family law of the People's Republic of China," in A. Bainham (ed.), *The International Survey of Family Law: 1995* (Bristol: Jordan Publishing (for The International Society on Family Law), 1997), pp. 107–16.

38 On these two systems, see Michael Palmer, "Controlling the state? Mediation in administrative litigation in the People's Republic of China," in Larry Backer (ed.), "China: law, finance and security," *Transnational Law & Contemporary Problems*, Vol. 16, No. 1 (2006), pp. 165–87.

39 See, for example, Thomas Scharping, *Birth Control in China 1949–2000: Population Policy and Demographic Development* (London & New York, Routledge, 2003), at p. 155.

term. A more specific issue is the severe shortage of girls that has developed in China over the past two decades, largely as a result of an intensification of the traditional preference for male children.[40] In addition to female infanticide and neglect of young daughters as causes of this growing problem, the increasing availability of amniocentesis testing and its use to ascertain foetal sex has encouraged sex-selective abortion.[41] From the late 1990s onwards provincial regulations specifically prohibited such misuse of pre-birth testing,[42] and then the 2001 Population and Birth Planning Law at Article 36 (b) stipulated that "identifying the gender of a foetus or aborting the pregnancy based on gender by using ultrasound technology or other technologies" without a specific and acceptable medical need is punishable by administrative warnings, a fine on illegal gains up to a level of six times the amount unlawfully acquired through the testing, and in more serious cases, withdrawal of practising certificate and even prosecution and imprisonment. Similar provisions were introduced into the 2003 Beijing Regulations at Article 37. Subsequently, in 2005, during the course of revisions to the Criminal Law 1997, the Standing Committee of the National People's Congress gave serious consideration to characterizing ultrasound testing for foetal sex (especially when followed by sex selective abortion) as a criminal offence, punishable by up to three years' imprisonment. However, a divergence of opinion amongst lawmakers undermined this possibility, with opponents asserting that pregnant women should have the right to know the sex of their child.[43]

The introduction of a national code of family planning is to be welcomed, as are its attempts to address some of the difficulties that the population control programme has created and exacerbated. But the 2001 Law has an ethos that is essentially administrative, demographic and policy orientated, with little room left for any statement of individual reproductive rights that might enable a citizen to secure redress through the courts for injustices as a result of official misconduct and mistakes. Although a key justification for the overall programme is that the demographic pressures on China are such that they threaten to undermine the economic reforms, the system that has been put in place is in a sense a curious relic of state planning. It rests uneasily with – and is often undermined by – the drift to greater individuality and more autonomous decision-making that are important features of socio-economic conditions in post-Mao China.

40 See, in particular, Judith Banister, "Shortage of girls in China today," *Journal of Population Research*, Vol. 21, No. 1, pp. 19–45.

41 Thus, Banister reports that China, with a population sex ratio of 106.7 males for every 100 females, is the most extreme example of overall imbalance, adding that among children aged 0–4 "China reports 120 boys per hundred girls" (p. 22) and concluding that demographic analysis shows that "by 1999, girls were permanently lost primarily through sex-selective abortion of female foetuses and secondarily through excess female infant deaths, due to infanticide, abandonment, ill-treatment or neglect of infant girls. The third factor was selective maltreatment of neglect of girls aged 1–3" (p. 27).

42 This development may explain one of the few rays of light in the data identified by Bannister, namely the puzzling fact that "the sex-ratio at 0–4 stabilised for the five years 1997–2001" (p. 27).

43 Josie Liu, "Changes to criminal law under NPC Review," *South China Morning Post*, 26 December 2005, p. A-4, cols. 2–3.

Reproducing – Adoption

In post-Mao China adoption (*shouyang* 收养) has been officially regarded as an important social and legal institution not only in its own right but also because of its contributions to the role of the family in providing care – especially for the elderly – and its relationship to population control.[44] Adoption was provided for in the 1979 Opinions of the Supreme People's Court Concerning the Implementation and Enforcement of Civil Affairs Policy and Law,[45] given major legislative support in the 1980 Marriage Law at Article 20, and then made the subject of a full national code in 1991: the Adoption Law (in force 1992). That Law was revised in 1998 and in the following year supplemented by new rules on adoption registration.

One of the most notable aspects of the 1991 Adoption Law is that the rights and interests of the adopting parents were defined as being nearly as important as those of the child. Thus, the main objective of the code was not one ordinarily ascribed to adoption in many modern jurisdictions, namely the welfare of the adopted child *per se*. Rather, the law offered protection to both adopted child and adopting parents, and to the "legitimate adoptive relations" between the parties (Article 1). In Article 2 of the 1998 revised Adoption Law, a clause has been inserted giving greater emphasis to the need to safeguard and promote the relations between the adopted person and the adopting parent or parents. In so doing, it further strengthens the policy emphasis on the reciprocal nature of the adoptive relationship in Chinese law, and thereby gives even greater weight to the adopting adults' wellbeing.

The basic conditions under which a child is considered to be suitable for adoption remain essentially unchanged under the revised Law. Article 4 stipulates that the adopted person should be a child under 14 years of age who is disadvantaged in one of three ways: as an orphan, a foundling or whose natural parents are untraceable or unable to raise the child as a result of unusual hardship. The requirement that an adoptant must be childless and "capable of rearing and providing education for the adopted child" also remains unchanged. However, the relatively stringent condition that adoptants must be 35 years or older has been relaxed in the 1998 revisions: they now need be only 30. This is an important shift, intended to make adoption easier.[46] Article 7 is amended in the revised Law to confirm that even with this reduced minimum legal age,

44 Thus, both the 1991 and revised 1998 version of the Adoption Law robustly declare at Article 3 that "adoption shall not contravene laws and regulations on family planning." For a comprehensive analysis of adoption, abandonment and orphanage care in post-Mao China see, in particular, Kay Ann Johnson, *Wanting a Daughter, Needing a Son: Abandonment, Adoption, and Orphanage Care in China* (St. Paul, MS: Yeong & Yeong Book Company, 2004).

45 "Zuigao renmin fayuan guanyu guanche zhixing minshi zhengce falü de yijian," 2 February 1979, in Liu Suping (ed.), *Hunyin faxue cankao ziliao* (*Reference Materials for Marriage Law*) (Beijing Zhongguo renmin daxue chubanshe, 1989), pp. 145–55 at p. 154.

46 An additional safeguard has also been introduced by the 1998 revisions at Article 6, namely, that the adoptant may not suffer from an illness considered inappropriate for the adoption of children. This parallels Marriage Law provisions which prohibit marriage if one party is deemed to be suffering from a disease rendering her or him unfit for marriage (Marriage Law 2001, Article 7).

continued recognition will be given in Chinese law to the customary practice of adoption of an agnatic nephew for the purpose of continuing a patriline that would otherwise be extinguished.[47] Changes to Article 8 are also intended to make adoption easier, and to enhance the family as a unit of care and welfare. They permit couples who already have a child (including an adopted child) to adopt an orphan, foundling or handicapped youngster in the care of a social welfare organ. In addition, Article 21 now regulates more clearly the processes by means of which foreign parties may adopt Chinese children, thereby encouraging greater overseas adoption.

The 1991 Adoption Law did not lay down specific formalities for the creation of lawful adoptive relations. In particular, it did not require registration of an adoption, even though adoption often necessitates changes under other systems of registration (such as household registration status). In order to regulate adoption better, however, subsequent regulations encouraged registration with the Civil Affairs Department[48] and Article 15 of the revised (1998) Adoption Law now stipulates that adoptions should be registered with civil affairs departments at the county level or above. Adoptive relations commence from the date of registration. Similarly, Article 28 encourages parties who wish to dissolve their adoptive relations to register the dissolution with a civil affairs department. The general direction of change throughout much of the 1990s was thus was towards a system of compulsory registration of adoption, one which would parallel that already in place for marriage. Finally, the revised Law at Article 31 strengthens the rules against abandonment and subsequent sale of children under the guise of adoption.

The trend towards greater bureaucratic control of adoption was continued in 1999, when attention was again given to issues of registration. The Measures for the Registration of Adoption of Children by Chinese Citizens[49] were introduced, in order to standardize the practice of registration (Article 1). The Measures assume that henceforth most, if not all, adoptions will be registered, following the basic requirement in Article 15 of the revised Adoption Law noted above, namely, that "adoptions should (*yingdang* 应当) be registered with the civil affairs departments at the county level or above, and adoptive relations are established on the day of registration." The Measures lay down strict rules on the provision of relevant documentation, including an undertaking in writing by the adoptants not to use adoption in any way to violate family planning

47 As noted above, n. 33.

48 "Minzhengbu, Zhongguo gongmin zai zhongguo banli shouyang dengji de ruogan guiding" ("Ministry of Civil Affairs, certain provisions [governing the] procedures for registration of adoptions by Chinese citizens in China"), promulgated 1 April 1992, in Liang Wenshu (ed.), *Zhonghua renmin gongheguo hunyinfa quanshi* (*Explanatory Notes on the Marriage Law of the People's Republic of China*) (Bejing: Renmin fayuan chubanshe, 1995), pp. 105–08.

49 "Zhongguo gongmin shouyang zinü dengji banfa," approved by the State Council, 12 May 1999 and in force 25 May 1999, in Zhonghua renmin gongheguo guowuyuan fazhi bangongshe (Office of the Legislative Affairs Office of the State Council) (ed.), *Zhonghua renmin gongheguo shewai fagui huipian 1999* (*Laws and Regulations of the People's Republic of China Governing Foreign-Related Matters 1999*) (Beijing, Zhongguo fazhi chubanshe, 2000), pp. 206–13.

provisions (Article 6); the procedures to be followed in difficult cases, such as when a child's biological parents cannot be found (Article 8); the system to be applied when the prospective adoptants are Chinese citizens resident in Hong Kong, Macau or Taiwan (Article 14); and the process by means of which an adoptive relationship may be ended by mutual consent (Articles 9 and 10). At exactly the same time, the Measures for the Registration of the Adoption of Children by Foreigners in the PRC were introduced in order to standardize the procedures necessary for foreign-related adoptions.[50] These require adoptions of Chinese children by foreigners to comply with the adoption laws of both China and the country of residence of the adoptants (Article 3), and also provide detailed rules on key practical aspects of the process. These include the requirement of a written adoptive agreement with the person placing out a child for adoption (Article 9), extensive documentation (Article 10), application examination formalities (Article 10), fees to be charged (Article 14) and supervision of the system as a whole (Article 15).[51]

Conclusions

In 2001, major revisions to the 1980 Marriage Law introduced clearer rules on void and voidable marriage, recognized the need for a system of retrospective registration of marriage, made efforts to deal with the increased social practice and problem of concubinage, reformed the grounds of divorce as well as the rules governing custody and property division at divorce, and attempted to promote a new approach to the treatment of domestic violence. These changes, which to a significant degree attempted to assist the position of women in the family context, were made in response, inter alia, to the rapid social and economic developments that have taken place in China in recent years. The reforms introduced by the amendments to the Marriage Law were further elaborated in two important interpretations of that law issued by the Supreme People's Court in 2001 and 2003, as well as by revised Marriage Registration Regulations (2003). The vigorous public debate that accompanied the process of amending the Marriage Law stands in stark contrast to the unheralded introduction of China's first national code of family planning, the 2001 Law on Population and Birth Planning. Unlike other areas of family law, the regulation of reproduction continues to be seen as a form of administrative rather than civil law. The Population Law lays down the basic policy norm of the single-child family, provides the possibility of a second child in certain circumstances, and serves as a consolidating code of basic principles that inform provincial birth

50 "Waiguo ren zai Zhonghua renmin gongheguo shouyang zinü dengji banfa," approved by the State Council 12 May 1999 and in force 25 May 1999, in *Laws and Regulations of the People's Republic of China Governing Foreign-Related Matters 1999*, pp. 213–23.

51 The system was further strengthened by the introduction of "Shouyang dengji dang'an guanli zanxing banfa" ("Provisional measures for the administration of adoption registration archives"), promulgated and in force 17 December 2003; available at http://www.mca.gov.cn/artical/content/WJYL_SYDJ/2004812163113.html.

planning regulations. It also embraces eugenics policies, designed to improve the quality of China's population. In 1998 and 1999 further reforms were introduced to China's legal framework for adoption, with a relaxation of rules on capacity and greater attention being given to the formalities of adoption registration.

In this process of reform, the relationship between the state and the family, and the role of individual choice in the processes of marriage and family, have changed and been made problematic in many important ways. Both substantively and procedurally, family law is, much more than it was in the 1980s, a matter of negotiation between the state and its increasingly vocal citizenry. Greater freedoms – in particular in respect of marriage and divorce – have been achieved and greater tolerance of social practice has been shown in the law. Significantly, marriage registration is now seen as being more of a civil responsibility of the individual than a purely an administrative act. Even more notably, a genuine freedom of divorce appears to have been established, with mediation no longer being used as a barrier to divorce even in contested cases in which the petitioner is a woman. Enhanced concern for individual rights has, in turn, led to debates about the appropriate boundaries for rights to privacy in the family context, especially in the areas of domestic violence and concubinage.

China has, in the reform of its family law, moved from a situation in 1980 in which the law governing marriage and family relations was still seen as a matter of control, an administrative instrument and a form of social engineering, to a contemporary situation in which these elements are significantly reduced and greater attention given to the technical and legitimating dimensions of law – in particular, there is a felt need to make law reflect popular social values as well as to change them. Procedurally, this has meant a decline in the use of mediation to resolve family disputes and a steady increase in reliance on the courts in such matters as divorce and domestic violence. But this acknowledgement of social practice is primarily true in terms of "family law" as officially understood within China itself. Birth limitation does not, except in terms of general principles, form part of family law. The continuing emphasis on law as a tool of administration and social engineering continues to manifest itself in the 2001 Population and Birth Planning Law which is considered to be a form of administrative law rather than civil law. Moreover, moral and ideological conservatism continue to complicate reform, restricting the pace of change and ensuring that debates about legal developments are kept within politically acceptable bounds. On the highly sensitive matter of birth control, very little debate was allowed even at the time of the promulgation of the first national law of family planning. Moreover, it is clear that those responsible for revising family law are also experiencing great difficulty in dealing with inter-generational conflicts of social values and conduct. The ever-growing disparity in social conditions between the Chinese littoral and its large metropolitan centres and the less well-developed areas inland, especially in the west, is another complicating factor, as is the demographic problem of the ageing population. The growing number of elderly, the associated increase in average life expectancy, and the physical and financial needs of older persons all mean that the state must continue for some time yet to rely on the family as a unit of care for the elderly. Relaxing the conditions of adoption and prohibiting adult children's interference in the re-marriage of parents are just two areas of family law reform that reflect this continuing reliance. Even family planning constraints are now the subject of public debate, as the authorities come to acknowledge the contradictions between population and social welfare policies which emphasize the role of the family as a provider of care.[52]

An important change is clearly taking place with respect to the treatment of women as victims of domestic violence. There has been, at the formal level, a shift from viewing this problem as a domestic or purely family dispute to be dealt with by means of mediation to seeing it as an issue of criminal justice to be dealt with by the public security organs, the procuracy and the courts in a manner that is more consistent with the PRC's international obligations under CEDAW. Elsewhere, in the revised Marriage Law (especially in its provisions on divorce), the 2001 Population and Birth Planning Law and the two Supreme People's Court interpretations on the Marriage Law, there is enhanced support for women's rights and interests, a matter of considerable importance in a society that was, and to a significant extent still is, strongly patriarchal in its family cultural values.

52 Alice Yan, "China's one-child policy questioned," *South China Morning Post*, 31 December 2005, p. A6, cols. 1–6.

Commentary on "Transforming Family Law in Post-Deng China"

Fu Hualing

Michael Palmer's article examines the development of three important aspects in Chinese family law: divorce, adoption and family planning. It is a commendable effort to approach Chinese family law broadly in order to bring family planning policy within its study. There remains a glaring gap in Chinese legal scholarship between the study of family law and the study of population. The disciplines are divided into two camps with little cross-fertilization. Palmer's article clearly demonstrates the importance and necessity of including family planning within the study of family law. The article is also a laudable attempt to examine the dynamic interaction between family law and socioeconomic changes.

Chinese legal reform largely follows a liberal paradigm. The ultimate goal of the reform is to separate the Chinese Communist Party from the state and to limit the role of the state in economy and the society. Viewed historically, the Chinese state is contracting while the private economy is expanding in size and importance, and civil society is emerging and becoming more autonomous. In a sense, Chinese legal reform is to institutionalize the circumscribed state. Notwithstanding fluctuations, the overall result of reform in the past 30 years has been an increasingly limited and accountable government and a growing importance in market, society and individual autonomy, as evidenced by a number of constitutional amendments entrenching the rule of law and the protection of human rights. In a society where Hayek is replacing Marx as the most influential writer, the state is now viewed with great suspicion, especially in matters relating to family life. If government is regarded as a hurdle on the road to freedom, then its role has to be limited and controlled. Palmer studies the development of Chinese family law in this particular political context.

In the area of family life in particular, the reform has been to rid the party-state from the bedroom. Family law in Communist China in general and the 2001 Marriage Law amendment in particular are liberal and progressive in enlarging individual autonomy, in protecting gender equality and in creating a realm which is relatively free of government interference. The 2001 Marriage Law amendment, for example, simplifies the procedures for marriage, and places effective limits on judicial discretion in granting or refusing to grant a divorce. The subsequent administrative rules enlarge individual freedom in matters relating to marriage and divorce. There is now much less political and institutional intervention in this particular realm. Increasingly, the law recognizes and treats marriage and divorce as private matters. People recognize and fully exercise these rights, as shown by the surge in the divorce rate in China.

 doi:10.1017/S030574100700166X

But the increase in freedom of choice in relation to marriage and divorce, while important, must be reviewed within the larger context, as Palmer cautions. One cannot merely discuss freedom and autonomy in marriage and divorce without considering family planning and its social consequences. When the family is understood from this broad perspective, freedoms are looked at differently. It is common ground that while family law (narrowly defined) is liberal, family planning as practised is repressive. It restricts people's reproductive rights, degrades women, reinforces gender discrimination, skews the gender ratio, and provides incentives for the abandonment of female infants and the neglect of the elderly. The policy has created many serious social problems and its implementation continues to be coercive and even brutal. Once the horizon of family law is broadened to include the family planning policy, the limited freedom in marriage and divorce pales and becomes marginalized. The irony is that, given the most intrusive family planning policies and the exposure of the family to the most meticulous scrutiny, it is difficult to imagine how autonomy and individuality can be genuinely respected and protected within the same legal framework. It is also difficult, though possible, to reconcile restrictive family planning with other freedoms in family matters.

The paradox in the Chinese political and legal reform is the contrast between severe repression in core policy areas and the lack of restrictions in peripheral areas. Thus, the government harshly suppresses critical political speeches but tolerates virtually uncontrolled commercial speeches and indecency; it executes the largest number of criminals in the world but is ready to ignore interpersonal violence; it invests great effort in combating corruption, but tolerates various forms of gift-giving and rebates. In family law, the state has been firm, extreme and brutal in its commitment to the birth quota and local implementation of family planning, but is willing to accept the social consequences, ranging from selective abortion, abandonment of female infants and neglect of the elderly to gender imbalance and gender discrimination. The clear lesson is that the state continues to exercise effective and firm control over the core policy areas, such as family planning and other politically sensitive matters, and is well-prepared and well-equipped to implement the policies at any cost. But at the same time it is prepared to tolerate, if not encourage, an expansive freedom outside these core areas, especially when the expansion of freedom does not incur much political and financial liability. But the vexing question is: will the enlarged freedom at the periphery eventually challenge the control at the core?

Under the market economy, freedom tends to be associated with people with resources and powers. Behind the limited freedom in China, the most vulnerable groups in society are left to the brutal force of the market with little government intervention. It makes little sense to talk about freedom in divorce without examining such well-documented gross neglect and abandonment.

This brings us back to the vexed issues of the role of state in promoting individual freedom and the need for a responsive state. The Chinese state in the post-Mao era has declined to play an active role in promoting social justice and

Chinese law continues to shift social burdens to families and society, even though the government recognizes the acute social problems it faces. Family desertion and domestic violence are examples. In cases of family neglect and family violence, the law continues to rely on villagers' and residents' committees, mechanisms which have been fundamentally weakened as a form of social control by the socioeconomic reform, to provide the primary intervention. As a result, vulnerable groups, largely the elderly, women and children, are left to the forces of market and society. Direct legal intervention remains secondary because victims are required first to approach their immediate and mostly dysfunctional communities.

Adoption is another sad example. China has abundant orphans lingering in its poorly run orphanages, but policy severely restricts domestic adoption. It is clear that the government chooses to promote international adoption; it is also clear that domestic demand for adoption exists had the government chosen to follow it. More flexible adoption conditions and procedures, a less greedy adoption bureaucracy, and a bit more sympathy and care would substantially alleviate the misery and suffering of the most innocent millions.

In conclusion, Michael Palmer's article serves as a reminder that autonomy in marriage and divorce and the decline in government intervention should also be seen in the larger context of the conspicuous failure of government, market and society to address certain social problems and social decay. It is misleading and superficial to claim that Chinese family law allows more individual autonomy and freedom, when the law fails to address the depressing social consequences of family planning and to provide an effective and meaningful mechanism to protect the interests of the vulnerable groups within the family. China needs an active and responsive state.

China and the International Legal System: Challenges of Participation*

Pitman B. Potter

ABSTRACT During the past decade, the Chinese government has pursued greater engagement with a range of international legal regimes. China's expanded participation in international regimes for trade and human rights, for example, can provide deeper understanding of the factors influencing China's international behaviour. Building upon scholarly perspectives about institutional compliance with treaty texts and the influence of local conditions on China's policies and practice, this article examines China's participation in international legal regimes for trade and human rights in light of dynamics of normative engagement and the paradigm of selective adaptation. Normative tensions help explain China's policies and practices on compliance with the WTO trade regime, while the imperative of normative engagement helps explain much about China's international human rights diplomacy.

When *The China Quarterly* published its last review of the Chinese legal system, China's participation in the international legal order was seen as uncertain and potentially problematic.[1] During the past decade, the Chinese government has pursued greater engagement with a range of international regimes, opening the economy more fully to foreign trade and investment, engaging in human rights diplomacy and intensifying participation in international institutions.[2] This has allowed China's international relations behaviour to be understood better, in terms of rational choice and self-interest, sovereignty concerns, cultural distinctiveness and victimization, and responses to globalization.[3]

* The author is pleased to thank Stanley Lubman for helpful comments and suggestions on an earlier draft of this article. The research on which this paper is based was supported by a Major Collaborative Research Initiatives (MCRI) research grant from the Social Sciences and Humanities Research Council of Canada, for which the author is deeply grateful.

1 James V. Feinerman, "Chinese participation in the international legal order: rogue elephant or team player?" in *The China Quarterly*, No. 141 (1995), pp. 186–210.

2 John Wong and Zheng Yongnian (eds.), *The Nanxun Legacy and China's Development in the Post-Deng Era* (Singapore: Singapore University Press and World Scientific Press, 2001). Samuel S. Kim, "Human rights in China's international relations," in Edward Friedman and Barrett L. McCormick (eds.), *What if China Doesn't Democratize? Implications for War and Peace* (Armonk, NY: M.E. Sharpe, 2000), pp. 129–62. Anne Kent, "China's international socialization: the role of international organizations," in *Global Governance*, Vol. 8 (2002), pp. 343–64; Mark Lanteigne, *China and International Institutions: Alternate Paths to Global Power* (New York: Routledge, 2005).

3 Alastair Iain Johnston and Robert S. Ross (eds.), *New Directions in the Study of China's Foreign Policy* (Stanford: Stanford University Press, 2006); Avery Goldstein, *Rising to the Challenge: China's Grand Strategy and International Security* (Stanford: Stanford University Press, 2005). Allen Carlson, *Unifying China, Integrating with the World: Securing Chinese Sovereignty in the Reform Era* (Stanford:

 doi:10.1017/S0305741007001671

China's expanded participation in international regimes also has the potential to support deeper understanding of the factors influencing its international law behaviour. Scholarly perspectives have tended generally to emphasize China's engagement with the international legal system in terms of compliance with treaty texts,[4] or to focus on local factors influencing China's behaviour.[5] These institutional and contextual perspectives come together through the paradigm of selective adaptation, which looks at the ways that interpretation of international rule regimes is mediated by local norms.[6] Focusing on the period since *The China Quarterly*'s previous review, this article will examine China's participation in international legal regimes for trade and human rights in light of the dynamics of normative engagement and the paradigm of selective adaptation.

Perspectives on China's Engagement with International Legal Regimes: The Role of Selective Adaptation

In contrast to expectations about convergence that suggest development towards a globally unified system of institutional practices and values,[7] selective adaptation explains variations in local reception of non-local standards by reference to the extent of normative consensus.[8] It suggests that local implementation of non-local rule regimes depends on the extent to which their underlying norms are received by local interpretive communities.[9] In the course

footnote continued

Stanford University Press, 2005). Rana Mitter, "An uneasy engagement: Chinese ideas of global order and justice in historical perspective," in Rosemary Foot, John Gaddis, and Andrew Hurrell (eds.), *Order and Justice in International Relations* (Oxford: Oxford University Press (2003), pp. 205–35; Anne-Marie Brady, *Making the Foreign Serve China: Managing Foreigners in the People's Republic* (Lanham MD: Rowman & Littlefield, 2003). Phillip C. Saunders, "China's global activism: strategy, drivers, and tools," Institute for National Strategic Studies Occasional Paper No. 4 (Washington: National Defense University Press, 2006); Yong Deng and Thomas G. Moore, "China views globalization: toward a new great power politics?" *Washington Quarterly*, Vol. 27, No. 3 (2004), pp. 117–36; Dwight Perkins (ed.), "A wary welcome: China and globalization," *Harvard China Review*, Vol. 5, No. 1 (2003).

4 On trade, see e.g. Deborah Cass, Brett G. Williams and George Barker (eds.), *China and the World Trading System: Entering the New Millenium* (Cambridge: Cambridge University Press, 2003); Donald C. Clarke, "China and the World Trade Organization," Freshfields (ed.), *Doing Business in China* (looseleaf) pp. I-11.1–I-1.30; on human rights see e.g. Ann Kent, *China, the United Nations, and Human Rights: The Limits of Compliance* (Philadelphia: University of Pennsylvania Press, 1999).

5 On trade see e.g. Kong Qingjiang, *China and the World Trade Organization: A Legal Perspective* (Singapore: World Scientific Publishing, 2002); on human rights see e.g. Karin Buhmann, *Implementing Human Rights Through Administrative Reforms: The Potential in China and Vietnam* (Copenhagen: Djof Publishing, 2001).

6 Pitman B. Potter, "Legal reform in China – institutions, culture, and selective adaptation," *Law & Social Inquiry*, Vol. 2, No. 4 (2004), pp. 465–95.

7 Ugo Mattei. *Comparative Law and Economics* (Ann Arbor: University of Michigan Press, 1997); David Trubek *et al.*, "Global restructuring and the law: the internationalization of legal fields and the creation of transnational arenas," *Case Western Reserve Law Review*, Vol. 44, No. 2 (1994), pp. 407–98.

8 For discussion of the intersection of norms with identity and community, see Roberto Unger, *Knowledge and Politics* (New York: Free Press, 1975). Also see Amitai Etzioni, "Social norms: internalization, persuasion, and history," *Law & Society Review*, Vol. 34, No. 1 (2000), pp. 157–78.

9 For discussion of interpretive communities, see Stanley Fish, *Is There a Text in This Class: The Authority of Interpretive Communities* (Cambridge MA: Harvard University Press, 1980).

of this process, interpretive communities selectively adapt non-local standards for local application in light of their own normative perspectives.

The process involves dynamics of perception, complementarity and legitimacy. Perception of the content and operation of international law standards determines the ways that communities will interpret and apply them.[10] This may involve relatively simple elements of translation of international trade and human rights standards, or reveal more complex factors of cognition, ranging from diversity of understanding to cognitive dissonance and denial. Complementarity describes how apparently contradictory phenomena are combined in ways that preserve the essential characteristics of each component, and yet may allow them to operate together in a mutually reinforcing and effective manner.[11] Complementarity between international and local practices and values informs the dynamics of local accommodation and resistance to international standards. Legitimacy concerns the extent to which members of local communities accept the purposes and consequences of selective adaptation.[12] This may involve factors ranging from personal preferences born of individual circumstances and interests, to broader social perspectives of idealism, nationalism and identity that inform responses to procedural or substantive dimensions of international law standards.

Applied to China, selective adaptation analysis permits understanding of local responses to international legal obligations. China's interpretation and implementation of international agreements in trade, such as the General Agreement on Tariffs and Trade (GATT) and agreements associated with the World Trade Organization (WTO), for example, will depend on the extent to which interpretive communities – comprising government officials, socio-economic and professional elites, and other privileged groups exercising authority borne of political and/or professional position, specialized knowledge, and/or socio-economic status – assimilate norms of trade liberalization.[13]

Influenced by their training and education, members of China's interpretive communities bring their perceptions about international law and relations to bear in responding to the requirements of international rule

10 See e.g. David Kennedy, "Receiving the international," *Connecticut Journal of International Law*, Vol. 10, No. 1 (1994), p.1.

11 Niels H. D. Bohr, *Essays, 1958–1962, on Atomic Physics and Human Knowledge* (New York: Interscience Publishers, 1963); Okifira Seliktar. "Identifying a society's belief system," in Margaret Herman (ed.), *Political Psychology* (San Francisco: Jossey-Bass, 1986).

12 Max Weber (ed. Roth and Wittich), *Economy and Society* (Berkeley & Los Angeles: University of California Press, 1978); Fritz W. Scharpf, "Interdependence and democratic legitimation," in Susan J. Pharr and Robert D. Putnam (eds.), *Disaffected Democracies: What's Troubling the Trilateral Countries* (Princeton: Princeton University Press, 2000); Stephen P. Turner and Regis A. Factor, *Max Weber: The Lawyer as Social Thinker* (London: Routledge, 1994).

13 On interpretive communities in China, see H. Lyman Miller and Liu Xiaohong, "The foreign policy outlook of China's 'third generation' elite," and Joseph Fewsmith and Stanley Rosen, "The domestic context of Chinese foreign policy: does 'public opinion' matter?" both in David M. Lampton (ed.), *The Making of Chinese Foreign and Security Policy* (Stanford: Stanford University Press, 2001), pp. 123–50 and 151–87.

regimes.[14] Perceptions contrasting China's colonial past and resulting weakness in foreign relations with its current strengths tend to encourage both a sense of grievance and of opportunities for correction and redress.[15] Perception dynamics are also evident in academic and policy assessments of the international legal system that acknowledge the challenges posed by globalization for sovereignty imperatives of the nation-state generally, and focus on the intrusive nature of international regimes whose underlying norms are seen as a challenge to China.[16] Such perceptions affect the reception of international legal standards by local interpretative communities, and ultimately China's responses of implementation.

Local analyses of China's participation in the international system tend to emphasize the need for compatibility with China's systemic and substantive requirements (complementarity).[17] In addition, the status of international law as a binding standard for Chinese domestic law remains the subject of intense debate, suggesting once again the link between complementarity and acceptance of international standards.[18] Dynamics of legitimacy are also evident. Although China's academic and policy discourses as well as its behaviour in international law are in some respects aimed at building legitimacy with local audiences, the pursuit of legitimacy in the international community explains much about China's engagement with international legal regimes.[19] Thus, understanding China's increased participation in the international legal system invites appreciation of issues of normative engagement, as international standards are selectively adapted by interpretive communities influenced by factors of perception, complementarity and legitimacy.

International regimes for trade and human rights offer useful examples of the ways that international standards are received by local interpretive communities. China's growing economic power seems to affirm support for its accession to the

14 See e.g. Zeng Lingliang, "21 shijie falu fuwu maoyi de fazhan qushi yu Zhongguo faxue rencai peiyang de yong you gaige" ("Development trends in 21st-century trade in legal services and needed reforms in training of China's legal talents)", *Faxue pinglun* (*Law Review*), No. 1 (2001), pp. 3–8; Xiao Yongping, "Falu de jiao yu xue zhi geming" ("Revolution in teaching and studying law"), *Faxue pinglun*, No. 3 (2003), pp. 153–60.

15 See e.g. Li Baojun, *Dangdai Zhongguo waijiao gailun* (*Treatise on Contemporary Chinese Foreign Policy*) (Beijing: People's University Press, 1999); Wang Yinzhou, *Quanqiu zhengzhi he Zhongguo waijiao* (*Global Politics and China's Foreign Policy*) (Beijing: World Knowledge Press, 2003).

16 Rao Geping and Huang Yao, "Lun quanqiuhua jincheng yu guoji zuzhi de hudong guanxi" ("On mutual impacts of globalization processes and international organizations"), *Faxue pinglun*, No. 2 (2002), pp. 3–13. Liu Shuguang, *Quanqiuhua yu fan quanqiuhua* (*Globalization and Anti–Globalization*) (Changsha: Hunan People's Press, 2003), esp. pp. 103–66. For response to such resistance, see He Qinghua, "Fa de yizhi yu fa de bentuhua" ("Legal transplanting and localization of law"), *Zhongguo faxue* (*Chinese Legal Studies*), No. 3 (2002), pp. 3–15.

17 See e.g. Li Dexi, Qian Zhen and Lin Zhe, *Quanqiu beijing xia de Zhongguo minzhu jianshe* (*Development of Democracy in China under the Global Background*) (Chongqing: Chongqing Press, 2005), based on a policy conference at the authoritative Central Party School. Also see Gao Gangjun, "Zhongguo de heping fazhan yu guoji fa de jiazhi tixi" ("China's peaceful development and the value system of international law"), in *Faxue pinglun*, No. 3 (2006), pp. 104–10.

18 See e.g. Zhang Shaodong, "Ye lun guoji tiaoyue zai woguo de shiyong," ("Again examining the application of international treaties in China"), *Faxue pinglun*, No. 6 (2001), pp. 73–79.

19 See e.g. Jiang Xiyuan, "An analysis on changing international system and its acceptance of China," *International Review*, Vol. 39 (2005), pp. 19–36.

WTO,[20] while its participation in international human rights regimes suggests the potential for expanded engagement.[21] However, in each of these areas, questions persist concerning China's compliance with international obligations, and the extent of the government's commitment to fundamental norms underlying international trade and human rights regimes. While one element of compliance centres on the capacity of regulatory institutions, normative engagement is also important and may be understood by reference to the dynamics of selective adaptation.

China and the WTO: Accession and Compliance

Begun in 1986, China's application for readmission to the WTO reflected a conflicting array of local policy priorities, including entrenchment of economic reforms and the pursuit of broader international institutional influence. China's accession to the WTO has not been without controversy domestically and internationally, however.[22] Questions about GATT/WTO accession within China pressured the government to resist concessions,[23] while internationally many WTO members expressed concerns over Chinese capacity to comply with GATT principles.[24] A core question involves normative engagement with the disciplines of the GATT/WTO system.

Reception of international governance norms

While China's accession to the WTO is often portrayed as a matter of economics and commerce, it also involves fundamental issues of governance. The WTO working party's final report on the accession of China, tabled at the Fourth Session of the WTO Ministerial Conference in Doha in November 2001 and using records from the 14 years since 1987, revealed the extent of the concern over numerous apparent conflicts and inconsistencies between Chinese trade policy and regulatory practice and GATT/WTO standards.[25] While the Protocol on the Accession confirmed China's entry to the WTO, the document also

20 See "Workshop on China and the world economy," Atlantic Council, 2006; UN Conference on Trade and Development, *China in a Globalizing World* (New York & Geneva: United Nations, 2005).

21 See Randall Peerenboom, *China Modernizes: Threat to the West and Model for the Rest?* (Oxford: Oxford University Press, 2007), ch. 3.

22 Sylvia Ostry, Alan S. Alexandroff and Raphael Gomez (eds.), *China and the Long March to Global Trade: The Accession of China to the World Trade Organization* (New York and London: Routledge, 2002). Council on Foreign Relations, *Beginning the Journey: China, the United States and the WTO* (New York: Council on Foreign Relations, 2001).

23 See e.g. "China sets deadline for GATT re-entry, slams US 'road blocks'," *Agence France Presse English Wire*, in *China News Digest* Online (10 July 1994); "Foot-stomping helps China in GATT bid," *South China Morning Post*, in *China News Digest* Online (1 August 1994); "China vows not to beg for WTO membership," *China News Digest* Online (23 September 1995).

24 See Draft Protocol on China (1997), prepared by the Working Party on the Accession of China to the WTO. While this document emerged from extensive negotiations between the WTO Working Party and the Chinese, it still contains useful examples of the concerns raised by the US and other OECD countries on issues such as transparency, enforcement, etc.

25 "Report of the working party on accession of China" WT/MIN(01)/31 (10 November 2001).

highlighted many challenges of institutional reform that would be needed to secure long-term sustainable compliance.[26]

Transparency and rule of law are among the most important of the GATT/WTO governance standards that have challenged norms and practices in China. GATT Article X requires publication of trade regulations, and uniform, impartial and reasonable administration of laws and regulations. These reflect liberal norms about government accountability and limits to state intrusion in private economic affairs.[27] In addition, the GATT places significant emphasis on state responsibility for ensuring local compliance. Article XXIV(12) requires each contracting party to take "necessary measures" to ensure observance of the GATT by regional and local governments and authorities.[28] These reflect assumptions about the capacity of national governments to ensure local level compliance through central legislation and regulatory edicts.[29]

Yet there has been conflicting reception of these governance standards in China.[30] On one hand, the government has enacted and revised legislation and administrative regulations in many economic sectors, including intellectual property, trade in services, investment and environmental protection, to accommodate WTO disciplines.[31] Recent efforts to establish systems of public hearings in anticipation of legislation at the central and provincial levels suggest increased efforts to build popular participation in rulemaking.[32] In addition, the government seems willing to rely on provisions of GATT Article XXIV to assert greater controls over local authorities, augmenting constitutional interpretations subordinating local autonomy to central authority under the principle of the unitary state.[33]

26 *Protocol of Accession of the People's Republic of China to the Marrakesh Agreement Establishing the World Trade Organization*, WLI/100 2 (10 November 2001).

27 See generally, John H. Jackson, *The World Trading System: Law and Policy of International Economic Relations* (Cambridge MA: MIT Press, 1989); John Braithwaite and Peter Drahos, *Global Business Regulation* (Cambridge: Cambridge University Press, 2000), pp. 507–11.

28 See *International Legal Materials*, 1994, Vol. 33, p. 1161. This provision has been amplified by the "Understanding on the interpretation of Article XXIV of the General Agreement on Tariffs and Trade" attached to the Uruguay Round, which requires signatory states to be "fully responsible … for the observance of all provisions of GATT 1994" and are required to "take such reasonable measures as may be available … to ensure such observance by regional and local governments and authorities."

29 See generally, Jeffrey S. Thomas and Michael A. Meyer, *The New Rules of Global Trade: A Guide to the World Trade Organization* (Scarborough ONT: Carswell, 1997), pp. 65–66; John H. Jackson, *The Jurisprudence of GATT & the WTO: Insights on Treaty Law and International Relations* (Cambridge: Cambridge University Press, 2000), ch.18.

30 Congressional-Executive Commission on China, *2005 Annual Report*, Section V(f): Commercial rule of law and the impact of the WTO; Susan Krause, "China's industrial policies conflict with WTO rules, experts say," *Washington Post*, 2 June 2005.

31 Zhang Guihong, "WTO dui Zhongguo falu de yingxiang" ("Effects of WTO on Chinese law"), *Zhongguo faxue* (*Chinese Legal Science*), No. 4 (2001), pp. 182–85.

32 National Democratic Institute, *Development of Legislative Hearings in China: A Report on NDI's Seminar on Local Legislative Hearings and Local Governance* (2003). Also see the US State Department Bureau of Democracy, Human Rights and Labor's "Human rights and democracy fund" project list, which includes a number of programmes accepted by China on public participation in rule-making (https://www.state.gov/g/drl/rls/57669.htm).

33 Gui Yushi and Chai Yao, "Guanyu woguo difang lifa de jige wenti" ("Several issues in our local legislation") in *Faxue pinglun*, No. 5 (2004), pp. 103–11 at p. 108; Zhuo Yue, *Difang renda jiandu jizhi yanjiu* (*Study of the Supervisory System of Local People's Congresses*) (Beijing: People's Press, 2002).

On the other hand, normative assimilation remains uncertain. Problems with transparency continue to recur in areas of public input to lawmaking, access to information on trade policy and regulation, and judicial review.[34] The resilience of non-transparent practices by administrative institutions and review agencies is acknowledged by Chinese observers.[35] China's governance norms expressed in the State Council's white paper on political democracy[36] raise questions as to whether principles about transparency and accountability will impose significant limits on conduct by government agencies. Reverence for principles of state sovereignty also works to limit the application of GATT/WTO dispute resolution mechanisms deemed in conflict with China's institutional arrangements.[37]

Questions about compliance with substantive standards

China's accession to the WTO also mandates engagement with substantive rules. Questions about China's performance of WTO market access commitments in areas of telecommunications, banking and insurance,[38] and the current WTO dispute with the European Union, Canada and the United States over China's imposition of high duties on imported car assembly kits,[39] suggest the influence of economic and bureaucratic interests. Yet an examination of intellectual property rights and anti-dumping suggests that additional factors of normative engagement are also involved.

The WTO Agreement on Trade-Related Aspects of Intellectual Property Rights incorporates into the WTO system provisions of the 1967 Paris Convention on Industrial Property, the 1971 Berne Convention on Copyrights and a number of other agreements.[40] Of particular importance is Part III on enforcement of intellectual property rights, which requires that member states ensure that enforcement procedures are available to permit effective action against infringements through civil and administrative procedures and remedies, injunctions, and the imposition of compensatory remedies. In furtherance of its obligations under this Agreement, China has enacted national and local

34 US Trade Representative, *2006 Report to Congress on China's WTO Compliance* (2007), pp. 96–98.

35 Shen Kaiju, "WTO yu woguo xingzheng caijue zhidu gongzhengxing yanjiu" ("Study of fairness in the administrative arbitration systems of the WTO and China"), *Zhongguo faxue*, No. 5 (2002), pp. 68–77 at pp. 73–74 and 76–77; Shi Youqi, "WTO dui Zhongguo xingzheng fazhi jianshe de yingxiang" ("Effects of WTO on development of China's administrative law system"), *Zhongguo faxue*, No. 1 (2001), pp. 11–24 at pp. 18–19.

36 State Council Information Office, *White Paper: Building of Political Democracy in China* (2005) (http://www.china.org.cn/english/features/book/145877.htm).

37 See generally, Zhang Naigen, "Lun WTO zhengduan jiejue jizhi de jige zhuyao guoji fa wenti" ("On several important international law issues in the WTO dispute resolution system"), in *Faxue pinglun*, No. 5 (2001), pp. 51–58.

38 Andrew C. Mertha and Ka Zeng, "Political institutions, resistance and China's harmonization with international law," *The China Quarterly*, No. 182 (2005), pp. 319–37.

39 "China 'regrets' auto parts decision," *China Daily*, 30 October 2006.

40 See Christopher Arup, *The New World Trade Organization Agreements: Globalizing Law Through Services and Intellectual Property* (Cambridge: Cambridge University Press, 2000). The text of the TRIPs Agreement appears in World Trade Organization (ed.), *The Legal Texts: The Results of the Uruguay Round* (Cambridge: Cambridge University Press, 1999), pp. 321–53. Also see *International Legal Materials*, Vol. 33 (1994), p. 1197.

legislation and regulations and strengthened central and local institutions for intellectual property rights enforcement.[41]

However, enforcement continues to be problematic.[42] Despite periodic public campaigns to improve it, an observed "epidemic" of pervasive intellectual property violations continues.[43] Industry estimates suggest piracy rates in China at between 85 and 93 per cent across all sectors, while internet piracy and end-user piracy of business software, books and journals continue: China's share of infringing goods seized at the American border is ten times that of any other US trading partner.[44] Problems range from lax enforcement of existing laws to use of pirated goods in government offices and corruption in the court system. Legal and policy analyses supporting integration of international intellectual property standards with local conditions reveal ongoing resistance to full assimilation of international regime norms.[45] While notable examples of enforcement have emerged, such as the decision of the Shanghai No. Two Intermediate People's Court upholding Starbucks' trademark rights, these appear to be the exception rather than the rule.[46] Despite repeated assurances of conformity from China,[47] the lengthy pattern of non-enforcement raises troubling questions about its commitment and capacity to comply with WTO disciplines.

As a second example, China has long been a regular target for anti-dumping and anti-subsidies actions by its trading partners.[48] Its admission to the WTO has had little apparent impact on this process, largely due to the difficulties in applying GATT disciplines to China's transitional economy.[49] Up to the end of

41 Volker Pasternak, "Introduction: China's intellectual property regime," in Freshfields, *Doing Business in China*, pp. III-10.1.1–III-10.1.28.

42 Comments of deputy Secretary of State Robert B. Zoelleck at Hearing of the House International Relations Committee (10 May 2006); Joseph A. Massey, "The emperor is far away: China's enforcement of intellectual property rights protection, 1986–2005," National Committee on US–China Relations (2005); Andrew Yeh, "China's piracy problems remain severe," *Financial Times*, 14 September 2005; Peter S. Goodman, "China a weak ally on piracy: country proves to be problematic partner in cutting theft," *Washington Post*, 4 June 2005; Jeffrey A. Bader, "China's implementation of its WTO commitments: mixed results after two years," Atlantic Council (October 2003).

43 "Oral remarks of Robert A. Kapp, President United States–China Business Council to the Trade Policy Staff Committee hearing on China's progress in implementing its WTO accession commitments," 23 September 2004.

44 "China's enforcement of intellectual property rights and the dangers of the movement of counterfeit and pirated goods into the Unites States" (prepared statement of Assistant US Trade Representative Timothy P. Stratford before the US–China Economic and Security Review Commission), 7 June 2006.

45 See e.g. Feng Jiehan, "Zhongguo zhishi chanquan baohu: Renzhong de daoyuan" ("Intellectual property protection in China: the burden is heavy and the road is long"), in *Faxue pinglun*, No. 1 (2006), pp. 80–85.

46 Geoffrey A. Fowler, "China: Starbucks wins China case over trademark," *The Wall Street Journal*, 3 January 2006.

47 Shi Jiangtao, "China: plea for understanding in war against piracy," *South China Morning Post*, 12 April 2006.

48 See e.g. Yang Guohua, "Respond to anti-dumping complaints vigorously," *Beijing guoji maoyi* (*Beijing International Trade*), 20 January 1998, in FBIS-CHI-98-077 (18 March 1998); Lei Wang, "China's difficulties and concerns as a respondent in antidumping proceedings," *World Competition Law and Economic Review*, Vol. 19, No. 3 (1996), pp. 55–58.

49 Julia Ya Qin, "WTO regulation of subsidies to state-owned enterprises (SOEs) – a critical appraisal of the China accession protocol," *Journal of International Economic Law*, Vol. 7, No. 4 (2004), pp. 863–919.

2005, China was the subject of 338 anti-dumping measures filed by WTO member economies.[50] Its response seems aimed mainly at strengthening its legal and regulatory framework to support defences against anti-dumping actions filed abroad. Under the Regulations on Responding to Anti-Dumping Suits (2001), the Ministry of Foreign Trade and Economic Co-operation (later made a division under the Ministry of Commerce) is authorized to co-ordinate legal defences against foreign anti-dumping suits, thereby ensuring that individual cases are subordinated to national trade policy.[51] In addition, China incorporated GATT/WTO provisions on subsidies and dumping into its own Foreign Trade Law (1994, revised 2004) and associated regulations,[52] to support retaliation against other economies in response to anti-dumping and anti-subsidy actions.

Local interpretations often portray the WTO anti-dumping regime as an effort to privilege state interests and promote protectionism.[53] Moreover, the close intersection between government and business in China's foreign trade sector heightens the potential for politicized interpretations of GATT restrictions on the permitted range of anti-dumping and countervailing duties available to China's trading partners.[54] Ongoing political pressure on trading partners to affirm China's status as a market economy seems aimed at altering the criteria for assessing anti-dumping and countervailing duties on Chinese exports.[55] The recent textile dispute with the EU exemplifies the difficulties in reconciling China's trade practices with its WTO commitments.[56] While China's official explanations tend to emphasize its natural low-cost production conditions,[57] its pricing practices, supported by state-controlled labour

50 WTO Statistics (www.wto.org/english/tratop_e/adp_e/adp_e.htm#statistics). Also see "China remains top anti-dumping target," *Xinhuanet*, 1 November 2004; "Anti–dumping," *The Economist*, 13 May 2006, p. 102.

51 "Regulations on responding to anti-dumping suits," *China Economic News*, 7 January 2002, pp. 11–13.

52 See "PRC Foreign Trade Law (Revised)," *China Law & Practice*, Vol. 18, No. 4 (2004), pp. 34–47. The earlier text of the law appears at "Foreign Trade Law of the PRC, 1994," *China Economic News*, 23 May 1994, p. 8 and 30 May 1994, p. 7. See "Anti-dumping regulations of the PRC," in *China Economic News* supplement No. 3 (2002) (supplanting "Anti-dumping and anti-subsidy regulations of the People's Republic of China, 1997"). Also see J. Shen, "A critical analysis of China's first regulation on foreign dumping and subsidies and its consistency with WTO agreements," *Berkeley Journal of International Law*, Vol. 15 (1997), p. 295; M. Zheng, "Regulations on antidumping, countervailing duties adopted," *East Asian Economic Reports*, 15 February 1997, pp. 9–13.

53 See e.g. Ling Huiming, "WTO fan qingxiao fa de hongguan fenxi" ("Macro analysis of WTO anti-dumping law"), in *Faxue pinglun*, No. 4 (2003), pp. 74–78.

54 See P.M. Norton and K.W. Almstedt, "Defending dumping claims: exporters to China beware," *China Law & Practice*, June 2000, pp. 32–39. Also see G. Han, "China learns how to deal with dumping charges," *Beijing Review*, 3–9 August 1998, pp. 12–14.

55 See e.g. Sun Liwen, "Lu shijie maoyi tizhi zhong wo guo feishichang jingji diwei wenti zhi xiaojie" ("On clearing up issues of China's non-market economy status in the international trade system"), in *Faxue pinglun*, No. 5 (2006), pp. 90–95.

56 "EU and China reach textile deal," *BBC News*, 5 September 2005; "China ups stakes in textile row," *BBC News*, 30 May 2005; "Textile row deepens as China revokes export tariffs," *Bridges Weekly Trade News Digest* (ICTSD), Vol. 9, No. 19 (1 June 2005).

57 "China slams EU anti-dumping charges on shoes," *China Daily*, 24 February 2006; "Chinese exporters fall victim to use of flawed WTO laws," *Business Weekly*, 18 June 2003.

conditions,[58] are seen internationally as working artificially to reduce export prices leading to market disruption elsewhere.

Selective adaptation in China's trade law regime

While the extent of China's compliance with WTO disciplines may well reflect factors of local interest and political will, conflicts of underlying norms also appear to play a role. Norms of liberal capitalism underlying the GATT/WTO system seem to operate in tension with imperatives of state-driven development in China.[59] Depictions of China's institutional conditions as a limit on imposition of WTO disciplines suggest resistance to GATT premises of universal minimum standards.[60] Selective adaptation elements of perception are also evident in policy and legal discourses that interpret GATT/WTO standards on governance, anti-dumping and intellectual property as purposefully unfair to China and/or as the result of US and international power politics.[61] Factors of complementarity arise in discussions about the compatibility of GATT/WTO disciplines with China's institutional arrangements and normative principles.[62] Elements of legitimacy are evident in discourses making acceptance of international rules conditional on preserving the authority of Party and government rule.[63] Thus, while assessment of China's compliance with GATT/WTO standards cannot be divorced from factors of economic and bureaucratic self-interest, selective adaptation also helps to explain the normative origins of compliance dilemmas.

China and Human Rights: Responses to International Standards

China's expanded engagement with international human rights discourses suggests the importance of normative engagement and selective adaptation. On one hand, the government has supported human rights research and scholarship

58 "Section 301 Petition of the American Federation of Labor and the Congress of Industrial Organizations," (8 June 2006) (http://www.afl-cio.org /issues/jobseconomy/globaleconomy/ upload/ china_petition.pdf).

59 See e.g. Wen Guanzhong, Zheng Zhihai, Wang Xinkui and Zuo Xuejin (eds.), *WTO yu Zhongguo: Zou jingji quanqiuhua fazhan zhi lu* (*WTO and China: Walking the Road of Economic Globalization Development*) (Beijing: Chinese People's University Press, 2001), pp. 16–21; Jin Xin, *Zhongguo wenti baogao: Xinshiji Zhongguo mianlin de yanjun taozhan* (*Report on China's Problems: Serious Challenges Faced by China in the New Century*) (Hong Kong: Liwen Press, 2001), pp. 237–42.

60 Jiang Wei and Wang Jingqi, "WTO xieyi yu Zhongguo minshi sifa zhidu de wanshan" ("The WTO agreement and perfection of China's civil judicial system"), *Zhongguo faxue*, No. 1 (2001), pp. 25–36.

61 On WTO for example, see Xie Kang, *Zhongguo yu WTO: Guize, taozhan yu yingzhan* (*China and the WTO: Rules, Challenges and Strategy*) (Guangzhou: Guangdong People's Press, 2001).

62 See Han Liyu, "WTO guize se shiyong yu Zhongguo guonei lifa," ("Application of WTO rules and Chinese domestic legislation"), in *Guoji jingji fa* (*International Economic Law*) No. 4 (2001),pp. 218–35.

63 See e.g. Wang Jiafu, "WTO yu Zhongguo shehui zhuyi shichang falu zhidu jianshe wenti" ("Issues of WTO and the establishment of China's socialist market legal system"), in *Zhongguo faxue*, No. 1 (2001), pp. 3–10 at p. 7.

at the highest levels.[64] International documents on human rights have been translated into Chinese and published with government support,[65] and the government has approved bilateral scholarly exchange programmes aimed at information sharing on human rights doctrine and practice.[66] China has signed both the International Covenant on Economic, Social and Cultural Rights (ICESCR) and the International Covenant on Civil and Political Rights (ICCPR), ratifying the ICESCR in 2001 and beginning the policy review process leading possibly to ratification of the ICCPR.[67]

Despite this, however, China continues to face criticism over its human rights practices in substantive areas such as labour, discrimination, health, gender and religious freedom.[68] There were hopeful expectations that participation in international regimes would improve protection for human rights, but institutional enforcement and reporting continues to lag.[69] Apart from familiar issues of torture and abuse of prisoners, extensive use of the death penalty, abuse of criminal process for political purposes, suppression of religious freedoms and denial of labour rights,[70] concerns have also been raised in the area of abuse of psychiatry for political purposes and the use of surveillance technology to

64 Wang Jiafu, Liu Hainian and Li Lin. (eds.), *Renquan yu 21 shijie* (*Human rights and the 21st century*) (Beijing: China Law Publishers, 2000); Xia Yong, *Renquan gainian qiyuan* (*Origins of Human Rights Concepts*) (Beijing: University of Politics and Law Press, 1997); Xia Yong (ed.), *Zuoxiang quanli de shidai: Zhongguo gongmin quanli fazhan yanjiu* (*Proceeding Towards an Era of Rights: A Study of the Development of Citizens' Rights in China*) (Beijing: University of Politics and Law Press, 1995).

65 CASS Law Institute (ed.), *Guoji renquan wenjian yu Guoji renquan jigou* (*International Human Rights Documents and International Human Rights Institutions*) (Beijing: Chinese Academy of Social Sciences Press, 1993).

66 Errol P. Mendes and A-M Traeholt (eds.), *Human Rights: Chinese and Canadian Perspectives* (Ottawa: Human Rights Research and Education Centre, 1997); P.R. Baehr *et al.* (eds.), *Human Rights: Chinese and Dutch Perspectives* (The Hague: Kluwer, 1996).

67 State Council Information Office, "China's progress in Human Rights in 2004" (13 April 2005), section VII (http://www.china.org.cn/e-white/20050418/VII.htm); Shi Jiangtao, "Beijing reviews key human rights treaty," *South China Morning Post* (6 September 2005).

68 US Congressional Executive Committee on China, *Annual Report 2006* (http://www.cecc.gov/pages/annualRpt/annualRpt06/index.php), Section V; Human Rights Watch, "China: events of 2006," in *World Report 2007* (http://hrw.org/englishwr2k7/docs/2007/01/11/china14867.htm); US Department of State, Bureau of Democracy, Human Rights and Labor, "Country reports on human rights practices: China (includes Tibet, Hong Kong and Macao) 2004" (28 February 2005). Also see Amnesty International 2005, "China: human rights – a long way to go before the Olympics" (5 August 2005); Amnesty International UK, "EU–China summit: EU must continue pressing for real progress on human rights in China" (2 September 2005).

69 Susan C. Morris, *Trade and Human Rights: The Ethical Dimension in U.S.–China Relations* (Aldershot: Ashgate, 2002). Leila Choukroune, "Justiciability of economic, social, and cultural rights" *Columbia Journal of Asian Law*, Vol. 19, No. 1 (2005), pp. 30–49.

70 UN Commission on Human Rights, "Civil and political rights, including the question of torture and detention: report of the special rapporteur on torture and other cruel, inhumane, or degrading treatment or punishment – mission to China" (10 March 2006). "High Commissioner for Human Rights highlights progress and challenges at end of visit to China" (Press Release, 2 September 2005). "Reviewing a quarter century of political crime," in *Human Rights Forum*, No. 2 (2003), pp. 54–57. Human Rights Watch, "China: a year after new regulations, religious rights still restricted" (1 March 2006); Congressional-Executive Commission on China, *2006 Annual Report*, section V(d) "Freedom of religion." "The WTO and Chinese labor rights," in *Human Rights Forum*, No. 3 (2005), pp. 39–41.

suppress freedom of communication and expression.[71] China's responses to these challenges have focused on normative engagement.

Participation and normative resistance

As China's participation in the international human rights system has expanded, official interpretations of international human rights discourses suggest an effort to resist and/or transform international standards and norms. As a signatory of and advocate for the 1993 Bangkok Declaration on Human Rights,[72] China has embraced the implications of what the Bangkok Declaration refers to as a "dynamic and evolving process of international norm-setting" as an opportunity to articulate and justify new standards for human rights that comport with its own policy priorities. Despite criticisms of the so-called "Asian values" discourse,[73] such alternative views on human rights have come to challenge liberal rights models.[74] The privileging of collective over individual rights remains a key element in China's rights discourse.[75] China also supports principles of the Bangkok Declaration on intrinsic hierarchies of rights, subordination of political and civil rights to socio-economic development, and the contingency of rights on local conditions, which depart from the principles established in the 1993 Vienna human rights declaration.[76]

In a series of white papers, the PRC government has articulated policy positions on human rights supporting the primacy of economic growth by stressing subsistence as the basic right upon which all others depend. The 1991 white paper asserted that economic development must take precedence over political rights.[77] The 1995 white paper conditioned civil and political rights upon achievement of development goals.[78] The 1997 white paper reiterated the theme that subsistence and development were paramount human rights.[79] The PRC human rights white paper of 2000 once again linked human rights to

71 Robin Munro, "Judicial psychiatry in China and its political abuses," *Columbia Journal of Asian Law*, Vol. 14 No. 1 (2000), pp. 1–128. Greg Walton, "China's golden shield: corporations and the development of surveillance technology in the People's Republic of China" (Montreal: International Centre for Human Rights and Democratic Development, 2001).

72 "Final declaration of the regional meeting for Asia of the World Conference on Human Rights" (Bangkok Declaration) (2 April 1993), *Human Rights Law Journal*, Vol. 14 (1993), p. 370.

73 David Kelly and Anthony Reid (eds.), *Asian Freedoms: The Idea of Freedom in East and Southeast Asia* (Cambridge: Cambridge University Press, 1998).

74 Peter Van Ness (ed.), *Debating Human Rights: Critical Essays from the United States and Asia* (London: Routledge, 1999).

75 For critical comment that underscores the prevalence of the collective approach, see Xu Xianming and Qu Xiangfei, "Renquan zhuti jie shuo" ("Speaking on the boundaries of the subject of human rights"), *Zhongguo faxue*, No. 2 (2001), pp. 53–62; He Zhipeng, "Ren de huigui: geren guojifa shang diwei zhi shenshi" ("The return of man: reflections on the status of the individual in international law"), *Faxue pinglun*, No. 3 (2006), pp. 56–63.

76 Compare Bangkok Declaration with "United Nations World Conference on Human Rights: Vienna Declaration and Programme of Action," UN Doc. A/CONF.157/24 (1993), *International Legal Materials*, Vol. 32 (1993), p. 1661.

77 "Text of human rights white paper," *FBIS Daily Report: China* (supplement), 21 November 1991.

78 State Council Information Office, "China's progress in human rights in 2004."

79 "Quarterly chronicle and documentation (April/June 1997)," *The China Quarterly*, No. 151 (1997), p. 698.

subsistence and development, even as the obligation to recognize and enforce civil and political rights was marginalized: "the Chinese government has always put the rights of the people to subsistence and development first."[80] The 2004 white paper formally integrated themes of subsistence with international discourses on the right to development,[81] confining civil and political human rights to the theme "political development with Chinese characteristics."[82] In these and other areas, the Chinese government seems to be orienting its participation in the international legal regime for human rights so as to challenge established norms that are contrary to PRC practice, thus diminishing the possibility that these might develop into some sort of *jus cogens* with greater binding authority.[83]

China appears comfortable to defend its human rights policies and practices by reference to its own interpretations of international legal standards. On particular subjects where it has faced criticism, the government has expanded its participation in bilateral and multilateral co-operation projects aimed at increasing the appearance of international law compliance. Thus, the 2004 human rights white paper noted the development of China's socialist legal system and emphasized constitutional arrangements for enforcement of human rights, asserting that China's provision of public health services, education, housing and its recognition of the right of religious belief were compliant with international law requirements.[84] In the area of minority nationalities where China has faced considerable criticism,[85] the government has publicized its efforts to incorporate international law standards into its minority policies, while also supporting institutional engagement with international agencies.[86] In the area of environmental protection and sustainable development where conditions in China have been roundly criticised,[87] government support for the China Council on International Co-operation in Environment and Development suggests an effort to highlight engagement with international law and policy norms.[88] In the area of

80 State Council Information Office, "White paper: 50 years of progress in China's human rights" (June 2000), section II (http://www.china.org.cn/e-white/3/index.htm).

81 Jack Donnelly, "In search of the unicorn: the jurisprudence and politics of the right to development," *California Western International Law Journal*, Vol. 15 (1985), p. 473.

82 State Council Information Office, "China's progress in human rights in 2004."

83 For discussion of the tensions between norms and practice in the development of *jus cogens* in international law, see Dinah Shelton, "Normative hierarchy in international law," *American Journal of International Law*, Vol. 100, No. 2 (2006), pp. 291–323.

84 State Council Information Office, "China's progress in human rights in 2004," section II.

85 Uradyn E. Bulag, *The Mongols at China's Edge: History and the Politics of National Unity* (Lanham MD: Rowman and Littlefield, 2002); Colin Mackerras, *China's Ethnic Minorities and Globalisation* (London: Routledge, 2003).

86 State Council Information Office, "National minorities policy and its practice in China" (20 May 2004). "2008 nian renleixue minzuxue shijie dahui xuanchuan ziliao" ("Information materials for the 2008 international conference on anthropology and ethnology") (May 2004), detailing international co-operation activities since 1992.

87 "Poor showing for China in 'environmental performance index'," *China Development Brief*, 9 February 2006 (www.chinadevelopmentbrief.com/node/455).

88 CCICED Secretariat, *China Council for International Cooperation on Environment and Development: Success Story* (2005) (www.harbour.sfu.ca/dlam/index.html and www.secretariat@cciced.org).

women's rights, even as its compliance with the Convention on Elimination of All Forms of Discrimination Against Women is challenged,[89] China has sought to justify its policies and practices on women's equality as consistent with international law standards.[90]

Patterns of normative resistance are also evident in China's participation in international human rights fora. Diplomatic initiatives are explained locally as an important avenue for influencing the application of international regime norms on human rights and democracy.[91] Thus, increased participation in international institutions (including NGOs) is seen as useful to prevent intrusion of international labour standards inappropriate to China's interests.[92] While reception of the UN High Commissioner for Human Rights Louise Arbour in November 2004 and the Special Rapporteur on Torture in November–December 2005 seemed to reflect increased willingness to accept international human rights scrutiny,[93] China also managed to avoid formal criticism at the UN's Commission on Human Rights, largely through a series of successful "no action" motions.[94] Similarly the effects of international monitoring of China's human rights record have seemingly been confined to areas of "technical co-operation" such as education and administration where the Chinese government is already embarked on reforms.[95]

Although China has participated increasingly in the UN's Human Rights Commission, this seems aimed as well at resisting international criticism. Thus, formal statements for the record are made to affirm China's resistance to use of country-specific criticisms, dismissing these as an exercise in "double standards and political motives."[96] In addition, China's participation works to advance its preferred interpretations of international human rights standards, such as the

89 Yin Sheng, "Zhongguo heping fazhan zhong funu renquan de guoji falu baohu" ("International legal protection of the human rights of women during China's peaceful development"), *Faxue pinglun*, No. 2 (2006), pp. 116–21; Amnesty International, *China Report 2005* (http://web.amnesty.org/report2005/chn-summary-eng). Also see Centre for Reproductive Rights, "Supplementary information on China" (letter to CEDAW Committee), 3 August 2006; Human Rights China, Asia Monitor Resource Centre, China Labour Bulletin, Hong Kong Christian Industrial Committee, *Report on Implementation of CEDAW in the PRC* (December 1998).

90 State Council Information Office, "White paper: gender equality and women's development in China" (August 2005) (http://news.xinhuanet.com/english/2005-08/24/content_3396107.htm).

91 Huang Deming, "Zhongguo heping fazhan zhong waijiao zhineng tiaozheng de qianyan falu wenti" ("The function of diplomacy in adjusting legal issues confronted in the course of China's peaceful development"), *Faxue pinglun*, No. 2 (2006), pp. 107–15.

92 Zeng Lijie, "Qiye de shehui zeren yu Zhongguo de heping fazhan" ("Corporate responsibility and China's peaceful development"), *Faxue pinglun*, No. 4 (2006), pp. 64–69.

93 "High Commissioner for Human Rights highlights progress and challenges at end of visit to China" (press release, 2 September 2005); "Civil and political rights, including the question of torture and detention: report of the special rapporteur on torture and other cruel, inhumane or degrading treatment or punishment, Manfred Nowak," Commission on Human Rights (10 March 2006).

94 "Attempt to block rights resolution, Beijing expected to counter Geneva offensive," *South China Morning Post*, 15 April 1997, p. 8. "Disappointed, not discouraged on China," *International Herald Tribune*, 17 April 1997, p. 4.

95 Office of the High Commissioner for Human Rights, "Mission report on China" (1999); Kent, *China, the United Nations, and Human Rights*.

96 "Statement by HE Ambassador Sha Zukang, on behalf of the like minded group, at the 61st session of the Commission on Human Rights" (14 March 2005) (http://www.china-un.ch/eng/rqrd/thsm/t187353.htm).

primacy of economic, social and cultural rights over other rights,[97] and restrictions on the application of international standards on self-determination to local national minority groups.[98] In discussions on implementation of international human rights instruments, China has challenged the credibility of the UN human rights process, suggesting that its ongoing support would depend on being insulated from criticism.[99] China's presence on the new UN Human Rights Council (replacing the Human Rights Commission) continues to serve as a vehicle through which to articulate preferred interpretations of international human rights standards – including principles on the right to development, deference to local subjective conditions as context for human rights assessments and state sovereignty in human rights enforcement.[100] In light of this, China's candidacy for the new Human Rights Council faced resistance from NGOs concerned with its human rights record.[101]

Selective adaptation in China's human rights discourse

Under conditions where international human rights standards do not have a uniform set of normative principles,[102] China's efforts to influence the content of international standards and norms reflect the importance of normative consensus as a basis for local reception of non-local standards. China's engagement with the international legal regime on human rights has combined institutional participation with normative resistance in furtherance of the "process of international norm-setting" referred to in the Bangkok Declaration. The selective adaptation paradigm seems particularly appropriate to further understanding of this behaviour.

Government statements on the human right to subsistence and development suggest normative tensions with international human rights standards that reject hierarchies of rights and question claims to conditionality based on local conditions. This emphasis reflects an insistence on a hierarchy of rights and on timetables for the granting of political and civil rights dependent on local conditions of development. China's reliance on the right to development discourse to justify its policies thus suggests a response to international norms that is grounded in the normative dynamics of selective adaptation.

97 "Statement by H. Ambassador Zhang Yishan, head of Chinese delegation, at ECOSOC substantive session of 2005 on human rights" (22 July 2005) (http://www.china-un.org/eng/xw/t204673.htm).

98 "Statement by Counsellor La Yifan of the Chinese delegation, at third committee of 60th UNGA session on elimination of racism and right to self-determination (Item 69, 70)" (7 November 2005) (http://www.china-un.org/eng/xw/t220137.htm).

99 "Statement by Mr La Yifan, alternative representative of the delegation of the People's Republic of China on Agenda Item 105(a): Implementation of human rights instruments at the third committee during the 59th session of the general assembly" (25 October 2004) (http://www.china-un.org/eng/xw/t167002.htm).

100 Yang Jiechi, "Work in cooperation for a new chapter in the cause of international human rights" (21 June 2006) (http://www.china-un.ch/eng/rqrd/thsm/t258933.htm).

101 PRC Foreign Ministry, "Aide memoire," 13 April 2006; China Rights Defenders, "Vote for the human rights council: is China qualified" (press release, 8 May 2006).

102 See generally, Henry J. Steiner and Philip Alston, *International Human Rights Law in Context: Law, Politics, Morals* (Oxford: Oxford University Press, 2000).

Factors of perception, complementarity and legitimacy are also evident. Perceptions that human rights criticism of China is driven by American or international power politics, for example, suggest important conditions for China's engagement.[103] In addition, official discourses suggest perceptions of human rights as constrained by China's constitutional system, limited to those expressly granted by the party-state and qualified by duties to uphold Party rule and protect the interests of the state and society.[104] Complementarity is evident in assertions that compliance with international human rights standards requires support for China's sovereignty imperatives, acceptance of the limits of local conditions and preservation of China's governance priorities.[105] In the case of China's compliance with the ICCPR for example, complementarity issues are to be resolved through legislative initiatives aimed to ensure that local priorities are preserved.[106] The importance of legitimacy is shown as China strives to present its legal and political system as fully honouring international human rights standards. Thus, international human rights norms of state responsibility are cited to support the primacy of Chinese government control in human rights enforcement.[107] Legitimacy dynamics are also evident in China's rebuttals of annual reports from the United States criticizing China's human rights record and its counter-reports on American human rights abuses, which seem aimed to establish a legitimate moral equivalent between China and the United States on human rights issues.[108]

Summary

China's participation in international legal regimes has increased substantially in the past ten years. Domestic policy priorities combined with the influences of

103 See e.g. Liu Jie, *Renquan yu guojia zhuquan* (*Human Rights and National Sovereignty*) (Shanghai: Shanghai People's Press, 2004), ch. 8.

104 Constitution of the People's Republic of China, Articles 1, 51. Also see Zhang Jiliang, *Zhonggong renquan lilun yu Zhongguo requan lifa* (*Party Policy on Human Rights and China's Human Rights Legislation*) (Beijing: Chinese Academy of Social Sciences Press, 2004).

105 See Li Wanqiang, "Lun quanqiuhua qushi xia guojifa de xin fazhan" ("New developments in international law under the trend of globalization"), *Faxue pinglun*, No. 6 (2006), pp. 55–62. Tang Tianri, "Zhongguo he xifang zai renquan wenti shang de yuanze fenqi" ("Divergence of principles between China and the West on human rights questions"), in China Human Rights Development Foundation (ed.), *Xifang renquan guan yu renquan waijiao* (*Western Human Rights Concepts and Human Rights Diplomacy*) (Beijing: New World Press, 2003), pp. 60–65. Wang Guangxian, "Diyue guo zai shishi guoji renquan tiaoyue fangmian de jingyan yu wenti" ("Experience and problems of signatory states implementing human rights treaties"), *Faxue pinglun*, No. 2 (2002), pp. 116–25.

106 See Liu Jian and Hao Jianyun, "Lun woguo laodong jiaopei zhidu yu guoji renquan gongyue de chongtu ji qi tiaozheng" ("On conflicts between our labour education and training system and international human rights treaties and their adjustment"), *Faxue pinglun*, No. 5 (2001), pp. 29–32.

107 See Zhou Chonghai and Xie Haibao, "Lun guoji fa shang de renquan baohu" ("On human rights enforcement in international law"), in *Zhongguo faxue*, No. 1 (2001), pp. 164–68; Sun Shichen, "Lun guoji renquan fa xia guojia de yiwu" ("On state responsibility under international human rights law"), in *Faxue pinglun*, No. 2 (2001), pp. 91–96.

108 "Human rights accusations refuted," *China Daily*, 29 March 1995, p. 4; State Council Information Office, "The human rights record of the United States in 2002" (Beijing: 2003); State Council Information Office, "The human rights record of the United States in 2001" (Beijing: 2002); Edward Cody, "China says US has double standard on rights," *Washington Post*, 3 March 2005.

globalization have seen increased internationalization of China's markets through WTO accession as well as increased participation in international organizations and discourses for human rights. Yet there are uncertainties about the extent to which China's increased engagement with the international legal regime has resulted in local assimilation of the normative underpinnings for international law standards in trade and human rights. To some extent, China's participation in the international legal regime reflects its "big power" aspirations[109] and suggests that participation remains contingent on unilateral assertions of state interest and the use of political power to achieve these interests.[110] However, selective adaptation analysis also helps to explain China's behaviour in terms of reception of international norms for trade and human rights. China's participation in the GATT/WTO can be understood in light of tensions between trade standards grounded in norms of liberalism and China's local governance norms. Similarly, China's participation in international human rights regimes can be understood in terms of normative engagement that ranges from resistance to pro-active norm-setting.

China's importance to the world mandates continued efforts to understand its participation in international legal regimes. The challenge remains to interpret China's formal references to international legal texts in light of questions about acceptance of underlying norms. Just as the *xieyi* (写 意) style of the great Chinese monk-painter Badashanren (八大山人) focused on the essence of a subject to express understanding of the details of surface appearance,[111] so too can observers of China's engagement with the international legal system attend to essential issues of normative consensus as a way to shed light on surface appearances of textual interpretation. China's participation in international legal discourses and institutions warrants such an approach, and invites the international community to consider its implications. As interpreted in light of selective adaptation, the details of China's interpretation and implementation of international standards in trade and human rights raise important questions about China's engagement with fundamental norms of international legal regimes.

109 Zhang Dengji, *Jianjiang Zhongguo: bu queding shijie zhong de daguo dingwei yu daguo waijiao* (*Writing China: Identity Formation and Big Power Diplomacy*) (Taipei: Yangzhi Wenhua Publishers, 2003).

110 China Mieville *Between Equal Rights: A Marxist's Theory of International Law* (Leiden: Brill, 2005), pp. 289–93.

111 Josef Hejzlar, *Chinese Watercolours* (London: Galley Press, 1987), pp. 19–21; Liu Mo, *Badashanren* (Shijiazhuang: Hebei Education Press, 2003), pp. 38–45.

Commentary on "China and the International Legal System: Challenges of Participation"

James Li Zhaojie

China's participation in the international legal system has long been a topic of academic inquiry both inside and outside China, and has produced a rich literature reflecting mainly two concerns. First, is China a help or a hindrance to the development of the international legal system? If China is a help, what impact has China made upon the contemporary international legal system and what can China contribute to its further development? Secondly, what impact has the international legal system in which China has participated had on China? In recent years, the context in which these questions are framed has changed greatly. After the founding of the PRC in 1949, China was seen as a potential rebel against the prevailing international legal system. Today, China is depicted, at least in the mind of US decision-makers, as a stakeholder of the world order.

What makes Pitman Potter's article unique among these inquiries is the theoretical paradigm he uses, namely "selective adaptation," for analysing and assessing China's participation in the international legal system. His article notes that China's participation in international legal institutions is by no means a passive response to outside initiatives. Instead, as Potter suggests, it represents a dynamic process of selectively adapting international norms to local conditions. In this process, he highlights such factors as perception, complementarity and legitimacy, all of which play an important role in influencing the degree of China's compliance with, and implementation of, rules of international law within China's domestic legal order.

Recent years have seen a profound transformation of China's mentality from a victim-minded underdog in the old international legal system to an active status quo keeper of the present international legal order. In the years following its founding, the PRC participated in a range of trade and diplomatic relations with states in Europe, the developing world, and the Soviet Union's sphere of influence. But that participation was characterized by doubt, mistrust and reservations which were reflected in the international law writings of Chinese scholars from the 1950s to the 1970s. The policy of reform and opening to the outside world that began in the late 1970s precipitated a fundamental change in this mind-set. With the continuing rapid expansion of China's engagement with the international community and its active involvement in the process of globalization in particular, international law provides a useful frame of reference for Chinese decision-makers in their assessment of internationally related facts and in the formulation of their policy of action as well. It plays an increasingly important role in the input, output and feedback processes of China's domestic and foreign policy system. Today China feels more confident in, and

 doi:10.1017/S0305741007001683

comfortable with, the international legal system, which as a whole is perceived to promote China's national interests.

At the same time, however, China's policy of integrating with the international system still follows a sovereignty-centred and state-empowering model. The logic is simple. China must participate in the international system in order to enhance its so-called "comprehensive national strength," but wishes to minimize the trade-off of its sovereignty. This perception of China's relationship to the international legal order, as noted by Potter, reflects to some extent China's "big power aspirations." National political independence and global economic interdependence have become two means towards the sovereignty-centred end. Such a perception obviously affects the reception of international legal standards by China and ultimately its response to their implementation in the Chinese domestic legal order.

What comes with this perception of international law are growing efforts made by China to have the Chinese domestic legal system live up to the requirements of international norms in a complementary manner. From a legal point of view, complementarity as such has at least the following normative strands. From the standpoint of compliance, most international legal norms cannot work without the constant help, co-operation and support of the national legal system. Thus, to faithfully perform its international legal obligations, China needs to incorporate rules of international law into its domestic legal order by making the latter compatible with the former. With China's active participation in international legal institutions, the inadequacies of its domestic legal system in this respect have become apparent. As noticed by Potter, the status of international law as a binding standard for Chinese domestic law remains the subject of intense debate among Chinese legal scholars. To a large extent, this is due to the phenomenal silence of China's Constitution on this matter.

However, progress has been made in the area of trade thanks to China's accession to the WTO. As a global organization based on free trade principles, the WTO places tremendous emphasis on compliance and regulatory transparency ensured by each contracting party's domestic legal system. To meet these obligations, China has not only made efforts to resolve conflicts and discrepancies between its existing trade policy and regulatory practice on the one hand and WTO standards on the other, but has also actively engaged itself in reforming fundamental norms of governance. In the implementation in its domestic legal system of the WTO-based obligation of transparency, for instance, China has committed itself to the publication and uniform enforcement of laws, regulations and other measures relating to trade. China has also promised to ensure that local laws and regulations conform to China's obligations under WTO.

Closely related to the factors of perception and complementarity is the question of legitimacy. Legitimacy as a legal term is often used to mean the quality of a rule which derives from a perception on the part of those to whom it is addressed that it has come into being in accordance with right processes. Thus, some rules in themselves seem to exert more pull to compliance than others simply because they are perceived to be legitimate by these rules' addressees. When used here by Potter, legitimacy as a dynamic factor concerns the extent to which members of local communities accept the purposes and consequences of selective adaptation. Therefore, the more legitimate an international legal norm is considered to be, the better chance it has of being accepted and ultimately implemented in a domestic legal order.

Furthermore, with the rapid expansion of its national interests on to the international plane, China is increasingly concerned with its ability to shape preferences of other nations so as to enhance the sense of legitimacy for its international behaviour. In a globalization and information age, not all hard power actions can bring about desired outcomes. In the words of Joseph Nye, the former dean of Harvard's Kennedy School of Government, "success depends not only on whose army wins, but also on whose story wins." This insight accords with the Chinese wisdom that a legitimate cause enjoys abundant support while an illegitimate one finds little. To China, this concern has been translated into an understanding that its national interests, whether in trade or in human rights, must be pursued within the international legal framework. A typical example in this respect is the recent discussion of reforms in China's criminal procedure law. Many proposals made and measures taken were actually informed by the established standards of international human rights law. As a result, China's participation in the international legal system has in turn served as a vehicle to push the development of rule of law in China.

While shedding great light upon understanding and explaining from a normative perspective China's participation in the international legal system, the paradigm of selective adaptation would be more powerful if other important dynamics – most prominently, institutional capacity – were involved.

As noted by Potter, while China's participation in the international legal regime has increased substantially in the past ten years, leading to China's ever closer integration within the international system, local assimilation of the normative underpinnings of international law is also marked by uncertainty and resistance – for example, in trade and human rights. If such a conflicted interplay between local and non-local norms results from selectively adapting international legal norms to local conditions, local institutional capacity should be seen as another significant factor affecting the dynamic process of selective adaptation.

This is particularly true in the case of enforcement of intellectual property rights (IPR). Since joining the WTO, China has strengthened its legal framework and amended its IPR and related laws and regulations to comply with international standards. A system of enforcement through criminal, civil, and administrative measures has been established. In recent years, China's leadership has made IPR protection a priority and has taken active measures to improve enforcement. Chinese authorities at the central and provincial government levels have launched numerous campaigns to crack down on IPR infringements.

Recently, China's Supreme People's Court has lowered the threshold for prosecuting manufacturers and vendors of counterfeit IP products.

Despite these efforts, however, China continues to be seen as a haven for counterfeiters and pirates, who target both domestic and foreign companies and nationals. Many believe that enforcement measures taken to date have not been sufficient to deter massive IPR infringements. There are, however, several factors that undermine enforcement measures, including corruption and local protectionism at the provincial level, limited resources and training available to enforcement officials, and lack of public education regarding the economic and social impact of counterfeiting and piracy. It is these obstacles that have diluted the strength of central legislation and the power of law enforcement. Therefore, the pattern of uncertainty and resistance with respect to IPR protection noted by Potter is, to a large extent, caused by insufficient institutional capacity.

In the human rights area, problems are much more complicated. First, there is a serious lack of universal consensus as to the concept of human rights: it is a dynamic and broad area ranging from civil and political rights to the so-called third generation of rights, which include the right to economic development and the right to health. Moreover, ideological and cultural differences coupled with the state of political, economic and social development have clearly influenced the discourse and inevitably affected the enforcement of the international standards for the protection of human rights. Against this background, the pattern of uncertainty and resistance remains apparent in regard to China's participation in international human rights institutions, and the paradigm of selective adaptation particularly appropriate.

Another important factor also shapes the process of selective adaptation in the field of human rights. In China, human rights are still seen as an essentially domestic issue. Only the people whose rights are affected, not foreign or international pressure, can force a government to respect human rights. International human rights institutions have only a secondary role to play. Experience shows that no state really respects human rights in the first place because it is internationally bound to do so. Rather, respect for human rights has to be entrenched in, and grow out of, the political and legal culture of a country in order to be stable and lasting. International law is mainly there to strengthen, secure, check, reinforce, encourage and harmonize domestic respect for human rights on a high, commonly agreed, level.

If human rights problems are confined to specific legal contexts of a given country, the challenge to China's performance of its international legal obligations for the protection of human rights comes also from the deficiency of its domestic legal system. Indeed, the international system for the protection of human rights depends, for its efficacy, on the domestic legal systems of states. In this connection, the enforcement of human rights forms part of a larger problem of belief in, and the maintenance of, the Rule of Law, including the existence of an independent judiciary, within the domestic legal system. For understandable reasons, China has a long way to go to solve these problems.

Trade, Investment and Beyond: The Impact of WTO Accession on China's Legal System

Julia Ya Qin

ABSTRACT This article assesses the impact of China's accession to the World Trade Organization on its foreign trade and investment regime. While the government had begun liberalizing the Chinese economy long before joining the WTO, the accession induced regulatory, institutional and normative changes that have transformed the landscape of trade and investment in China. The profound impact of the WTO stems directly from the extensive commercial and rule commitments China undertook in its accession. Focusing on the most significant of these commitments, the article examines their implications for Chinese constitutional law and their effect on the regulation of foreign trade, foreign investment, intellectual property rights and domestic governance. Additionally, it looks at the impact of WTO disputes on Chinese law and practice. It concludes that China's accession has made its foreign trade and investment regime far more liberalized and less opaque than a decade ago. More importantly, the accession has institutionalized the process of China's domestic reform externally through the force of WTO obligations. Although much uncertainty remains concerning the future direction of government policies, WTO membership ensures that the course of China's economic development will be charted within the disciplines of the WTO system.

China's foreign trade and investment regime has changed profoundly in the past decade. It is today far more liberalized and less opaque. Much of the progress occurred as a result of China's accession to the World Trade Organization (WTO), which, after 15 years in the making, finally took place on 11 December 2001. In its accession agreement (the Protocol), China made extensive commitments to lower its trade and investment barriers, deepen economic reforms, and improve its domestic governance, many of which exceeded the requirements of the WTO agreements.[1] To implement these commitments,

1 *Protocol on the Accession of the People's Republic of China*, WT/L/432 (10 November 2001), which incorporates by reference selected paragraphs of *Report of the Working Party on the Accession of China*, WT/MIN(01)/3 (10 November 2001) (WPR). For WTO agreements see: Agreement Establishing the WTO (15 April 1994) and its annexes, including the General Agreement on Tariffs and Trade 1994 (GATT) and its related agreements, the General Agreement on Trade in Services (GATS), the Agreement on Trade-Related Aspects of Intellectual Property Rights (TRIPS), and the agreements on dispute settlement and trade policy review.

 doi:10.1017/S0305741007001695

China has conducted a legislative overhaul: thousands of laws and regulations relating to WTO matters have been scrutinized, revised or repealed. Meanwhile, the central government has gradually shifted its role in the economy from exerting direct control to being a regulator in the marketplace. Moreover, WTO norms, such as market economy, nondiscrimination and transparency, have gained wide acceptance among the Chinese public. These regulatory, institutional and normative changes brought about by the WTO accession have transformed the landscape of trade and investment in China.

Corresponding to these changes, China's foreign trade and investment has grown tremendously. From 1996 to 2005, foreign trade increased nearly fivefold, with more than three-quarters of that growth taking place after WTO accession.[2] During the same period, China became one of the top destinations for foreign direct investment (FDI). The FDI inflow since 2001 accounted for more than one-third of the total amount of actually utilized foreign investment since 1979.[3] This FDI expansion has in turn fuelled external trade, as nearly 60 per cent of China's imports and exports have been conducted by foreign-invested companies.[4]

Meanwhile, an increasingly globalized Chinese economy has created new issues. The rapid economic growth powered by foreign trade and investment has been at the cost of severe environmental degradation and widening income disparities. As the government rebalances its development policy, it has heightened state intervention in the economy. With foreign competition intensifying in the Chinese market, protectionism and economic nationalism arise. There are signs that the government is tightening control over foreign businesses and dragging its feet in implementing some of the more difficult WTO commitments. It seems uncertain, therefore, whether China will progressively liberalize its trade and investment regime in the post-accession era.

China pursued WTO membership because it was consistent with its domestic reform agenda. For more than two decades before WTO accession, China had engaged in economic liberalization unilaterally. A primary reason for Chinese leaders to accept the many onerous obligations of WTO membership was so they could use external pressures to overcome domestic obstacles in furthering the reform. In the grand scheme of China's development strategy, therefore, WTO accession was only one step, albeit a critical one, in the reform process. And China's reform agenda is much broader than that called for by its WTO commitments.

Nevertheless, WTO accession marks the formal integration of China into the global trading system. The accession has institutionalized China's systemic reforms through the force of international legal obligations. Since joining the WTO, whether China stays on the course of reform and how it chooses to

2 The total value of China's imports and exports was $289.9 billion in 1996, $509.5 billion in 2001 and $1,422.1 billion in 2005 (China National Bureau of Statistics).

3 WTO Trade Policy Review, *Report by the People's Republic of China*, WT/TPR/G/161 (17 March 2006), paras. 3 and 4.

4 WTO Trade Policy Review, *Report by the Secretariat – People's Republic of China*, WT/TPR/S/161/ Rev.1 (26 June 2006) (TPR Report), p. 2, n. 7.

pursue its economic development is no longer purely a domestic policy matter; instead, it has become a matter subject to the scrutiny of the WTO. While in theory China can always break away from the WTO or in practice find ways to evade its WTO commitments, it cannot do so without incurring considerable political and economic costs. It is in this sense that WTO membership performs a constitutional function for its members.[5]

This article assesses the impact of WTO accession on China's legal system. It introduces the nature and scope of China's WTO commitments, examines their constitutional implications, and surveys the major changes they have brought about in the regulation of foreign trade, foreign investment, intellectual property rights and domestic governance. It then discusses the impact of WTO disputes on China law and practice. The article concludes with some thoughts on the future prospects of China and the WTO.

Nature and Scope of China's WTO Commitments

The WTO represents a liberal trading system that aims to increase the welfare of nations by reducing government restrictions on trade. WTO jurisdiction extends to trade in goods and services, trade-related investment, and intellectual property. It prescribes two types of obligations for its members: market access obligations, which are commitments by each member to open up domestic markets to goods and services produced by other members; and rule obligations, which are rules of conduct for international trade. Market access commitments vary from member to member and can be renegotiated periodically. Rules of conduct, on the other hand, are uniform and cannot be changed easily. These rules cover not only border measures, such as customs tariffs and import restrictions, but also internal measures affecting trade, such as domestic taxation and regulation, health and technical standards, government subsidies, investment requirements, and intellectual property protection. All WTO obligations are enforceable through the WTO dispute settlement mechanism, which features compulsory jurisdiction and binding decisions. Failure to implement dispute settlement rulings may lead to trade sanctions authorized by the WTO. The WTO also monitors its members' trade practices through notification requirements and trade policy reviews.

As an acceding member, China must make market access commitments of its own and accept all WTO rules of conduct. In terms of market access, the scope and depth of China's commitments is unprecedented in WTO history. For instance, China agreed to bind all tariffs at low statutory rates, a commitment few countries ever made[6]; and its commitments in service sectors are much more

5 This constitutional function of the world trading system is commonly understood. See generally, Frieder Roessler, "The constitutional function of the multilateral trade order," in *Essays on the Legal Structure, Functions & Limits of the World Trade Order* (London: Cameron May, 2000), pp. 109–53. See also "Ten benefits of the WTO trading system," at www.wto.org.

6 Nicholas R. Lardy, *Integrating China into the Global Economy* (Washington, DC: Brookings Institution Press, 2002), p. 79.

extensive than those offered by any other group of countries, including high income ones.[7] This level of trade liberalization is particularly remarkable considering that China is still a developing country.[8] Even more remarkable, however, is the fact that China accepted a whole set of special rule obligations in addition to the generally applicable WTO rules.[9] These China-specific rules fall into two categories. The first prescribes obligations that exceed the requirements of generally applicable WTO rules. These "WTO-plus" obligations address primarily matters concerning market economy conditions, foreign investment and domestic governance. The second category authorizes discriminatory treatment of Chinese exports. These "WTO-minus" provisions permit an importing member to lower WTO standards in applying trade remedies (antidumping, anti-subsidy and safeguard measures) against Chinese products. While some of the WTO-minus rules have built-in expiry dates, all WTO-plus provisions are permanent. Additionally, China agreed to forgo much of the special treatment the WTO grants to its developing country members.

All the market access and rule obligations undertaken by China are enforceable through the WTO dispute settlement mechanism. In addition, a special transitional review mechanism was set up to monitor China's compliance with its extensive commitments. Under this, annual review of China's practice is conducted during the first eight years of its accession, followed by a final review before the end of the tenth year. No other member is subject to such special surveillance within the WTO.

In sum, China has undertaken extraordinary obligations exceeding those of any other WTO member. In fact, the Protocol is the first treaty of the People's Republic that contains explicit discriminatory terms. But why was the Chinese government willing to take on such onerous burdens? The question seems even more puzzling considering that most of China's exports already enjoyed WTO tariff rates by virtue of the most-favoured-nation treatment clause contained in its bilateral agreements with all major trading partners.[10] While the motives of Chinese leaders may never be fully known, one thing has become clear: they

7 Aaditya Mattoo, "China's accession to the WTO: the service dimension," *Journal of International Economic Law*, Vol. 6, No. 2 (2003), pp. 299–339, at 302–04.

8 Developing countries typically maintain a relatively high level of trade barriers to protect their domestic industries from foreign competition. For instance, the average statutory tariffs on industrial products in Argentina, Brazil, India and Indonesia are respectively 30.9%, 27%, 32.4% and 36.9%, as compared with 8.9% set by China. Lardy, *Integrating China into the Global Economy*, pp. 79–80. For a comparison in the coverage of services commitments between high-income, low and middle-income countries, large developing countries and China, see Mattoo, "China's accession to the WTO," p. 303, Table 1.

9 See generally, Julia Ya Qin, "'WTO-plus' obligations and their implications for the WTO legal system – an appraisal of the China accession Protocol," *Journal of World Trade*, Vol. 37, No. 3 (2003), pp. 483–522.

10 China could expect two major improvements in market access from WTO accession. One was to secure permanent MFN treatment by the US, which had been subjecting China's MFN status to annual Congressional approval. The other was in textile trade, where the decades-old global quota system was scheduled to be replaced by a tariff-based system for all WTO members at the end of 2004, which would benefit more competitive textile exporters such as China. But the discriminatory textile safeguard put a limit on the expansion of China textile exports. See n. 24 and text.

intended to utilize external forces – the enhanced foreign competition inherent in market access commitments and the multilateral disciplines imposed by the WTO – to transform the ailing state sector in the economy.[11] In order to achieve this strategic objective, the government was willing to accept certain discriminatory and unfair treatment as part of the cost. In other words, WTO accession was, first and foremost, a strategic decision on the part of the leadership to further liberalize China's economy. The tremendous growth in trade and investment following the accession is the direct result of such liberalization. This essential character of China's WTO accession is not always well understood.

Impact of WTO Accession on the Chinese Legal System

The WTO is the first international organization China joined that is vested with the authority to police a wide range of domestic policies of its members. It is also the first international organization China joined whose dispute settlement mechanism has compulsory jurisdiction over all its members. WTO accession, therefore, presents many new challenges to the Chinese system.

A basic issue encountered by the Chinese system, for example, is the domestic legal effect of the WTO agreements. The PRC Constitution is silent about the status of treaties under Chinese law and whether an international agreement can be directly applied in China without enabling domestic legislation. The issue had not commended much attention previously because no prior treaty contained such a large number of obligations requiring domestic implementation. After much debate, a consensus has emerged: the WTO agreements will not be applied in China directly; instead they must be implemented through domestic legislation.[12]

Constitutional Implications

A number of "WTO-plus" obligations undertaken by China bear directly upon the fundamental aspects of its economic system and are therefore constitutionally significant. They include the commitments, first, to let market forces determine prices of all goods and services except for a few specified categories such as tobacco, pharmaceuticals and public utilities; secondly, to allow any Chinese or foreign entity to engage in the import-export business within three years of accession, and to limit state trading to a list of specified products; and thirdly, not to influence, directly or indirectly, commercial decisions of state-owned enterprises (SOEs) except in a manner consistent with the WTO agreements.

11 For an insightful analysis, see Lardy, *Integrating China into the Global Economy*, pp. 9–21.

12 This view has been confirmed by the Supreme People's Court. See *Guanyu shenli guojimaoyi xingzheng anjian ruoganwenti de guiding* (*Provisions on Several Issues concerning the Adjudication of Administrative Cases Relating to International Trade*), 27 August 2002, effective 1 October 2002. For a detailed analysis, see Donald C. Clarke, "China's legal system and the WTO: the prospects for compliance," *Washington University Global Studies Law Review*, Vol. 2 (2003), pp. 99–104.

These "market economy" commitments went beyond the requirements of the then-existing Chinese law. For instance, the Price Law of 1997 merely declared that the state should gradually move to a market-based pricing system. While in practice most price controls were removed before WTO accession, the government is not required by domestic law to refrain from price-setting. Similarly, although the Constitution recognizes the right of SOEs to autonomous management, it does not impose any obligation on the government to refrain from interfering with SOE operations. As for trading rights, under the Foreign Trade Law of 1994, the government still controlled the allocation of all rights to conduct imports and exports. It was the WTO commitment that has finally rid China of this legacy of a centrally-planned economy.

Furthermore, these "market economy" commitments cannot be altered by China unilaterally, whereas Chinese domestic legislation including the Constitution can be, and has been, revised from time to time. So long as China remains a member of the WTO, it may not negate these commitments without incurring the consequences of breaching WTO obligations.[13] In effect, therefore, China has committed itself to a particular economic system – a matter of constitutional importance – through the force of WTO law.[14]

Foreign Trade Law

In the past decade, liberalization and making China's foreign trade regime WTO-compliant has been the main theme in the development of foreign trade law. During this period, China reduced its tariff and non-tariff barriers across the board and opened up important service sectors to foreign competition. Institutionally, the government has gradually moved away from direct control over trade and increasingly assumed the role of a regulator. Major legislation governing trade, including the Foreign Trade Law, the Customs Law, and laws and regulations on technical and safety standards, intellectual property and administrative procedures, has all been revised to ensure WTO consistency.[15] Consequently, China's foreign trade regime today is considerably more liberal than that of other major developing countries. However, recent years have also seen a rise in protectionism, reflected mostly in China's extensive use of trade remedy and other non-tariff measures.

13 In fact, one of these market economy commitments – liberalization of trading rights – has become the subject of a WTO complaint. See n. 52.

14 Although its rules are premised upon market economy assumptions, the WTO does not prescribe any particular economic system for its members, which is consistent with the principle that sovereign nations may freely choose their own political and economic system. Since other members have not undertaken such systemic obligations, they may, at least as a formal matter, change their economic regime without breaching WTO obligations.

15 For a list of Chinese legislation relating to foreign trade, see TPR Report, Appendix, Table A.II.2. For a general study of China's foreign trade regulation, see Xin Zhang, *International Trade Regulation in China* (Hart Publishing, 2006).

Trading rights

To implement its WTO commitment on liberalization of trading rights, China amended the Foreign Trade Law of 1994, which took effect on 1 July 2004, six months ahead of schedule. The amendment replaces the previous approval system with a registration system for operating import-export businesses in China. Under this new scheme, any firm or individual (domestic or foreign) wishing to engage in imports and exports of goods or technologies may do so upon completing certain registration procedures with the Ministry of Commerce (MOFCOM). Documents required for registration are mostly for identification purposes, and MOFCOM must complete the registration within five days of receipt of the required documents. This new system is a primary example that the government has shifted its role from direct control over foreign trade operations to functioning as a regulator in the marketplace. The liberalization of trading rights works hand-in-hand with the opening of domestic distribution sectors to foreign investment, as discussed below.

Tariffs, quotas and state trading

China has substantially reduced its tariff and non-tariff barriers over the last decade. Pursuant to its WTO commitments, all tariffs are now bound at newly lowered statutory rates. As of 2005, the average applied most-favoured-nation rate for imports was 9.7 per cent, compared to 39.5 per cent in 1994.[16] Before WTO accession, China used quotas and licences extensively to restrict trade flow. Following accession, import quotas are abolished and the number of tariff lines subject to licences is cut by half.[17] While state trading activities remain, their operations have become much more transparent: all goods subject to state trading are listed in the Protocol; the adjustments of that list and the firms authorized to trade in those goods are published by MOFCOM and notified to the WTO.

Technical standards

One area where non-tariff barriers may have risen in China, however, is the use of technical and health standards. While these standards are meant to ensure product quality and to protect health or environment, they can also be used to restrict imports and exports. The WTO, therefore, has detailed rules on standards, requiring that domestic technical and health regulations not be more trade-restrictive than necessary to fulfil a legitimate objective and not be applied arbitrarily or discriminatorily. To that end, WTO members are obliged to use relevant and available international standards as the basis for their national standards. Although China has revised relevant laws and regulations to ensure WTO consistency, its practice in setting and applying standards has become an

16 See TPR Report, pp. 4 and 277, Table AIII.1.
17 *Ibid.* pp. 77–79.

increasing concern for its trading partners. At present, a majority of the Chinese standards are not based on international standards.[18] And traders have complained about a variety of unnecessary and burdensome procedures for product registration, licensing and certification that effectively hinder imports and exports.

Moreover, China has attempted in recent years to develop its own unique standards in areas where internationally recognized standards already exist, a well-known example of which is the Chinese WAPI security standard for wireless LAN.[19] Such attempts raise the issue of consistency with WTO requirements and are viewed as a strategy to benefit Chinese domestic industries at the expense of their foreign competitors.

Trade remedies

Trade remedies refer to antidumping, anti-subsidy and safeguard measures used by an importing country to remedy injuries caused by imports to its domestic industries. Dumping (selling below normal value) and certain government subsidies are considered "unfair" trade practices, and a WTO member may levy antidumping and countervailing duties on dumped and subsidized imports respectively if they are found to cause or threaten material injury to a domestic industry. A member may also take safeguard measures (tariffs and quotas) against imports when there is a sudden surge in imports that causes or threatens serious injury to domestic producers, even when no "unfair" trade practice is involved. Because these remedies raise trade barriers and can easily be abused by protectionist forces, the WTO imposes strict disciplines on their use. WTO trade remedy rules are extremely complex, and complaints about violations constitute a large number of WTO disputes.

The past decade witnessed the establishment of a trade remedy regime in China. The first Chinese antidumping and anti-subsidy regulation was issued in 1997 (superseded by two separate regulations on antidumping and anti-subsidy measures in 2001), and the first safeguard regulation in 2001. These regulations generally follow WTO standards, but contain much less detail than WTO provisions. MOFCOM is designated as the chief regulatory authority for conducting all relevant investigations and making determinations on trade remedies. Despite its nascent trade remedy regime, China has quickly risen to be one of the top users of antidumping measures in the world.[20] Japan, South

18 As of 2004, only 32% of the 21,342 national standards were equivalent to international standards. For the numerous sectoral, local and enterprise standards used in China, no data on their conformity with international standards is available. TPR Report, p. 90. Direct comparison with practices of other countries, however, is difficult. The US, for example, does not maintain centralized statistics on the extent to which its technical regulations conform with international standards. About two-thirds of the standards developed at the EU level were reportedly based on international standards. WT/TPR/S/136 (23 June 2004), p. 60.

19 See Scott Kennedy, "The political economy of standards coalitions: explaining China's involvement in high-tech standards wars, *Asia Policy*, No. 2 (2006), pp. 41–62.

20 During the first four years of WTO accession, China initiated 103 antidumping investigations and took final measures in 68 cases, which made it the third largest antidumping user after India and the United States (WTO Antidumping Statistics).

Korea, the United States and the European Union are among the most frequent targets of China's antidumping investigations. It is however notable that foreign respondents won a partial or complete victory in more than 40 per cent of the concluded cases.[21] To date, China has used safeguard measures only once, and has not initiated any anti-subsidy investigation.

China's aggressive use of antidumping measures is not surprising. Typically, when tariff and non-tariff barriers are significantly lowered, domestic industries will seek protection through more frequent resort to trade remedies. Besides, China's own experience as the "victim" of discriminatory trade remedies has unavoidably affected its position. For years, China has been by far the most frequently targeted country in antidumping actions.[22] The designation of China as a non-market economy by the United States, the EU and certain other countries has made it easier for them to find dumping by Chinese producers and impose high antidumping duties on Chinese products.[23] WTO accession did not end this practice; instead, the Protocol permits WTO members to treat China as a non-market economy till December 2016 for antidumping purposes, and indefinitely for anti-subsidy purposes. Furthermore, contrary to the WTO principle on non-discriminatory application of safeguards, the Protocol allows an importing member to single out Chinese products for safeguard measures. The China-only safeguards consist of two kinds: the general one may be used against any Chinese products till December 2013; the specific one against Chinese textile products till the end of 2008. Both kinds have been utilized in practice.[24] Such discriminatory treatment cannot help but motivate China to pursue its own trade remedies aggressively.

Foreign Investment Law

WTO accession provided a spur to foreign investment in China – the FDI inflow between 2001 and 2005 accounted for more than one-third of the total utilized foreign investment since 1979. This major expansion in foreign investment has in turn contributed to a tremendous growth in foreign trade. Since WTO accession, China's foreign trade has more than doubled in value, of which nearly 60 per cent is attributable to imports and exports by foreign-invested enterprises (FIEs).[25] Given that the WTO agreements provide only limited disciplines on

21 For an excellent analysis of the dynamics in China's antidumping practice, see Scott Kennedy, "China's porous protectionism: the changing political economy of trade policy," *Political Science Quarterly*, Vol. 120, No. 3 (2005), pp. 407–32.

22 From 1995 to 2005, WTO members initiated a total of 2,840 antidumping investigations, of which 469 involved Chinese products; of the 1,804 final measures taken by the members during this period, 338 were against Chinese products (WTO Antidumping Statistics).

23 See Chad Bown and Rachel McCulloch, "US trade policy toward China: discrimination and its implications" (June 2005), http://ssrn.com/abstract=757124, for a comparison between antidumping duties facing China and those facing all other countries involved in the same investigations in the US.

24 More than a dozen proceedings have been initiated against China under the special safeguard provision by the US, Canada, India, Colombia, Peru, Ecuador, Turkey and Chinese Taipei. The special textile safeguards have been invoked by the US, EU, Argentina and Turkey, following the expiration of the global quota system in textile trade at the end of 2004.

25 See n. 4.

investment activities, the impact of the WTO on foreign investment in China stems mostly from its accession commitments – particularly its extensive market-access commitments in service sectors, unique rule commitments on treatment of FIEs, and special pledges on market economy practices and domestic governance, which boost the confidence of business in the overall investment environment in China.

Against this backdrop, however, there are signs of a new trend of tightened government controls over foreign investment along with protection of domestic industries. Some of the new regulations and measures taken by the government call into question China's compliance with its WTO commitments, while others raise issues that cannot be easily addressed by WTO rules.

Easing entry restrictions

Ever since China opened up to foreign investment in 1979, the government has maintained control over the entry of foreign capital through an elaborate examination and approval system. For more than a decade, foreign investment projects have been classified by sector into the categories of encouraged, permitted, restricted and prohibited. The sectoral restrictions imposed include straight bans, equity limits and various other conditions on investment. The government maintains the Industry Guidance Catalogue for Foreign Investment, which provides a detailed list of specific industries under each category. The Catalogue has been substantially revised following WTO accession. The number of encouraged industries has increased from 186 to 262, while restricted industries decreased from 112 to 75. About 75 per cent of foreign investment in China is now in wholly foreign-owned companies.

It should be noted that market access for foreign capital is not subject to WTO rules except to the extent covered by the General Agreement on Trade in Services (GATS). Under GATS, members negotiate market access commitments in services, which include services supplied through the "commercial presence" of foreign service suppliers in their territories (that is, foreign investment in service sectors).[26] Once a member makes a commitment in a particular service sector, it is obliged to provide national treatment to the service suppliers in that sector from other members, subject only to the conditions specified in its service schedule attached to GATS. The scope and terms of market access for foreign investment in service sectors, therefore, vary from member to member.

As previously noted, China made extraordinary market access commitments in services. Of the 12 service sectors classified under GATS, China is bound by specific commitments in nine, including crucial areas in distribution, construction, transport, communication and financial services.[27] Take the opening of the

26 GATS covers trade in services supplied in four different "modes," of which mode 3 is "commercial presence."

27 No commitment was made in health related and social services, and recreational, cultural and sporting services.

distribution sector as an example. Previously, FIEs were not permitted to sell products in China other than those of their own production, and FDI in retail business was strictly restricted. After accession, the distribution sector has been liberalized according to a specified timetable. Today, FIEs can engage in wholesale and retail of all kinds of products, without limitation on the percentage of ownership or geographical location. Distribution rights, which work hand-in-hand with trading rights, are arguably the most important gains for foreign producers, as most of them are interested in selling directly into the vast Chinese market. Another critical area of liberalization is banking services. To stimulate its ailing state-owned banking sector, China made a bold commitment to allow foreign banks to operate fully in its territory – without geographic, client or ownership restrictions – within five years of accession. The ongoing implementation of this commitment may result in profound changes in domestic finance in China.[28]

It is worth mentioning that China also made several commitments regarding FDI in the automobile industry, including the removal upon accession of the 50 per cent foreign equity limit for joint ventures manufacturing motor vehicle engines.[29] China's car industry commitments are unique, as WTO members are not required to make market access commitments on investment in non-service sectors.

Eliminating performance requirements

Apart from GATS, the WTO has only a narrow set of rules regulating investment activities. Under the Agreement on Trade-Related Investment Measures (TRIMs), WTO members must eliminate certain performance requirements imposed on investment, including those relating to export performance, local content (import substitution) and foreign exchange balancing. These performance requirements are prohibited because of their distorting effect on trade in goods.

Before WTO accession, China imposed many performance requirements on FIEs of the kind prohibited by the TRIMs. In the Protocol, China promised that it would, upon accession, comply with the TRIMs without recourse to the transitional period available to developing country members. Remarkably, China also pledged not to condition approval of foreign investment on "performance requirements of any kind," including not only those covered by TRIMs but also "the transfer of technology" and "the conduct of research and development in China." This commitment to abolish any and all performance requirements is one of the WTO-plus obligations that no other country has undertaken.

28 China issued a new regulation in November 2006 to implement this commitment, which requires that foreign banks establish Chinese subsidiaries, instead of operating as foreign branches, in order to engage in the full range of RMB business with local clients.

29 WPR, paras. 204–07. See generally Eric Harwit, "The impact of WTO membership on the automobile industry in China," *The China Quarterly*, No. 167 (2001), pp. 655–70.

To implement these commitments, China has revised foreign investment laws to eliminate all mandatory performance requirements for FIEs. In addition, it has reduced control over cross-border technology transfers. The previous system requiring government approval of every technology transfer agreement has been replaced with a system under which approval is required only of those transfers involving a prohibited or restricted technology identified by a government catalogue. Despite these reforms, however, China has not eliminated all performance requirements in practice. For instance, the 2004 automobile industry development policy issued by the National Development and Reform Commission requires newly established automobile enterprises to set up their own research and development institutions. And tax benefits and other incentives are still offered to FIEs and domestic enterprises contingent upon the use of domestic over imported equipment. Such measures have given rise to challenges at the WTO as discussed below.

National treatment

WTO accession has significantly expanded China's obligations to accord national treatment to foreign investment. Traditionally, China grants national treatment only to foreign investors of selected countries through bilateral investment treaties, and the scope of the national treatment clause in those treaties is typically limited to the protection of investment against expropriation or nationalization.[30] While the accession protocol does not require China to extend all-around national treatment to foreign investors, it enlarges the traditional scope considerably by requiring that foreign investors be given national treatment with respect to China's market access commitments in services, the right to engage in the import-export business, and the conditions affecting FIEs' production and sales in China, such as the prices and availability of public utilities and other factors of production. The latter two aspects go beyond the scope of WTO national treatment provisions and are therefore special WTO-plus obligations for China.

Interestingly, China's WTO-plus obligations on national treatment of foreign investors has led to a demand for "national treatment" (or more precisely, equal treatment) of *domestic* enterprises. Historically, China has maintained different treatment between foreign and domestic enterprises, and between state-owned and private enterprises. To attract foreign investment, the government has provided FIEs with substantial tax benefits and other privileges that are not available to domestic enterprises. On the other hand, SOEs traditionally enjoyed more favourable treatment than FIEs and domestic private enterprises with respect to market access, performance requirements, supply of production inputs and state bank credits. With China's entry into the WTO, FIEs have

30 Of the more than 100 bilateral investment protection agreements of China, only a minority contain a national treatment clause. Historically, China preferred the "fair and just treatment" standard to the "national treatment" standard in dealing with foreign interests.

gained national treatment in new areas, whereas SOEs have lost many of their privileges, and domestic private enterprises, which are fast growing in number, continue to receive less favourable treatment than both FIEs and SOEs in terms of market access, bank financing and access to capital markets.

Under WTO national treatment provisions, China is obliged only to accord foreign interests treatment "no less favourable" than that accorded to domestic interests, and is therefore not prohibited from providing preferential treatment to foreign interests.[31] Nevertheless, publicity about the national treatment principle of the WTO has made the Chinese public keenly aware of the issue of unequal treatment of enterprises in China. There have been increasing calls to remove FIE preferences and to level the playing field for all players in the economy. In March 2007, the National People's Congress adopted the new Enterprise Income Tax Law that provides for a uniform income tax system for domestic and foreign-invested enterprises. Once fully implemented, the new law will end the decades-long preferential tax treatment of FIEs.

Rise of protectionism

In recent years, there has been a growing perception in China that decades of economic reform and opening up have benefited foreign interests more than domestic ones. Critics have sounded an alarm that foreign investors have bought out name-brand Chinese companies or acquired valuable Chinese assets at bargain prices, leading to foreign domination in industries and the disappearance of domestic brands. They also claim that foreign investment has not resulted in significant technology transfers to China and instead has diverted Chinese domestic resources from research and development to low-end manufacturing sectors.

Partially responding to these concerns, the government began to readjust its foreign investment policy in 2006. Recent months have seen a host of new regulations and policies that aim to tighten controls over foreign investment and to promote domestic industries. For example, a new regulation in August 2006 provides MOFCOM with broad discretion to block foreign acquisition of domestic companies involved in a "key industry," holding famous Chinese brands or otherwise affecting "national economic security."[32] In November 2006, the National Development and Reform Commission issued an important policy document outlining the foreign investment plan for the next five years.[33] While affirming that China will continue to open up service sectors and improve the business environment for foreign investment, the document indicates that

31 While preferential treatment of FIEs is well within the perimeter of WTO national treatment provisions, FDI incentives provided by China have been challenged as inconsistent with WTO subsidy rules. See n. 50.

32 See *Guanyu waiguo touzizhe binggou jingnei qiye de guiding* (*Provisions on Mergers and Acquisitions of Domestic Enterprises by Foreign Investors*), jointly issued by MOFCOM and five other central government agencies, 8 August 2006, effective 6 September 2006.

33 NDRC, *Liyong waizi "shiyi wu" guihua* (*The 11th Five-Year Plan for Utilizing Foreign Investment*), November 2006.

China will focus on the quality rather than the quantity of FDI, and select new investments that will bring technology or otherwise fit into China's development strategy. These new policies and rules have already made a difference in practice, holding up a number of foreign acquisitions.[34]

After nearly 30 years of encouraging foreign direct investment, China is entering a stage where it no longer needs to rely on foreign capital to generate growth and employment. Against this economic reality, the tightening of government control over FDI, while evidently a response to a variety of concerns,[35] may signal the rise of a protectionist trend. It remains to be seen to what extent China's WTO commitments can serve as a check on this trend.

Intellectual Property Rights

The development of intellectual property (IP) rights in China has been closely related to the development of foreign trade and investment. Since adopting the Trademark Law in 1982, China has enacted numerous IP laws and regulations, and acceded to most of the major IP treaties.[36] In building up China's IP regime, WTO accession has played an important role.

The WTO's Agreement on Trade-Related Aspects of Intellectual Property Rights (TRIPS) provides a comprehensive legal framework for the protection of IP rights. It does so by incorporating the principles and rules of other major IP conventions, setting out minimum standards on substantive IP rights, and prescribing certain civil, administrative and criminal procedures and remedies that WTO members must adopt into their domestic legislation.

To ensure compliance with TRIPS, China has made great efforts on both the legislative and institutional fronts. Legislatively, new amendments have been made to all major IP laws, including the Patent Law (2000), the Trademark Law (2001) and the Copyright Law (2001), and new regulations have been issued on the protection of computer software (2001), layout-designs of integrated circuits (2001) and new plant varieties (2001). In addition to administrative and civil remedies, specific crimes of IP violations have been added to the criminal code.[37] Institutionally, an elaborate government apparatus has been set up to administer and enforce IP laws, and a special IP adjudication division has been established

34 According to Bloomberg, almost 70% of the $19.5 billion of acquisitions in China announced by foreign investors in 2006 were not completed, whereas all but 25% of the $34.4 billion in purchases were cleared in 2005. See "China's buyout backlash stalls investments by Carlyle, Ewing," Bloomberg.com (30 November 2006) (suggesting that China's tougher stance on foreign takeovers may be a backlash from the aborted acquisition in 2005 of California-based Unocal Corp. by Cnooc. Ltd., China's biggest offshore oil producer, due to a threatened veto of the deal by the US Congress on the ground of national security).

35 Among other things, accelerated inflows of foreign capital have contributed to a massive accumulation of foreign exchange reserves for China, which puts tremendous pressure on the Chinese currency to appreciate – a matter of serious concern to the Chinese government.

36 For a list of the IP conventions acceded by China, see TPR Report, p. 147, Table III.16.

37 A section on IP violations was added to the Criminal Law in 1997, imposing up to seven years of imprisonment for counterfeits, piracy and violations of trade secrets.

within the People's Courts. As a result of these efforts, China today has an extensive and basically WTO-compliant legal framework for IP protection.

Despite this, IP violations remain rampant in China. The main problems identified by China's major trading partners include: lack of co-ordination among the large number of government agencies responsible for IP enforcement; local protectionism and corruption; inadequate deterrence provided by the system of administrative, civil and criminal penalties; and insufficient training of government personnel.[38] Although in recent years the government has stepped up enforcement efforts, weak protection of IP rights remains one of the main complaints of the foreign companies doing business in China.

Inadequate enforcement of IP rights in China has prompted the United States to file a formal WTO complaint, charging China for failure to protect IP rights according to TRIPS standards.[39] Among other things, the United States claims that China's criminal law sets inadequate thresholds for criminal procedures and penalties for trademark counterfeiting and copyright piracy. While the outcome of the case remains to be seen, this long-threatened WTO complaint has put great pressure on the Chinese government to enhance IP law enforcement. Indeed, merely days before the United States filed the complaint, the Supreme People's Court and the Supreme People's Procuratorate jointly issued a judicial interpretation, lowering certain thresholds for criminal punishment for copyright piracy by 50 per cent.[40]

Domestic Governance

The Protocol sets out a number of special obligations concerning the transparency, uniformity and impartiality of the Chinese system. The need for implementing these obligations has stimulated significant changes in domestic governance.

Transparency

Transparency is one of the basic values of the WTO system, given that open markets require transparent rules and procedures. The WTO obliges members to publish all trade-related laws, regulations and other government measures of general application before their implementation and enforcement, and to notify the WTO of any change in such laws, regulations or measures. Because of its historical lack of transparency, China was asked to undertake additional transparency obligations that are more stringent than the general requirements.

38 TPR Report, p. 153.

39 See n. 51.

40 The Supreme People's Court and the Supreme People's Procuratorat, *Guanyu banli qinfan zhishichanquan xingshi anjian juti yingyong falü ruogan wenti de jieshi* (*Interpretation on Several Issues of Concrete Application of Law in Handling Criminal Cases of Infringing Intellectual Property (II)*), adopted 4 April 2007, effective 5 April 2007 (reducing the threshold for copyright piracy punishable by imprisonment of less than three years from 1,000 to 500 illegal copies, and that between three and seven years from 50,000 to 25,000 illegal copies).

It is required, for instance, to designate an official journal dedicated to publication of all measures affecting trade, to establish enquiry points where traders may obtain information about such measures, to provide a reasonable comment period before implementation of such measures, and to translate all such measures into one of the official languages of the WTO and make such translation available to WTO members within 90 days.

China has taken concrete steps to implement its transparency commitments. These include efforts to open up the rulemaking process to more public participation and to standardize the procedures for granting administrative permissions. For instance, the Law on Legislation (2000) mandates that government agencies solicit public comments during the drafting of administrative rules. And the Law on Administrative Permissions (2003) forbids government agencies from using unpublished documents as the basis for granting administrative licences. In addition, most central government agencies and local governments have launched their own websites, and many of them allow the public to provide input directly. Increasingly, laws, regulations, administrative rulings, judicial interpretations and court decisions have become generally available on the official websites.

In sum, transparency in the Chinese regulatory system has improved markedly in connection with WTO accession. The government has yet to implement its WTO commitments on transparency fully,[41] and lack of transparency still ranks among the top concerns for foreign businesses operating in China. However, the present condition is a far cry from the days when "internal documents" ruled government administration, and there is reason to expect further improvement as the Chinese public embraces transparency as a norm for good governance.

Judicial review

To ensure that government measures affecting trade are administered fairly, the WTO requires members to maintain independent tribunals and proper procedures for the review of administrative decisions relating to trade. The Protocol specifies that judicial or administrative tribunals in China shall be impartial and independent of the agency entrusted with administrative enforcement and shall not have any substantial interest in the outcome of the matter. And it further requires that China provide private parties affected by administrative action the opportunity for appeal "in all cases" to a judicial body – a standard exceeding WTO general requirements[42] – and that the reasons for the decision on appeal must be provided in writing.

41 For instance, as late as March 2006, the State Council was still instructing its ministries and local governments to notify their trade-related regulations to MOFCOM so as to enable their timely publication in the designated official journal.

42 While judicial review of final administrative decisions is guaranteed under TRIPS, appeal to a court of the decision by an independent tribunal is merely referred to as a possibility under GATT and not mentioned in GATS.

Previously under Chinese law, administrative decisions on certain trade-related matters were excluded from judicial review, including decisions concerning the validity of patents and trademarks, and determinations in antidumping and countervailing cases.[43] To implement its WTO commitments, China has amended relevant legislation so as to provide the right to appeal to courts in all such WTO-related matters. In 2002, the Supreme People's Court issued three judicial interpretations to clarify the scope of and standards for judicial review of WTO-related administrative decisions. It also designated courts at the intermediate or higher level as the first-instance trial courts for international trade cases – a move aimed to ensure impartiality and quality of judgement in the adjudication of WTO-related cases, given that judges in upper level courts tend to be less vulnerable to external interference and are generally better qualified than judges in the basic courts. It is, however, still too early to assess the situation of judicial review in WTO-related cases since few such cases have been reported.

On a broader scale, WTO requirements on judicial review provided a fresh impetus to the development of administrative law and judicial reform in China. Important legislation was adopted, including the Law on Administrative Review (1999), Law on Legislation (2000) and Law on Administrative Permissions (2003), which set boundaries for the exercise of government powers and provide the legal basis for judicial review of specific administrative actions. WTO accession has also inspired intensified efforts by the Chinese judiciary to improve the competency level of its judges and to strive for judicial independence. Although substantive judicial independence in China cannot be achieved without political reform, the WTO requirements on impartiality and independence of tribunals have lent legitimacy and support to the call of the Chinese judiciary for freedom from local and departmental interferences.[44]

Uniform administration

In the Protocol, China undertook to administer all its laws, regulations and measures, including those issued at the sub-national level, in a uniform, impartial and reasonable manner. Specifically, China promised to annul all local laws and measures inconsistent with China's WTO obligations, and to establish a complaint mechanism under which private parties can bring to the attention of national authorities cases of non-uniform administration. These special commitments target local protectionism, which has become a major concern for foreign businesses.

It is unclear to what extent China has implemented these commitments. Many problems China faces today are associated with entrenched localism. From early

43 The Administrative Litigation Law (Article 12) excludes from judicial review administrative decisions that are declared to be final by any other laws.

44 See generally, Veron Mei-Ying Hung, "China's WTO commitment on independent judicial review: impact on legal and political reform," *American Journal of Comparative Law*, Vol. 52, No. 1 (2004) pp. 77–132.

on, China adopted decentralization as a core reform strategy. Local governments have been given power to adopt measures necessary to boost local GDP growth and are allowed to benefit directly from such growth.[45] As a result, they have been heavily involved in the investment in and operations of local enterprises. To promote their economic interests, local governments often provide subsidies to local firms or otherwise protect them against outside competition. They may have little incentive to enforce IP laws if local enterprises profit from violations of IP rights. Their control over local courts means that it may be impossible to obtain independent and impartial judicial review of matters involving local economic interests. Moreover, the close ties between local officials and firms make it extremely difficult to combat official corruption, which has been plaguing the Chinese system and undermining the legitimacy of the regime.

In principle, WTO rules apply to the entire territory of each member, and a member is responsible for WTO violations by its political subdivisions. The WTO agreements specifically permit a member to bring WTO complaints against measures taken by the local authorities of another member. Hence, if the Chinese government lacks the political will to rein in local protectionism, other members do have the means available at the WTO to compel it to take action.

Normative impact

Potentially more significant than the legislative and institutional improvements are the normative changes brought about by the WTO accession. During the years leading up to and following the accession, the government and academia engaged in an unprecedented scale of public education on the WTO, portraying it as mostly a progressive force for China.[46] As a result, WTO principles and concepts, such as nondiscrimination, transparency, due process and judicial review, have gained wide acceptance in China as the norms for good governance in a modern society. The public's appeal to WTO norms often goes beyond the technical scope of their application; a notable example was the popular demand for "national treatment" of domestic enterprises discussed above. There is also a tendency among academics to construe WTO concepts liberally and expansively so as to give them meanings in a larger political and constitutional context.[47] As WTO principles and concepts acquire a normative force in China, their overall impact on the construction of rule of law may well be more profound in the long run than the WTO-conforming changes at the legislative and institutional level.

45 See Kenneth Lieberthal, "Completing WTO reforms," *The China Business Review* (September–October 2006), pp. 52–57, for a perceptive analysis of this strategy and its positive and negative consequences.

46 During this period, the number of books and articles published in China on WTO-related topics may have exceeded that in the rest of the world combined.

47 For example, legal scholars interpreted "market economy" as a WTO norm requiring the protection of economic rights of citizens under the Chinese Constitution. See Xin Chunying and Feng Jun (eds.), *WTO yu Zhongguo xingzhengfa gaige* (*WTO and the Reform of Chinese Administrative Law*) (Beijing: Social Sciences Academic Press, 2005), ch. 1.

Enforcing China's Commitments

With the power to issue binding decisions and authorize trade sanctions against noncompliance, the WTO arguably has the most effective enforcement system of all international organizations. In the case of China, the WTO also adopted the special transitional review mechanism (TRM) to monitor compliance. The enforcement of China's commitments through these mechanisms has already had an impact on the Chinese system.

Transitional review mechanism

The annual TRM reviews put China's practices under the constant scrutiny of other members, and give them the opportunity to raise many of their concerns with China in a timely manner. During the review in 2006, for example, members requested clarification and explanation from China on WTO consistency of its new automobile policy, the new regulation on mergers and acquisitions, and the new banking regulations. Even though China resents the TRM as discriminatory, it has accepted the annual exercise. As the Chinese government is compelled to address member concerns, the process has added transparency to the Chinese system.

Dispute settlement

To date, China has encountered eight WTO complaints, of which five were brought by the United States, and one each by the EU, Canada and Mexico. The eight complaints involve five sets of disputes. The first, *China – Value Added Tax*, was filed by the United States in 2004, alleging that China's policy of refunding value-added taxes to domestically-produced integrated circuits discriminated against imported circuits.[48] China settled the case through consultations and withdrew the measures in 2005.

All other disputes are currently pending. The second, *China – Auto Parts*, involves three complaints brought by the EU, the United States and Canada in 2006.[49] At issue are Chinese regulations that impose a surcharge on imported automobile parts used in manufacturing vehicles for sale in China, effectively raising the tariff on parts from 10 to 25 per cent, the same rate as for imports of complete vehicles. The third dispute, *China – Subsidies*, was initiated by the United States in February 2007, later joined by Mexico.[50] The complaints charge that China has been subsidizing domestic firms (including FIEs) through various tax breaks that are WTO-illegal. The fourth and fifth disputes were brought by the United States on the same day in April 2007. The fourth, *China – Intellectual Property Rights*, claims that China's criminal law does not provide sufficient punishment for IP violations, and that the denial by China's copyright law of

48 WTO: *China – Value-Added Tax on Integrated Circuits*, DS/309 (March 2004).

49 WTO: *China – Measures Affecting Imports of Automobile Parts*, DS339, DS340, DS342 (April 2006).

50 WTO: *China – Certain Measures Granting Refunds, Reductions or Exemptions from Taxes and Other Payments*, DS358, DS359 (February 2007).

protection for works under censorship reviews is inconsistent with TRIPS requirements.[51] The fifth, *China – Trading Rights*, raises issue with China's implementation of its commitments on trading rights and distribution services for publications and audiovisual products.[52] It complains that, contrary to its commitment to fully liberalize trading rights, China has continued to reserve the right to import foreign cultural products to designated SOEs.

These pending disputes challenge important aspects of China's industrial policy and legal regime. The automobile-parts case and the subsidy case target tax incentives and local content requirements which China has used for decades as part of its development strategy. Although on its accession China agreed to comply with all WTO rules and even accepted more stringent obligations on subsidies than any other member,[53] the government has not fundamentally changed its policy. The IP case is legally most significant because it challenges WTO-consistency of two important pieces of Chinese legislation: the Criminal Law, an area traditionally reserved for national jurisdiction, and the Copyright Law in the context of government censorship. The trading rights case also raises sensitive issues of government control over importation and distribution of foreign cultural products. If China loses in these cases, it will have to change its law and policy to comply with WTO rulings.

At least in the initial period, China responded well to all WTO complaints against it, actual or threatened. As noted above, it settled its first WTO dispute with the United States by withdrawing the VAT measures in question. In 2004, the EU threatened to bring a WTO complaint against China over its export restrictions on coking coal used in European steel production. Although China claimed that the restrictions were necessary to reduce severe pollution caused by excessive coke production, it soon backed down and agreed to maintain the level of coke supply to the EU.[54] In late 2005, when the United States threatened to initiate a WTO case against China's antidumping determination regarding linerboard, MOFCOM quickly repealed that decision.[55] China's accommodating attitude, however, appears to have changed in 2006 when it refused to settle the automobile-parts case through consultations. And it has recently vowed to fight the IP case till the end. This change of attitude is significant for China, which has never been sued, let alone lost a case, in any other international court.

51 WTO: *China – Measures Affecting the Protection and Enforcement of Intellectual Property Rights*, DS362 (16 April 2007).

52 WTO: *China – Measures Affecting Trading Rights and Distribution Services for Certain Publications and Audiovisual Entertainment Products*, DS363 (16 April 2007).

53 See Julia Ya Qin, "WTO regulation of subsidies to state-owned enterprises (SOEs): a critical appraisal of the China accession protocol," *Journal of International Economic Law*, Vol. 7, No. 4 (2004), pp. 863–919.

54 BNA, WTO Reporter, "EC threatens WTO suit against China unless it lifts coking-coal restrictions" (25 May 2004); "EC, China reach agreement on continued Chinese shipments of coking coal to Europe" (2 June 2004).

55 BNA, WTO Reporter, "China lifts dumping duties on linerboard in face of US' threat of WTO proceedings" (11 January 2006).

It suggests that China has finally accepted a rule-based approach, instead of relying on diplomacy exclusively, in settling its international disputes.

The number of WTO cases brought against China is still small compared to those brought against other major trading powers during the same period.[56] This may be in part a result of the "honeymoon effect" – trading partners were willing to give China some leeway in light of its recent accession – and in part because of China's willingness to compromise in threatened disputes as discussed above. This situation, however, is changing. Both the United States and the EU have indicated an intention to bring more WTO cases against China. Judging from the numerous concerns raised during the TRM reviews, there is no shortage of issues that could evolve into formal complaints.

Relying on WTO litigation to enforce China's WTO obligations undoubtedly has its limits. The dispute settlement process is time-consuming and resource-intensive, and complaints can target only selected measures. Moreover, WTO rules do not effectively regulate all government policies affecting trade – the Chinese currency controversy is an example. Nevertheless, given that China's economy is so heavily reliant on trade and that its practice is so closely monitored by other members, it is reasonable to expect that WTO process will be effective in enforcing China's obligations.

Future Prospects

WTO accession has brought about extensive changes to China's foreign trade and investment regime. As a result, the Chinese system today is far more open and less opaque than a decade ago. But what does WTO membership hold for China in the next decade? The reason that the accession had such a major impact on China is because it served the agenda of domestic economic liberalization set by Chinese leadership in the 1990s. Now that China has substantially implemented its market access commitments and the government has achieved the main objectives of the accession, will China continue to liberalize its economy beyond what was called for by the WTO? The answer will of course depend on the vision of the current leadership and its future agenda. Given the widening income gap and severe environmental degradation in China, the government is compelled to adjust its development strategy to pursue more balanced and sustainable growth. This adjustment, however, may slow the process of further economic reform and liberalization.[57]

In the next few years, the impact of the market access commitments made in the accession will wane as the domestic economy adapts to the new level of foreign competition. The impact of WTO rule obligations, by contrast, may be

56 From 2002 to 2006, more than 40 WTO complaints were brought against the US and more than 20 against the EU, although only three against Japan.

57 Indeed, China has declared that, given its extensive accession commitments, it should not be required to make substantial new concessions in the Doha Round. BNA, WTO Reporter, "China, other new WTO members seek special terms on farm tariff, subsidy cuts" (14 March 2007).

felt more acutely. With the continuing expansion of its trading power, China will be likely to find itself a frequent target of WTO complaints. When China loses a case, the government will feel the external constraints imposed by the WTO directly as it must change the offending law and practice or face possible trade sanctions. The Chinese public may then develop an image of the WTO quite different from the positive one promoted by the leadership during the accession era. The issue of sovereignty and domestic regulatory space will be raised. Other issues that have long generated controversies about the WTO and globalization in other parts of the world, such as the relationship between trade and environment, trade and labour rights, and trade and other social policies and values, will also attract greater attention in China.

Thus, when the dust settles from the accession commitments, the impact of the WTO on China will become comparable to that on other major trading nations. That, however, will not diminish the historic significance of the accession. WTO membership has integrated China into a multilateral system which, through its extensive rules and enforcement mechanisms, will impose meaningful disciplines on China in charting its future course of economic development.

Commentary on "Trade, Investment and Beyond"

Huang Dongli

In her article, Julia Ya Qin draws conclusions from the accession of China to the WTO which reflects the effects of WTO obligations on China's constitutional law, the development of foreign trade law, the foreign investment regime, intellectual property rights protections and general rule-of-law conditions. With respect to foreign trade law, the foreign investment regime and intellectual property rights protections, it is not difficult to observe the legal consequences the accession has brought and will bring to China. However, Qin's article goes beyond these general observations and provides profound insights on significant effects of the WTO obligations on China's economic reforms as well as rule of law processes. This essay comments on arguments she has presented on these issues.

The Significance of the WTO Obligations to China's Economic Reform

Public ownership was the political foundation of the Chinese Communist Party. Before the open-door policy in 1978, all enterprises, by and large, were owned by the government and private business transactions were illegal. The government controlled the market completely by enforcing a national uniform price policy, conducting strict trade control and making all commercial decisions on behalf of enterprises. During the years from 1978 to the third amendment of China's Constitution in 1993, there were heated political and theoretical debates over whether or not China would allow partial private ownership. These debates reflected the political struggle between the reformers and the conservatives within the Communist Party. Although the 1993 Constitutional Amendment replaced a planned economy with a socialist market economy, domestic economic policies may still be altered for political reasons. However, the accession of China to the WTO has, as Qin points out, made a market-based economy "no longer merely a matter of [China's] domestic policy, but also a matter of international legal obligation" and "so long as China remains a WTO member, it may not negate its market economy commitments without incurring the consequences of breaching WTO obligations."

The Impact of the WTO Accession on China's Rule of Law Processes

As pointed out by Qin, the WTO accession has played a positive role in improving the rule of law conditions of China. However, her article gives insufficient explanation of the WTO impact on China's rule of law aspect.

 doi:10.1017/S0305741007001701

The notion of the rule of law has never been part of traditional Chinese culture. In over 3,000 years, Chinese people have not imagined a possible contractual relationship with their governments. The relationship between the governments and the people has always been that of master to servants. The WTO accession has somehow forced the Chinese government to change the way it manages the country and, more fundamentally, it has actually helped to change how the Chinese people view their relationship with the government. This is an overturning of the traditional national consciousness. It makes possible a true understanding by the Chinese people of the meaning of the rule of law, forming the foundation to the possibility of democracy in China.

Whereas rule of law is not an abstract concept, its realization depends upon certain indispensable conditions including transparency, uniformity and impartiality. These principles are in conflicts with the routine practice of the Chinese government. Thus, any change of status would not be without opposition. It is well accepted that political considerations formed part of China's rationale to accept the harsh demands for WTO accession. The reformers in the Communist Party hoped that external forces would ease opposition to the reforms. And the accession did achieve that goal. Both before and after WTO accession, China made great efforts towards institutional reforms in order to comply with WTO obligations. These included amending and revoking over 2,000 trade-related laws and enacting new laws. Many of the intellectual property laws were enacted just before or immediately after China's accession. At the same time, WTO accession was utilized as an opportunity to promote the rule of law concept. Nationwide education regarding the WTO, including its principles and requirements, was conducted, especially among government officials. Today, such education is still ongoing among government officials working in trade-related fields. Among these efforts, the most important steps the government has taken are measures on "nondiscrimination, fair competition, transparency, due process and judicial review." As pointed out by Qin, "as WTO principles and concepts acquire a normative force in China, their overall impact on the construction of rule of law may well be more profound in the long run than the WTO-conforming changes at the institution level."

In addition, WTO accession makes two other contributions to rule of law construction in China. First, the WTO judicial review requirement helped the Chinese to realize the importance of judicial independence. The requirement triggered intensive nationwide discussions on issues related to domestic judicial review immediately after accession. Secondly, the WTO dispute settlement decisions demonstrate to China how a non-common law system can develop a system in which case law matters. In China, professional incompetence causes technical problems in adequate applications of laws which seriously impede uniformity and predictability of the law and thus the authoritativeness of the judicial system. Some scholars argue that this makes the Chinese judiciary incapable of functioning independently. However, the WTO quasi-precedent and dispute settlement practice has provided a successful model for China, countering the argument that Chinese courts cannot adopt a precedent system because China has a civil law system. Respect for precedents and emphasis on case law will require courts to be more careful about their legal reasoning, which may help Chinese courts to gain judicial independence.

Index

Lightning Source UK Ltd.
Milton Keynes UK
UKOW06f0510040516

273529UK00010B/445/P

9 780521 719292